Season

WITH LOVE

A RECIPE COLLECTION FROM AUDREY BENNER

COMPILED BY
KAY WORDSWORTH WILDER

BEACON HILL PRESS OF KANSAS CITY
Kansas City, Missouri

Copyright 1985
by Beacon Hill Press of Kansas City

ISBN: 083-411-061X

Printed in the
United States of America

Design: Royce Ratcliff
Inside Illustrations: Bob Holloway
Cover Photo: Ron Howard

10 9 8 7 6 5 4 3 2 1

CONTENTS

MINISTERING HOSPITALITY
by Gloria Ramquist Willingham

Genuine hospitality is a gift from God. It bespeaks good things like

love

friendliness

receptivity

compassion

sensitivity

and generosity.

Anyone can have this gift, though it must be accepted and used. The more you practice the gift of hospitality, the more accomplished you will become.

Does this sound easy? It really is.

- "But I can't entertain until we get a larger home."
- "I'll do my entertaining after the children have grown up."
- "To tell you the truth, I don't know how to cook anything but plain, down-home food. It's just not good enough for company."
- "If I can't do it up right, then I won't even try to entertain. After all, there are so many others who can do it better than I."

Hospitality: what is it?

Hospitality is the art of caring enough about others that you are willing to become a servant to them. This sometimes requires sacrifices, but these are usually far outweighed by the unexpected benefits of pleasure derived from doing it. Many times the most costly ingredient is your own personal time. Since everyone has 24 hours in each day, setting priorities and managing your time become keys to success.

But in ministering through hospitality, time is not the only consideration. It also takes an open spirit, an attitude that doesn't judge others and that is not afraid to be judged by other people.

God's written Word gives clear directives:

- "Use hospitality one to another without grudging" (1 Pet. 4:9).
- "Be not forgetful to entertain strangers: for thereby some have entertained angels unawares" (Heb. 13:2).

Here is an interesting phenomenon: a new person enters your circle of friends. Subconsciously, perhaps, you wonder how the relationship will benefit *you.*

Actually this is a self-centered attitude, and it is at the heart of the world's point of view. It is directly opposite from the *others*-centered position of Christ's followers. Hospitality, God's style, requires looking at the individual and wondering how you can make him feel more at ease, more comfortable, more at home.

"Tit for tat," another worldly view, creeps in to make Christian hospitality a burden, rather than the joy it *should* be. One young mother, after making a major move from one city to another, exclaimed, "Oh, when I get settled I want to have dinner for the Browns who helped us move in, the Rogers who got us a job, and the Harps who helped with our kids."

The "you-do-something-for-me-and-I'll-do-something-for-you" scene is loaded with obligation. Although planning "thank you" occasions is appropriate, the model for Christians is to stretch beyond that

> *. . . seek out strangers*
> *those who are poor or in need*
> *the lonely folk*
> *the aged . . .*

Serve those who need support and encouragement with a sense of love, His love working through you, with no concern about a return on your efforts or of being paid back.

How wonderfully freeing this is! To serve with love is to minister! There is no sense of obligation on anyone's part. And what is beautiful is the overflow of joy that causes the recipient to find someone to whom *he* can minister!

Does hospitality mean formality?

Hospitality means "generous and cordial reception of guests." God said to Moses, "What is that in thine hand?" And as we accept the gift of hospitality and seek ways to minister, He asks the same question of us. What do you have? Use it for His glory!

Hospitality inspired by Christ's love often bypasses formal introduction. It allows you to take action, to introduce yourself, and to invite the guests to your home and serve them in the manner most comfortable for you, your family, and them. Some people feel that hospitality must mean a full dinner around a dining table with linen, china, silver, and crystal. What a mistake!

How does one begin?

Practicing the gift of hospitality begins with friendship. You make the first move, you find an area of mutual interest, and you help the other person feel at ease. You introduce your new friend to others: your family, your pastor.

The hospitable act of greeting leads to the offer of friendship, and friendship leads to invitation. It can take place anywhere, in a moment, or over a period of time. It is accepting others into your life just the way they are, without judgment. Much of your personal fear vanishes as you realize that through this simple act, you are serving the Lord you love. He gives us power to extend warmth and acceptance. He shows us how to care.

Hospitality: what is the purpose?

Who does not like to be the recipient of hospitality! It requires both a giver and a receiver, who may be a teenager, a grandparent, a single person, a new family in the church, someone in need—or a longtime friend. A few of the ways God uses the ministry of hospitality come to mind:

Support during stress: Sensitivity to special needs during the tough times people encounter is developed through friendship. Death, severe illness, job loss, accidents, or broken home relationships tend to cause withdrawal on the part of the one who is hurting. Special outreaches of love demonstrate acceptance, love, and a willingness to help. If you are tempted to shy away from tender times like these, remember you are doing it in the name of the Lord.

Food, calls, letters, cards, and books are usual avenues to express concern. But an invitation to your home for lunch, dinner, or after evening service may turn things around for the person(s) in need. And if bringing them to your home won't work, try serving a meal or dessert at their house, for fellowship, as well as financial help.

Help for the needy: Thank God for the charitable acts of agencies whose interest is in helping the poor! But it is neither enough nor reason to withhold further assistance. Groceries, donations of money, purchases of clothing, and transportation are all concrete ways to alleviate some of the suffering.

The best way to show Christian charity is through hospitality. Which would you rather have done for you? Check one:

☐ A grocery sack of used clothing handed to you by an usher at church.

☐ An invitation to a casserole supper, and a casual offer of "Johnny's outgrown clothing."

Whatever you are giving is best given in the warmth of your own home.

The art of encouragement: Who doesn't need it? But using the gift of hospitality to encourage others who are serving the Lord rates high in His estimation.

Who are these people? The pastor, of course, and . . .

missionaries,

Sunday School teachers,

seminary students,

musicians . . .

the church janitor . . .

People outside the church will also be grateful for your hospitable gestures. Your home can become a pleasant oasis for those who are pressing hard in the service they render for God, and your act of hospitality—perhaps a fresh pie delivered to them—could give them renewed vigor.

Evangelism: "Christ has no hands but our hands . . ." wrote Annie Johnson Flint. So hospitality rates highest among the effective means to evangelism. Friendship evangelism includes role modeling, mutual acceptance, conversational witness, involvement, invitations to church, and decision making. Once a person has been led to Christ, hospitality continues, providing a natural platform for discipleship—nurturing the babe in Christ—all in the comfort of your own home!

Fellowship of the saints: Christ was entertained in many homes. One can sense in the Gospels His delight in being in a home, and the ease with which He carried on His ministry in these settings.

The serendipity of entertaining Christian friends is that more happens than what was expected. In the setting of your home, lessons are learned, examples rub off, decisions fall into place. Visiting and relaxing together are supportive, whether or not a mini-church service is included. Sharing arts, music, literature, and delicious food can become an avenue of inspiration and praise to God. Open your home! It's a beautiful way of life!

Hospitality: where?

You need a large, spacious home with well-matched furnishings? A football-field size recreation room? Matching dishes?

No! Hospitality takes place wherever you are and with whatever you have. An invitation can be to any place: a park, a restaurant for coffee or a Coke, a fast-food or carry-out place, a parade, a ball game, a potluck at church, or to your home.

If the thought of bringing someone to your home causes tremblings, relax in the truth that John Howard Payne wrote in 1852:

'Mid pleasures and palaces though we may roam,
Be it ever so humble, there's no place like home. —your home!

When you invite someone to your home, rest in the confidence that it is your castle. Put forth your own best spirit, be organized, have your home clean, let your family relax and show a natural warmth that spells welcome, and leave the rest to God.

All of the material possessions you have belong to God. You are the steward, the caretaker. He has plans to use what He has entrusted to you in a unique way, perhaps reaching people no one else can reach, or being a blessing to fellow believers who need your special touch.

- Every roast you prepare for a guest is prepared as a love gift to Christ.
- Every vegetable you peel, you peel for Him.
- Every pie crust you roll out, is rolled out with Him in mind.

Even in the midnight hours of preparation, excitement builds when you realize that you are serving Christ when you invite strangers to your home. The task becomes easier, the wallpaper looks less tacky, the food seems to stretch. Your creative ideas blossom and develop new and different ways to be hospitable.

On the spur of the moment

One of the most valid reasons for developing good housekeeping habits and stocking the kitchen with goodies is that you are freed to ask others over without planning ahead.

"How about coming to my house after church tonight for popcorn and lemonade?" you can blurt out. What do you need to pull off a successful invitation? Frozen lemonade and popcorn—both easy to stock and ridiculously inexpensive.

Or how about this?

"Hey, I've got hamburger at home" (two pounds you were hoping would last two weeks). "Come on over and let's make sandwiches." And who can resist a good hamburger?

Ooops! There goes your budget. Remember the promise "Give and it shall be given to you." If you have to live on jelly sandwiches for a while, you will reap benefits that far outweigh your sacrifice!

Making cookies? Or you wish you could, if you had a little child to enjoy them hot out of the oven! You can always adopt a child to give a tired mother a rest. Ministry to children is dear to the heart of Christ, who said, "Suffer little children, and forbid them not, to come unto me." When we include children in our ministry of hospitality, we are making an investment in precious lives!

Spur-of-the-moment invitations require the cooperation of the whole household. The pace is set by whoever assumes the responsibility for the invitation. To be ready for such occasions, others involved must be tuned in to what you are doing. If you are relaxed and have the house in order and the kitchen stocked with whatever you have in mind, your family will enjoy having guests. Shop and bake with invitations in mind, and straighten up the house before leaving for church!

The well-planned occasion

Regardless of the number of people you invite, this is more demanding. A small dinner party can be as expensive and wearing as a Sunday School class party of 30! Planning is the key, with as much of the work done in advance as possible.

Is rejection possible?

Yes! One of the most difficult things to handle in hospitality is rejection. You invite someone, and that someone says no.

This can be a touchy time. When your best efforts are thwarted, it is easy to feel frustration and tempting to say, "Well, I won't bother to invite him again!"

Jesus continues to keep asking. He never stops loving. He never gives up. The best advice for a beginner in the ministry of hospitality is to hang on. Keep planning, keep inviting, and keep loving those who, for whatever their reason may be, do not accept your invitations.

Hospitality: unexpected benefits

If you accept the gift of hospitality, you will need to use your time, your money, your home, your possessions, and your creative ideas to carry it out successfully. But it is worth it! Your goal is to serve Him joyfully, and your rewards will be immense both in heaven . . . and on earth.

Here are some of the unexpected benefits you may receive:

- An effervescent joy will arise in your heart when you realize you have succeeded in ministering to others.
- Because your life will be a bit more complicated when it is entwined with other lives, you will find yourself more organized and able to achieve for yourself, your family, your church, and your Savior.
- As you meet new friends your circle of influence will widen. Christ's message will be made more real. You will gather to yourself and your family, friends from many areas of interest: warriors

of the Cross, saints with unique ministries, children, the poor and needy, people with problems, the sick—and many, many folk just like yourself.

- As you encourage others, you will find yourself encouraged. No one is without some valleys to travel through, and your circle of friends will be there when you need them.
- Hospitality is made up of actions and reactions. While you do not expect to be paid back, there is a contagious element about the warmth of hospitality. The best payback is when you hear that someone you've ministered to by having them in your home, has turned around and given similar loving care to someone else.

*   *   *

Hospitality is the extension of your day-to-day routine. If boredom has set in, one remedy is the ministry of hospitality. It makes life more interesting, more challenging, full of meaning, and full of change.

Your style of hospitality will develop as you practice your gift, but it can start out simply. Through determined effort and the helps found in this fascinating collection of recipes, you can become a real minister for Him.

A good scripture to remember is: "Whatsoever ye do in word or deed, do all in the name of the Lord Jesus, giving thanks to God and the Father by him" (Col. 3:17).

PORTRAIT OF A HOSTESS

To serve graciously! If this is your goal as a Christian host or hostess, read on. For Audrey Carroll Benner, who was the creative heart and talent behind this collection of recipes and hospitality ideas, was a woman whose ways with food and style you can adapt to your own situation with good success.

Helping others develop their hospitality skills in the light of ministry is an important consideration behind the gathering of these recipes. Well mixed with every ingredient this book offers is the strong conviction that

good food,

warm fellowship,

and God's Spirit

can provide an atmosphere in which friends and strangers will better relate to one another and to God.

Hostess Audrey Benner was a woman of varied interests and talents. She loved art, beauty, and well-prepared food. Living in various parts of the United States with her minister husband, Hugh C. Benner, and traveling throughout the world, she was exposed to many cultures. Audrey was able to use these experiences to enhance her understanding and love of people, and to create a special warmth in the houses she called home.

Mrs. Benner knew and appreciated her middle-American upbringing. She particularly loved the foods of that region. She often said, "I think the best cooking in the United States can be found in the Midwest."

An evening at the Benners was a time one could never forget. Audrey Benner had a gift for making guests feel at home. She chose to love people by feeding their bodies, minds, and spirits. The reason for the occasion didn't matter; she was always a *ministering* hostess. She entertained in a variety of ways; sometimes a night of games (she loved Scrabble), a special birthday or anniversary meal, a winter-night dinner next to the fireplace on a small intimate table, or a simple family meal. Part of the Benner style was always to plan well; every meal or social occasion was important to her.

A meal prepared by Audrey was an event of beauty. It usually combined, to near perfection, flavors, textures, and colors that were complementary and compatible. Not only was Mrs. B. careful in her preparation, but she was also an organized manager. Often after developing a successful menu she would create variations on the theme and preserve her idea in an ever-present recipe file.

Audrey Benner's standard for food preparation was exemplary. She continually experimented with new recipes; researching many variations until she discovered "just the right one." It was well known that Mrs. Benner did not like convenience food. When asked about it, she rather disdainfully replied, "I never use mixes." That generally settled the issue right there.

Food preferences and the comfort of family and guests were important to Audrey Benner. As an expedience to diners, the salad was always placed on the right side of the place setting, because she felt it was a more sensible serving style; "One didn't need to worry about getting one's sleeve in the dinner plate."

Simplicity with elegance describes the table decorations preferred by Mrs. Benner. She loved to create flower arrangements, and the understated simplicity of a Japanese arrangement seemed to be most appealing to her. Her love for oriental beauty was heightened through a series of lessons she received on a trip to Japan. Her centerpieces and other arrangements made use of fresh flowers, sticks, leaves, fruit, and vegetables.

Audrey Benner was known for a number of dishes that became "specialties." Family and friends happily remember her raisin-stuffed apple dumplings, her gloriously light biscuits, flaky pie crusts, and her memorable chicken and dumplings. Daughter-in-law Patricia Benner describes her recollection of the popular main dish:

> Mother Benner usually cooked the chicken a day ahead of the dinner. The sauce was a rich white sauce made with real butter, cream, milk, and chicken broth from the stewing hen. She added a few drops of yellow food coloring to make it look as rich as it tasted. She seasoned the stewing hen with celery, carrot, a small bit of onion, and parsley. The dumplings were incredibly light and fluffy. Part of her secret for scrumptious dumplings was to cook them in a simmering, low boil; not too hot and not too deep. The chicken broth (from the stewing hen) was placed in a tall pan with a tight lid. The broth should be no more than two inches deep, and you must not peek while the dumplings are cooking. After they were cooked, small bits of parsley were placed on top and carefully placed on the cream sauce and chicken. All of this was encased in a wonderful tureen, that seemed to add to our joy of eating.

When all is said and done, to hostess Audrey Benner, hospitality was more than flaky biscuits and calorie-laden sauces; hospitality was (and always will be) the bringing together of resources that make guests feel cared for and receptive. And through this hospitality there were times when the Benner dining room became a sanctuary.

That will always be the goal of the Christian host and hostess; to allow God's Spirit to flow through in encouragement to others.

In dedication . . .
　To the loving memory of Audrey Benner, my friend
　and
　to Anne Elizabeth, my joy.
In acknowledgment . . .
　A special thank-you to
　my parents for their love
　my dear friends for their encouragement
　Janet Benner Miller, Richard Benner, and Patricia Benner
　　for their advice and support
　Marilyn Hills, Linda Black, Kathy Ellis, Carol Heasley, and Judy Corbin
　　for their diligent work.
　　　　　　　　　　　　　　　　　—Kay Wordsworth Wilder

SOUPS & STEWS

Seasoning with love...

*W*ill I ever forget the lonely old man whom my husband brought home with him one day for lunch? Our first parsonage was in the basement of the church. There was little money to spare and the going was tough both for us and for the church. Taking me to one side, Harry suggested that we invite the man to stay and eat with us. I looked bewildered and not a little chagrinned. But it seemed to be the thing to do; so I borrowed a few dollars from the piggy bank and went to the next-door grocery store for some bread, baloney, and a can of soup. The lunch was a success.

When I cleared the table to wash the dishes, imagine my surprise at finding $40.00 neatly folded beneath a plate. That was a lot of money in those days! No wonder I smile whenever I read the Scripture: "Be not forgetful to entertain strangers: for thereby some have entertained angels unawares" (Heb. 13:2).

—Marion K. Rich
Dollard des Ormeaux, Quebec

Five-Hour Beef Stew

2 pounds beef chuck, cut in 1" pieces
1 cup tomato juice (or 1 cup cream of celery soup)
2 tablespoons quick tapioca
1 teaspoon salt
pepper to taste
1 tablespoon sugar
5 carrots, cut in 1" pieces
5 stalks celery, diced
2 medium-size onions, sliced
1 ten-ounce package frozen peas (optional)

Combine ingredients, using tomato juice or soup depending on color and flavor you prefer. Bake at 250° 4½ to 5 hours, adding peas in the last hour.

One-Pot Oven Stew

2 to 3 pounds stewing meat, cut into chunks
3 large carrots, diced
1 medium-sized onion, chopped
1 one-pound can tomatoes with juice
1 No. 2 can peas with liquid
1 ten-ounce can undiluted onion soup
4 tablespoons Minute tapioca
1 four-ounce can mushrooms
2 tablespoons brown sugar
½ cup bread crumbs
1 can whole potatoes, quartered (optional)
2 bay leaves
salt and pepper to taste

Mix all ingredients in a covered Dutch oven or large baking pan with lid. Bake 6 to 7 hours at 250°. Serves 6.

Janet's* Meatball Stew

1½ pounds ground beef

1 cup soft crumbs (bread or crackers)

¼ cup finely chopped onion

1 egg, beaten

1 teaspoon salt

½ teaspoon marjoram

¼ teaspoon thyme

2 tablespoons oil

1 can tomato soup, undiluted

1 can beef broth

4 medium potatoes, pared and quartered

4 carrots, cut in chunks

8 small white onions

2 tablespoons chopped parsley

Combine the first 7 ingredients and shape into 24 meatballs. Brown them in oil in a 4-quart Dutch oven. Remove as they brown. Combine the soup and broth; then add meatballs and vegetables. Bring to a boil, cover, and simmer until vegetables are tender, about 30 minutes. Add parsley and serve. Serves 6-8.

*Mrs. Janet Benner Miller, Leawood, Kans.

Best Chili

2 pounds ground beef

⅓ cup chicken fat

1½ teaspoons chili powder

¼ teaspoon cayenne powder

2 tablespoons cumin seeds, crushed

2 cloves garlic, minced

1 two-pound can tomatoes

1 one-pound can red kidney beans

In a large saucepan fry meat in hot fat and drain. Combine remaining ingredients. Simmer slowly for 3 to 4 hours. Serves 6.

Steak Soup

½ cup butter
½ cup flour
4 ten-ounce cans beef consommé
½ cup diced carrots
½ cup diced celery
½ cup diced onion
1 eight-ounce can tomatoes, chopped
1½ teaspoons Kitchen Bouquet
2 beef broth cubes
½ teaspoon pepper
1 teaspoon Accent
1 ten-ounce package frozen mixed vegetables
1 pound beef steak, cubed and browned

Melt butter in large saucepan. Add flour and stir until smooth. Cook over medium heat without browning for 3 minutes, stirring constantly. Add consommé and beef broth cubes, cook until slightly thickened. Bring to full boil, add fresh vegetables, seasonings, and tomatoes. Bring to boil, reduce heat, and simmer 30 minutes. Add remaining ingredients and simmer 15 minutes. Serves 8.

Sausage Soup

½ pound bulk sausage
1 cup chopped onion
1 can tomatoes (2 pounds, 3 ounces)
3½ cups chicken broth
1 teaspoon dried basil
½ cup macaroni, uncooked
¼ teaspoon salt

Cook sausage until done, breaking up meat as it cooks with spoon; add onions and sauté until soft; add rest of ingredients; boil; lower heat and simmer for about 20 minutes or until tender. Taste and adjust seasoning if necessary. Serves 8.

Slow Cooker Soup

1 to 2 pounds stew beef, cut in 1" cubes

3 carrots, sliced

1 small onion, chopped

3 stalks celery, sliced or chopped

3 medium potatoes, cut in bite-sized chunks

1 ten-ounce package frozen peas or baby lima beans

1 quart tomato juice or 1 large can tomatoes

1 teaspoon salt

1/4 teaspoon pepper

1 bay leaf

1 clove garlic

1/4 teaspoon basil leaves, crushed

1/4 teaspoon rosemary leaves, crushed

1/8 teaspoon thyme leaves, crushed

1/2 teaspoon dried parsley flakes, crushed

water

Trim fat from meat. Combine all ingredients in 3½-quart crockery slow cooker and mix thoroughly. Add water until liquid almost reaches top of pot. Cover and cook on low 12 hours or high 5-6 hours. Serves 6 to 8.

Pacific Chowder

4 slices bacon

1/4 cup chopped onion

2 tablespoons chopped green pepper

1 can frozen condensed cream of potato soup

2 cups milk

1 can tuna fish (6½ or 7 ounces), drained

Cook bacon till crisp. Drain, reserving 2 tablespoons drippings. Cook onion and green pepper in reserved drippings. Cook onion and green pepper until tender but not brown. Add soup and milk; heat just to boiling. Break tuna in chunks and crumble bacon; add. Heat. Dash with paprika or mace. Serves 4.

Clam Chowder

¹/₂ cup diced ham or bacon

1 medium onion, diced

2 eight-ounce cans minced clams, drained to reserve liquid

3 tablespoons cornstarch

4 large potatoes, diced (about 4 cups)

1 tablespoon salt

¹/₄ cup chopped celery

¹/₄ teaspoon pepper

4 cups milk

2 tablespoons butter or margarine

In large saucepan or Dutch oven cook ham or bacon over medium heat until lightly browned. Add onions and celery and cook until tender, about 5 minutes. Add enough water to clam liquid to make 2 cups. Mix cornstarch in the clam and water liquid. Add potatoes and clam liquid to onion and celery mixture, stirring constantly until mixture is slightly thickened. Cover and cook about 10 minutes. Add clams, milk, and butter. Cover and cook until heated through, about 5 minutes more, stirring occasionally. Serves 6 main dish servings or 12 first course servings.

Oyster Soup

1 pint oysters

2 cups milk

sprig of parsley

¹/₂ bay leaf

1 slice onion

2¹/₂ tablespoons butter

1¹/₂ tablespoons flour

salt to taste

Remove any bits of shell from oysters. Strain oyster liquid through cheesecloth. Cook in liquid until edges curl, 3 to 5 minutes. Scald milk with parsley, bay leaf, onion. Strain. Melt butter, add flour, add milk. Cook till thick. Combine with oysters, and heat; season and serve immediately. Put butter in soup dishes or soup tureen, about 1 teaspoon in each bowl, then pour soup. Serves 4.

Salmon Chowder

6 medium potatoes, cut into ½″ cubes
1 cup sliced carrots
3 teaspoons salt
3 cups water
1 ten-ounce package frozen peas
⅓ cup butter
⅓ cup chopped onion
¼ cup flour
1 cup thinly sliced celery
5 cups milk
1 one-pound can red salmon, skin and bone removed
½ teaspoon Worcestershire sauce

Cook potatoes and carrots in salt and water. Add peas, bring to boil, cook 1 more minute. Do not drain, remove from heat. In a frying pan sauté onion in butter. Add flour, stir until smooth. Cook 1 minute. Add half of the milk, stirring constantly. Cook over low heat until mixture boils and thickens. Add to vegetables salmon, white sauce, celery, Worcestershire sauce, and remaining milk. Heat thoroughly. Serve at once. Serves 10 to 12.

Potato Soup

1 large potato, peeled and diced
1 small onion, diced
2 to 3 cups water
1 large egg
1 cup flour
1 quart milk
butter and green onions, if desired

Boil potato and onion in water until tender. Work flour into egg until crumbly. Mash potato and sprinkle egg mixture over boiling water with potatoes and onion in it. Boil 5 minutes and add milk. Bring to boiling and add salt and pepper to taste. Do not drain off water. Butter and green onions may be added if desired. Serve with home-made bread, crackers, and cheese. Serves 4 to 6.

Turkey Soup

bones from a leftover turkey

tops from celery stalks

handful of parsley

2 large potatoes, peeled and cut up

1 large onion

3 or 4 carrots

water

2 cups fine noodles, cooked and drained

salt to taste

nutmeg to taste

Remove all meat and dressing from the turkey bones. Put bones in a large soup kettle. Add all vegetables. Cover ingredients with water. Bring them to a boil and then simmer for 1½ hours. Remove bones. Run soup through a colander, until all vegetables are well strained. Heat soup and add cooked noodles. Season with salt and nutmeg. Makes 4 to 5 quarts. Serves 12.

Delicious Bean Soup

2 cups navy beans

2 stalks chopped celery

1 onion, chopped

1 package dry onion soup mix

2 beef bouillon cubes

2 teaspoons Worcestershire sauce

3 teaspoons molasses or sorghum

8 cups water

¼ teaspoon salt

½ teaspoon sugar

2 cooked, smoked ham hocks

dash paprika

Wash beans and drain well. Mix all ingredients together in large pot or kettle. Let simmer all day, stirring and adding more water if necessary. Serves 6.

Vegetable Soup

1½- to 2-pound round steak; trim fat, cut into 1″ cubes, brown and drain
4 carrots, sliced in circles
3 or 4 potatoes, quartered and cut up
1 sixteen-ounce can green beans
1 sixteen-ounce can stewed tomatoes
1 beef bouillon cube
2 stalks celery, cut in circles
salt to taste
2 to 3 cups water
Optional:
fresh canned green beans and tomatoes
½ head cabbage, quartered

Put all ingredients into slow cooker. Stir to mix well. Cover and set control on low for 10 to 12 hours or high for 6 to 7 hours. "Serve with warm bread slices and tossed salad. It will make a nourishing and delicious meal."

Cream of Potato Soup

1 large potato, peeled and diced
1 large onion, thinly sliced
2 cups boiling water
2 slices bacon, cut in small pieces
3 cups evaporated milk
1½ teaspoons salt
⅛ teaspoon pepper
2 or 3 generous dashes of nutmeg

Add potato and onion to boiling water; cook covered, until vegetables are tender; mash mixture with a wooden or wire potato masher until smooth. Add bacon; simmer covered, 15 minutes longer. Add evaporated milk and seasonings; heat thoroughly, but do not boil. Serve with croutons. Serves 6.

Corn and Chicken Chowder

½ cup diced salt pork
1 medium onion, chopped
½ cup chopped celery
¼ cup green pepper, chopped
2 cups chicken broth
1 medium potato, cubed
1½ cups half-and-half
chopped parsley
½ bay leaf
¼ teaspoon paprika
½ teaspoon salt
3 tablespoons flour
½ cup milk
2 cups canned whole kernel corn
2 cups cooked diced chicken

Brown salt pork in skillet. Remove and reserve. In pork fat sauté onion, celery, and green pepper. Add chicken broth, potato, bay leaf, paprika, and salt. Simmer until potato is tender. Blend flour with milk. Add to soup. Boil 1 minute. Add corn, chicken, half-and-half, and reserved pork. Garnish with parsley. Serves 6.

SALADS & SALAD DRESSINGS

Seasoning with love...

It was in 1962 that Frank and I realized it was possible to reach out and touch many nations by opening our home to foreign students. Tuesday evenings we began having get-acquainted times, with fun and games followed by a Bible study. Some came to be in an American home; others to practice their English. There were those who had little knowledge of the Bible or Christianity, and they came to learn. We offered to pick up any who wanted to visit our church on Sunday mornings, with an invitation to Sunday dinner after church.

What a great privilege—exceptional people from many countries seated around our large table. The food and menu were never elaborate, but because we always asked our Heavenly Father's blessing on each guest before the meal, it was very special indeed!

—Frank and Nettie Rice
Oklahoma City, Okla.

Antipasto Salad for Four

1 head lettuce, cut up
chopped onion
1 can anchovies
sliced pepperoni
2 tomatoes, sliced
2 hard-cooked eggs, quartered
sweet cherry peppers
hot olives
sliced green pepper
grated Romano cheese to sprinkle over top

Combine ingredients in a salad bowl and top with grated cheese. Serve with salad dressing. Serves 4.

SALAD DRESSING

¾ cup olive oil
¼ cup wine vinegar
1 teaspoon salt
¼ teaspoon pepper
3 teaspoons paprika
½ teaspoon sugar
1 teaspoon lemon juice

Mix ingredients and pour over antipasto.

Mrs. Jenkins'*
Uncooked Cranberry Sauce

1 pound cranberries
2 cups sugar
¾ large orange (peeling and all)
⅛ teaspoon powdered cloves
pinch nutmeg
pinch salt

In electric blender put cut-up orange first, then add cranberries, sugar, and spices. Add 3 or 4 tablespoons of water. Use wooden spoon to push cranberries down in blender, blend well until chopped fine. Keep refrigerated in a covered jar. Will keep 3 or 4 months.

Mrs. Louise (Orville) Jenkins, Kansas City, Mo.

Cherry Relish Salad

1 No. 2 can red pie cherries
1/2 cup brown sugar
1/2" stick cinnamon
2 whole cloves
1/8 teaspoon grated nutmeg
1 three-ounce package cherry gelatin
1 cup boiling water
1/2 teaspoon salt

Simmer cherries, sugar, and spices for 20 minutes. Remove cinnamon and cloves and cool cherry mixture. Dissolve gelatin in boiling water. Add salt and chill until almost firm. Fold in cherry mixture. Pour into serving dish.

Mustard Dressing

2 tablespoons flour
4 tablespoons vinegar
4 tablespoons sugar
6 tablespoons cream
1 teaspoon mustard
1/2 teaspoon pepper
pinch salt

Cook, stirring constantly. When serving, thin with cream.

Strawberry Salad—1

1 cup boiling water
2 three-ounce packages strawberry gelatin
1 can crushed pineapple (1 pound, 4 ounce), drained
2 ten-ounce packages frozen strawberries
3 bananas, mashed
1 cup chopped walnuts
1 pint dairy sour cream

Dissolve gelatin in boiling water. Mix in strawberries, pineapple, bananas, and nuts. Pour half of the mixture into a 13″ x 9″ pan. Chill until firm. Spread with sour cream, cover with remaining gelatin mixture. Chill.

Strawberry Salad—2

1 can crushed pineapple (13¼ ounce), reserve juice
2 ten-ounce packages frozen strawberries
1 cup miniature marshmallows
1 cup heavy cream, whipped
2 beaten eggs
½ cup sugar
⅛ teaspoon salt
2 tablespoons lemon juice—fresh, frozen, or bottled
1 three-ounce package strawberry gelatin, prepared and partially jelled
water

Drain pineapple, reserving the juice and adding water if needed to make ½ cup. Combine eggs, sugar, salt, lemon juice, and pineapple juice in saucepan. Cook over low heat until thick, stirring constantly. Chill. Fold in drained pineapple, strawberries and their juice, marshmallows, whipped cream, and partially set gelatin. Pour into a 2-quart casserole and cut into squares. Serve on lettuce cups. Serves 10 to 12.

Orange Perfection Salad

1 cup boiling water
1 three-ounce package lemon gelatin
2 tablespoons sugar
¼ teaspoon salt
½ cup orange juice
1 tablespoon vinegar
1 orange, sectioned and diced
1 cup shredded cabbage
¼ cup finely chopped celery

Dissolve gelatin, sugar, and salt in 1 cup boiling water. Add ½ cup cold water, the orange juice, and vinegar; chill until partially set. Fold in remaining ingredients; turn into 3-cup mold. Chill until set; unmold. Trim with lettuce and an orange twist, if desired. Serves 6.

Frozen Fruit Salad—1

1 three-ounce package cream cheese, softened
⅓ cup mayonnaise
1 teaspoon lemon juice
2 egg whites, beaten
⅓ cup sugar
1 cup heavy cream, whipped
6 large marshmallows, cut up
¼ cup mandarin oranges, drained
1 sixteen-ounce can fruit cocktail, drained
2 tablespoons chopped maraschino cherries
1 tablespoon chopped walnuts

Blend together cheese, mayonnaise, lemon juice. Beat in sugar to beaten egg whites a tablespoon at a time, beat until it forms stiff peaks. Fold whipped cream into egg whites. Fold in cheese mixture. Gently blend in the remaining ingredients. Pour into 8″ square pan. Freeze. Serves 6 to 8.

Frozen Fruit Salad—2

1 three-ounce package cream cheese
2 tablespoons cream
½ cup mayonnaise or salad dressing
2 tablespoons lemon juice
⅛ teaspoon salt
2 tablespoons sugar
1 cup canned pineapple tidbits
1 cup diced orange sections
¼ cup chopped maraschino cherries
¾ cup quartered and pitted Royal Anne cherries
½ cup chopped pecans
1 cup heavy cream, whipped

Prepare up to 6 weeks ahead: Blend cream cheese with 2 tablespoons cream; add mayonnaise, lemon juice, salt, and sugar. Drain fruit well. Combine with next 5 ingredients; fold in whipped cream. Pour into freezer mold or containers, cover tightly, then place level in freezer. To serve: Remove salad from container by dipping in and out of warm water and turning onto plate. May be garnished with salad greens, fresh strawberries, or nut halves. Serves 6.

Texas-Style Molded Cherry Salad

1 sixteen-ounce can dark sweet cherries
1 nine-ounce can crushed pineapple
cola soft drink
1 three-ounce package cherry gelatin
1 three-ounce package cream cheese

Reserve the juice from the cherries and pineapple. Add enough cola drink to the fruit juices to equal 2 cups. In a bowl dissolve gelatin in the boiling 2 cups of fruit-cola liquid. Crumble cream cheese over gelatin. Chill until partially set. Fold in the pineapple and the cherries that have been stuffed with pecans. Place in an 8″ square pan. Chill and serve on greens with salad dressing.

Favorite Perfection Salad

½ cup sugar
2 envelopes unflavored gelatin
1 teaspoon salt
½ cup cider vinegar
2 tablespoons lemon juice
1½ cups finely shredded cabbage
⅔ cup diced celery
1 four-ounce can pimientos, drained and diced
celery leaves for garnish
mayonnaise (optional)

Early in day: In small saucepan over low heat, stir sugar, gelatin, salt, and 1 cup water until gelatin is dissolved. Remove from heat and stir in vinegar, lemon juice, and 1½ cups water. Pour into large bowl and refrigerate until mixture is the consistency of unbeaten egg white. Then add cabbage, celery, and pimientos. Pour into mold. Chill until firm.

Aunt Kate's Salad

1 cup coffee cream or evaporated milk, undiluted
1 cup sour cream
1 tablespoon butter
juice of one lemon
1 tablespoon flour
1 ten-and-one-half-ounce package miniature marshmallows
1 No. 303 can pineapple tidbits, well-drained
1 cup walnut meats, not chopped

Cook cream, sour cream, butter, lemon juice, and flour in top of double boiler until mixture starts to boil. Add marshmallows. Cook until marshmallows are dissolved, stirring constantly. Add pineapple and nutmeats. Place in bowl and refrigerate overnight. Serves 8.

Frozen Strawberry Salad

½ pound marshmallows
2 tablespoons milk
1 cup crushed strawberries, fresh or frozen
1 cup crushed pineapple, well drained
1 three-ounce package cream cheese
½ cup mayonnaise
1 cup whipping cream, whipped

Melt marshmallows in milk in top of double boiler. Cool. Add fruits. Mash cheese with a fork, blending until creamy. Blend mayonnaise and whipped cream with cheese. Fold into fruit-marshmallow mixture. Pour into refrigerator tray and freeze until firm. Serve in slices on lettuce. Serves 8 or 10.

Double Cheese Frozen Fruit Salad

5 ounces cream cheese, softened
½ cup mayonnaise
1 teaspoon lemon juice
2 egg whites
⅓ cup sugar
1 cup whipped topping
½ cup small marshmallows
½ cup mandarin oranges, drained
½ cup crushed pineapple, drained
½ cup grated cheddar cheese
½ cup chopped pecans

Blend together cream cheese, mayonnaise, lemon juice, and whipped topping. Beat eggs until fluffy, add sugar, whip 1 minute. Stir in cream cheese mixture and remaining ingredients. Mix well. Wash and dry one large can, leaving one end connected. Fill can. Freeze overnight. Thaw 10 minutes before serving. Open bottom with electric can opener and use to push salad through. Slice 1″ thick, serve on lettuce leaf.

Janet's Caraway Cole Slaw

3 cups finely shredded cabbage

1 teaspoon minced onion

2 teaspoons caraway seeds

3/4 cup mayonnaise

1/2 teaspoon salt

1/8 teaspoon pepper

1 tablespoon lemon juice

1/2 cup diced green pepper

1/2 cup thinly sliced carrots

Combine shredded cabbage, minced onion, and caraway seeds. Combine mayonnaise, salt, pepper, and lemon juice. Let stand while preparing green pepper and carrots. Add mayonnaise mixture, green pepper, and carrots to cabbage. Toss thoroughly. Chill in the refrigerator at least 1 hour before serving. Serves 6.

Hot Potato Salad

4 medium potatoes (4 cups sliced)

8 slices bacon, diced

1/4 cup chopped onion

1 tablespoon flour

1 tablespoon sugar

1 1/2 teaspoons salt

1/2 teaspoon pepper

1/3 cup vinegar

1/4 cup water

3 boiled eggs, sliced

1 tablespoon chopped parsley

1/2 teaspoon celery seed

Cook potatoes in jackets until tender; peel and slice. Fry bacon crisp, add onion; cook 1 minute. Blend in flour, sugar, salt, and pepper; add vinegar and water and cook until thick. Pour mixture over hot potatoes, add eggs, mix. Sprinkle with parsley and celery seed. Serve warm. Serves 6.

Fresh Spinach Salad

1 ten-ounce package fresh spinach

1/2 teaspoon salt

1 1/2 teaspoons vinegar

1/2 teaspoon Tabasco sauce

3/4 cup finely chopped celery

1/4 cup finely chopped onion

3 hard-cooked eggs, chopped

3/4 cup diced sharp cheese

1/3 to 1/2 cup mayonnaise

2 tablespoons horseradish

Wash spinach and remove stems, chop. To chop in blender, place half of spinach loosely in container, cover with cold water, process at "chop" two seconds. Repeat. Drain in colander, squeeze to remove all water. Use this method to finely chop celery and onion. Drain well. Sprinkle spinach with salt. Blend vinegar and Tabasco sauce. Mix with spinach. Add celery, onion, chopped eggs, and cheese. Blend in mayonnaise, stirring until well coated. Serve on lettuce leaf with chopped egg and horseradish. Serves 6 or 8.

Poppy Seed Salad Dressing

3/4 cup sugar

1 teaspoon dry mustard

1 teaspoon salt

1/3 cup white vinegar

1 1/2 tablespoons onion juice

1 cup salad oil

1 1/2 teaspoons poppy seeds

Mix first four ingredients. Add onion juice, slowly add salad oil; beat, then add poppy seeds as the last ingredient. Mix well before serving.

Asparagus Salad

wedges of lettuce

cooked asparagus

tomato wedges

avocado slices

3 hard-cooked eggs, sliced

Arrange on salad plates. Cover with the following dressing.

DRESSING

½ cup mayonnaise

1 cup dairy sour cream

2 tablespoons oil

2 tablespoons wine vinegar

2 teaspoons of tarragon vinegar

1 clove garlic, crushed

dash chives and parsley

Blend together thoroughly.

Mandarin Orange Molded Salad

2 eleven-ounce cans mandarin oranges, drain and reserve syrup

2 three-ounce packages of orange gelatin

1 pint orange sherbet

1 thirteen-ounce can crushed pineapple

Dissolve gelatin in boiling 1½ cups liquid (reserved orange syrup and remainder water). Add orange sherbet and stir until melted. Chill until it is slightly set, then add orange sections and pineapple. Place in a 2-quart tube-type mold. Chill. Before serving fill the center and arrange the edge of the salad with a mixture of fresh fruits. Serves 8 to 10. "I use fresh strawberries, pineapple chunks, mandarin orange slices, flaked coconut, sour cream, and miniature marshmallows."

Seven-Layer Salad

6 cups chopped iceburg lettuce
¼ cup sliced green onion
salt (to taste)
Lawry's seasoned pepper (to taste)
1 tablespoon sugar
6 hard-cooked eggs, sliced
1 ten-ounce package frozen peas, thawed
1 four-ounce can water chestnuts
1 pound bacon, cooked crisp, drained, crumbled
2 cups shredded natural baby Swiss cheese
1½ cups mayonnaise
cheddar cheese
American cheese
green grapes

Put three cups lettuce in bottom of a large salad bowl. Add layer of ¼ cup green onions. Sprinkle with salt, pepper, and sugar. Add layer of eggs; sprinkle with salt again. Add in layers the thawed, uncooked peas, water chestnuts, remaining 3 cups of lettuce, bacon, and Swiss cheese. Seal salad with mayonnaise. Cover and refrigerate for 24 hours. Before serving, garnish with cheddar and American cheese and green grapes when available. Salad may be served layered or tossed as desired. Serves 20 as an accompaniment, 8 to 12 as luncheon dish.

Purple Lady Salad

1 six-ounce package raspberry gelatin
1 cup boiling water
1 one-pound can blueberries with syrup
1 small can crushed pineapple, not drained
1 cup chopped pecans
½ cup heavy cream, whipped

Dissolve gelatin in boiling water, add blueberries and syrup, and pineapple. Refrigerate until almost set. Add pecans. Fold in whipped cream. Pour into mold. Chill. Serves 8 to 10.

24-Hour Salad

3 beaten egg yolks
2 tablespoons sugar
2 tablespoons vinegar
2 tablespoons pineapple syrup
1 tablespoon butter
dash salt
2 cups drained pitted white cherries
2 cups drained pineapple tidbits
2 oranges, peeled and sectioned, cut in pieces
2 cups quartered marshmallows or use miniature
1 cup heavy cream, whipped

Beat yolks, add sugar, vinegar, pineapple juice, butter, and salt in top of double boiler. Cook over hot (not boiling) water until thick, stirring constantly. Cool. Add whipped cream to dressing, fold in marshmallows and fruits that have been well drained. Chill 24 hours. Add nuts over top. Serves 8 or 10.

Gooseberry Molded Salad

2 cups sweetened gooseberries, fresh or canned
2 three-ounce packages lemon gelatin
1/2 cup sugar
2 cups orange juice
2 cups chopped celery
1/2 cup chopped nuts
water

Drain gooseberries and reserve syrup. Add enough water to syrup to make 1¾ cups. Heat 1 cup syrup mixture to boiling. Add gelatin and sugar. Dissolve. Add remaining syrup mixture and orange juice. Chill until partially set. Add celery, nuts, and gooseberries. Place in a 10″ x 6″ x 1½″ dish or in a mold. If using fancy mold, reduce liquid slightly. Chill. Serves 8.

Sesame Seed Salad Dressing

1 tablespoon butter

¹/₂ cup sesame seeds

¹/₄ cup grated Parmesan cheese

¹/₂ cup mayonnaise

1 cup sour cream

1 tablespoon tarragon vinegar

1 tablespoon sugar

¹/₄ cup green pepper, chopped

2 tablespoons onion, chopped

³/₄ teaspoon salt

¹/₄ teaspoon garlic salt

salad greens

Melt butter. Add sesame seeds. Cook over moderately low heat, stirring until sesame seeds are lightly browned. Cool at room temperature. Add cheese, mixing well. Combine mayonnaise, sour cream, vinegar, sugar, pepper, onions, and salts, mixing well. Toss any mixed green salad with as much dressing as desired and about three-fourths of the sesame seed mixture. Sprinkle remaining sesame seed mixture over the top of the salad.

Creamy Italian Dressing

¹/₂ cup mayonnaise

¹/₂ cup sour cream

¹/₄ teaspoon oregano

¹/₈ teaspoon garlic powder

¹/₈ teaspoon white pepper

¹/₄ teaspoon dry mustard

¹/₂ teaspoon chives

¹/₂ teaspoon parsley flakes

1 teaspoon minced onion

¹/₂ teaspoon sugar

Mix all the ingredients and chill for about 2 hours. About 70 calories per tablespoon.

Molded Chicken Salad

4 tablespoons gelatin

1 cup cold water

3 cups hot chicken broth

2 cups mayonnaise

2 cups diced celery

1 cup chopped pimiento

4 cups coarsely diced chicken

¾ cup sliced, stuffed olives

1 teaspoon grated onion

salt and pepper to taste

Soak gelatin in water. Dissolve in hot chicken broth. Cool to room temperature. Stir in mayonnaise. Stir in celery, pimiento, chicken, olives, onion, salt, and pepper. Pour into an oiled 13″ x 9″ x 2″ pan. Chill until firm. Serves 20.

24-Hour Slaw

1 large head cabbage (about 2 pounds), coarsely shredded

2 medium-sized onions, chopped

2 green peppers, grated

14 tablespoons sugar

½ cup vinegar

1 cup vegetable oil

1 tablespoon dry mustard

1 teaspoon salt

1 teaspoon celery seed

Mix the cabbage, onions, and green pepper together. In a large container spread a layer of the vegetable mixture. Sprinkle 2 tablespoons sugar over it. Add another layer of the vegetable mixture and the same amount of sugar until all of the vegetable mixture has been used, about four layers. Add remaining sugar. Mix the vinegar, oil, mustard, salt, and celery seed together and bring to a boil. Pour over the vegetable mixture and stir well. Cover. Refrigerate for at least 24 hours. Serves 15 to 20.

Creamy Frozen Salad

2 cups dairy sour cream
2 tablespoons lemon juice
3/4 cup sugar
1/8 teaspoon salt
1 can crushed pineapple (8 1/2 ounce), drained
1/4 cup maraschino cherries, sliced
1 banana, sliced
1/4 cup chopped pecans

Blend together sour cream, lemon juice, sugar, and salt. Stir in pine-apple, cherries, banana, and pecans. Pour into 1-quart mold or paper-lined muffin pan. Cover and freeze. Thaw 15 minutes at room temperature. Serve at once. Serves 8.

Wilma's* Blue Cheese Dressing for Tossed Salad

2 cups mayonnaise
1 cup dairy sour cream
3/4 cup buttermilk
1/2 teaspoon Accent
1/2 teaspoon salt
1/4 teaspoon sugar
1 tablespoon fresh lemon juice
1/2 teaspoon white pepper
4 ounces blue cheese

In a large bowl of an electric mixer add all the ingredients except the blue cheese. Mix at medium speed for 5 minutes. Crumble in blue cheese, blend slightly. Chill five days before serving, for flavors to blend well. Thin with half-and-half if too thick. Makes 1 quart.

*The "Wilma" cited in this recipe and others is Wilma Lloyd of Littleton, Colo., sister of Mrs. Benner.

Yum-yum Salad

1 three-ounce package cherry gelatin
1 three-ounce package lime gelatin
1 three-ounce package lemon gelatin
1 cup miniature marshmallows
1 cup cream, whipped
1 three-ounce package cream cheese
1 cup salad dressing or mayonnaise
1 small can crushed pineapple, not drained

Prepare lime gelatin according to package directions. Pour into a 9″ x 13″ x 2″ glass baking dish. Allow to congeal completely. Dissolve lemon gelatin in 1 cup boiling water. While hot, dissolve marshmallows in it. Whip in softened cream cheese and salad dressing. Add pineapple. Fold in whipped cream. Spread on top of green layer and allow to congeal completely. Prepare cherry gelatin according to package directions. Pour on top of yellow layer and let congeal overnight. Serves 12.

Cherry Salad Supreme

1 three-ounce package raspberry gelatin
1 twenty-one-ounce can cherry pie filling
1 three-ounce package lemon gelatin
1 three-ounce package cream cheese
⅓ cup mayonnaise
½ cup whipping cream
1 cup miniature marshmallows
1 can crushed pineapple (8¼ ounce)

Dissolve raspberry gelatin in 1 cup boiling water; stir in pie filling. Pour into 9″ square pan. Chill till partially set. Dissolve lemon gelatin in 1 cup boiling water in small mixing bowl. Add cheese and mayonnaise; beat at low speed. Chill until partially set; then beat until light. Whip cream. Fold whipped cream, undrained pineapple, and marshmallows into whipped gelatin. Spread on cherry layer. Chill at least 4 hours or overnight. Serves 9 to 12.

Frozen Pineapple Dessert Salad

| 1 eight-ounce package cream cheese, softened |
| 1 cup mayonnaise |
| 1 can pineapple tidbits (20½ ounce), drained |
| ½ cup chopped walnuts |
| ¾ cup maraschino cherries, chopped |
| 1 cup heavy cream, whipped |

Combine cream cheese with mayonnaise in medium bowl; beat with mixer until smooth. Add pineapple, walnuts, and cherries; then stir until well mixed. Beat cream in small bowl just until stiff enough to hold its shape. Gently fold into cream cheese mixture until well combined. Turn mixture into 1½-quart ring mold that has been rinsed with cold water. Freeze.

Raspberry-Cranberry Salad

| 2 three-ounce packages raspberry gelatin |
| 1 sixteen-ounce can whole cranberry sauce |
| 1 can crushed pineapple (8½ ounce), undrained |
| ½ cup water |
| ⅓ cup chopped walnuts |
| orange and grapefruit sections |

Dissolve gelatin in two cups of boiling water. Stir in cranberry sauce, undrained pineapple, and water. Chill until partially set. Stir in nuts. Pour into 6-cup mold. Chill until firm. At serving time, surround mold with orange and grapefruit sections.

Jellied Cranberry Salad

| 1 tablespoon lemon juice |
| 1 three-ounce package cherry gelatin |
| 1 cup hot water |
| 1 cup crushed pineapple |
| 1 ten-ounce package frozen cranberry relish, thawed |
| ⅓ cup diced celery |

Dissolve gelatin in hot water. Drain pineapple, reserving syrup. Add water to syrup to make ¾ cup, add to gelatin along with relish. Chill till partially set. Stir in pineapple and celery. Put in six small molds or in 1-quart mold. "Especially nice served with chicken or turkey."

Cranberry Salad

1 pound raw cranberries
2½ cups sugar
1 cup pecans
1 cup seeded grapes, quartered
8 large marshmallows, cut in pieces, or 1 cup miniature marshmallows
1 pint whipping cream, whipped

Grind cranberries; add sugar and let stand several hours or overnight. Add nuts, grapes, and marshmallows to cranberries. Fold whipped cream into cranberry mixture. Freezes well. Serves 12.

Raspberry Molded Salad

1 three-ounce package raspberry gelatin
1 three-ounce package lemon gelatin
2 cups hot water
1 package frozen raspberries
1 regular size can applesauce (approximately 16 ounces)
1 regular size can crushed pineapple, drained (approximately 16 ounces)
desired topping of mayonnaise or sour cream

Dissolve gelatin with hot water. Add thawed raspberries with juice, applesauce, and the drained pineapple. The raspberry juice and the moisture in the other fruits provide remaining liquid needed for gelatin. Stir gelatin and fruit mixture and refrigerate. When molded, serve with topping of mayonnaise or sour cream. Flavor topping with lemon juice to taste. This mold has a pleasing texture, heavy and smooth, with a sweet-tart taste. Serves 6 to 8.

Caesar's Salad

1 bud fresh garlic
1 anchovy fillet
salt
¼ cup olive oil
¼ cup corn oil
3 long dashes of wine vinegar
½ fresh lemon, squeezed
4 long dashes of Worcestershire sauce
3 turns of coarsely ground pepper
3 shakes of red hot pepper sauce
coddled egg
Romano and Parmesan cheese
romaine lettuce

Crush garlic into a wooden salad bowl. Add anchovy fillet and crush until smooth. Add next 8 ingredients. Blend thoroughly. In a separate bowl, blend romaine lettuce with coddled egg and some Parmesan cheese. Transfer to bowl containing dressing and mix, adding some Romano cheese. Serves 8.

Reception Salad

1 three-ounce package lemon gelatin
1 large can crushed pineapple, drain and reserve syrup
2 small packages cream cheese
small jar of pimientos (mashed with the cream cheese)
½ cup chopped celery
⅔ cup nuts (any kind except peanuts)
½ pint whipped cream
pinch of salt

Mix gelatin with boiling pineapple syrup. When it begins to jell, add the crushed drained pineapple and the cream cheese that has been mashed with a small jar of pimientos. Then add the celery, nuts, whipped cream, and salt. Let stand in refrigerator until set. Serve on lettuce leaf.

Frozen Pineapple Salad

1 cup heavy cream, whipped

1 twelve-ounce package dairy sour cream

1 tablespoon lemon juice

³/₄ cup sugar

¹/₈ teaspoon salt

1 nine-ounce can crushed pineapple, drained

¹/₃ cup maraschino cherries, chopped

¹/₄ cup chopped walnuts

2 bananas, sliced

Fold sour cream into whipped cream. Add lemon juice, sugar, and salt. Gently fold in remaining ingredients. Spoon into a 9″ square pan. Freeze.

Roquefort Cream Dressing

¹/₃ cup Roquefort cheese, crumbled

1 tablespoon minced onion

¹/₂ clove garlic, minced

¹/₂ cup mayonnaise

¹/₂ cup sour cream

1 tablespoon lemon juice

1 tablespoon vinegar

dash pepper

Mix all ingredients with an electric mixer for 4 minutes or until smooth. Makes 1¹/₂ cups dressing.

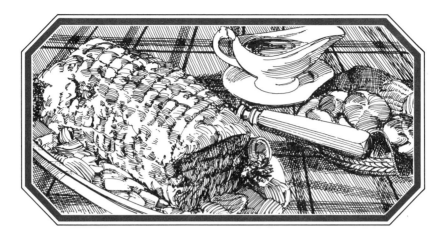

MEAT AND MAIN DISHES

Seasoning with love...

While we were in Lincoln, Nebr., where my husband was assigned to Lincoln Air Force Base, we invited a captain and his wife to Sunday dinner. They attended the morning worship service in which Dr. Ralph Earle, who was also our dinner guest, was the revival speaker. Over dinner our friends had opportunity to ask questions of Dr. Earle and to learn more about the plan of salvation. That night at the end of Dr. Earle's sermon, they both accepted the Lord.

Captain Morris was transferred and assigned to a B-52 wing. Shortly after this assignment, the B-52 he was flying crashed and all aboard were killed. We were so thankful for the opportunity we had been given to minister through hospitality, to know that he had accepted the Lord and was prepared for death.

—Edna Minor
Olathe, Kans.

Roast Sirloin Tip

4 to 5 pounds sirloin tip
¼ cup melted butter
2 teaspoons salt
1 teaspoon coarsely ground pepper
½ cup coarsely chopped onions
½ cup coarsely diced celery
1 cup water

Heat oven to 450°. Place meat on rack in shallow pan. Brush with melted butter. Sprinkle with salt and pepper. Roast for 25 minutes or until browned on all sides. Reduce oven to 375°. Add vegetables. Continue to roast, allowing a total time of 25 minutes per pound. Remove roast from pan for 15 minutes. Meanwhile pour off fat from pan and place over high heat. Add water and bring to boil. Strain and serve with roast. Or after straining liquid, add 3 tablespoons flour and 1 more cup water, cook until thick. Season to taste. Serves 8.

Standing Rib Roast of Beef

Season meat with salt and pepper. Place in open roaster, fat side up. If you have a roast-meat thermometer, make hole in center of roast with metal skewer; insert thermometer so bulb reaches center of roast but does not rest on fat or bone. Roast, using either of the following methods:

For an even color all through: Roast in moderate oven (325°) until done, using these time periods as a guide: 18-20 minutes per pound for rare; 22-25 minutes per pound for medium; 27-30 minutes per pound for well done.

For extra crispness and brownness outside with rarer slices at the center: Using same time periods as above, put roast into hot oven (500°); roast 15 minutes. Reduce heat to moderate (325°) for remaining time.

The trick lies in moderate temperature, which makes it possible to use an open roaster and eliminate the need of water. Basting is unnecessary if the meat is placed in the roaster fat side up. This way it bastes itself and has more flavor. A hot oven for the entire cooking period dries meat, shrinks it, and makes it stringy.

Not Just Steak

3 pounds beef tenderloin, cut into 6 steaks
2 cloves garlic
2 tablespoons clarified butter
salt and pepper to taste
½ pound fresh mushrooms
3 tablespoons butter
½ cup catsup
¾ cup beef broth
6 slices of white bread
⅓ pound liverwurst
2 tablespoons chopped parsley

Place clarified butter in pan and rub pan with 1 clove of garlic. Discard clove. Sear steaks on both sides, turning with tongs. Salt and pepper to taste. Remove steaks from pan. Place in a 140° oven to keep warm. Wash and slice mushrooms. Place them in same pan with one crushed clove of garlic. Add 3 tablespoons butter and simmer until mushrooms are lightly sautéed. Add catsup and let simmer while constantly stirring for 5 minutes. Add beef broth and simmer gently until sauce thickens. If sauce still appears thin, add a little arrowroot to thicken.

Cut rounds the size of the steaks out of bread slices. Toast, butter, and spread generously with liverwurst. Place steaks on top of liverwurst. Pour sauce over all and sprinkle with parsley before serving. Serves 6.

Chicken Fried Steak

2 pounds round steak ½" thick, pounded and cut into serving pieces
2 eggs, beaten
2 tablespoons milk
1 cup crushed soda crackers
¼ cup fat

Mix together egg and milk. Dip meat slices into egg mixture and crackers. Brown steak in hot fat on low heat. Season with salt and pepper. Cover skillet tightly. Bake at 300° for 1½ hours. Serves 6.

California Steak

| ¼ cup enriched flour |
| 1 teaspoon salt |
| ¼ teaspoon pepper |
| 2 pounds round steak, about ¾″ thick |
| 2 tablespoons fat |
| 1 medium onion, thinly sliced |
| 1 can condensed beef broth |
| ½ cup water |
| ½ cup dairy sour cream or evaporated milk |
| 2 tablespoons enriched flour |
| poppy-seed noodles |

Combine ¼ cup flour, the salt, and pepper. Cut meat into 6 serving pieces and dredge in flour mixture; brown in hot fat. Add onion slices, beef broth, and water. Cover and simmer 1 hour or until tender. Remove steak and onions to serving platter. Blend sour cream and 2 tablespoons flour. Remove broth from heat and add sour cream mixture; stir to blend. Cook, stirring constantly, just until gravy thickens. Serve with poppy-seed noodles: Cook 4 ounces (2 cups) medium noodles in boiling salted water until tender; drain. Add 2 tablespoons butter or margarine and 2 tablespoons poppy seeds; toss. Serves 6.

Minute Steak Scramble

| 4 cube steaks, cut in julienne strips |
| ¼ teaspoon garlic salt |
| ¼ teaspoon ginger |
| ¼ cup salad oil |
| 2 green peppers, cut in julienne strips |
| 1 cup bias-cut celery slices |
| 1 tablespoon cornstarch |
| ¼ cup cold water |
| 3 tablespoons soy sauce |
| 2 tomatoes, peeled and cut in eighths |

Season meat with garlic salt and ginger. Heat half of oil in skillet; add meat and brown quickly on all sides. Remove meat. Add remaining oil; heat. Add peppers and celery; cook just until slightly tender (about 3 minutes). Mix cornstarch, water, and soy sauce. Add to skillet; cook and stir until mixture thickens. Add meat and tomatoes; heat. Serve with hot rice. Provide soy sauce. Serves 4.

Beef Stroganoff

¼ cup flour
1½ teaspoons salt
¼ teaspoon pepper
1 pound sirloin steak (cut ¼" thick)
¼ cup butter, margarine, or salad oil
½ cup diced onion
¼ cup water
1 can undiluted cream of chicken soup
1 pound fresh mushrooms, sliced
1 cup sour cream
chopped parsley or dill

Combine flour, salt, and pepper. Pound seasoned flour into sirloin steak. Cut meat into strips 1½" x 1". Melt butter, margarine, or salad oil in deep fry pan and brown meat strips, turning frequently. Add diced onion, water, chicken soup, and mushrooms. Cook uncovered over low heat until mixture thickens and meat is tender (45 minutes to 1 hour). Just before serving, stir in sour cream. Transfer to serving dish and garnish with chopped parsley or dill. Serve over fluffy beds of rice. Serves 6.

Steamed Beef Brisket

6- to 10-pound beef brisket
2 tablespoons Liquid Smoke
3 tablespoons water
1 package dried onion soup mix

Wipe brisket dry and lay in a roasting pan. Pour Liquid Smoke and water in the bottom of pan. Spread onion soup mix over top of brisket. Tightly cover with foil. Bake at 250° for 5 hours.

Pepper Steak

1½ pounds round steak
2 tablespoons cooking oil
2 tablespoons vinegar
1 tablespoon sugar
2 green peppers, cut in chunks
salt and pepper to taste
½ cup beef broth
5 tablespoons soy sauce
1 cup water
1½ tablespoons cornstarch
2 tomatoes, cut in chunks
½ pound fresh mushrooms
1 large onion, cut in chunks
cooked rice

Cut steak in very thin strips; brown in oil. Add vinegar, sugar, soy sauce, and 1 cup water. Add beef broth. Cook over low heat 1 to 2 hours. Add green peppers, mushrooms, and onion. Cook 10 minutes. Blend in cornstarch. Add tomatoes. Cook 10 minutes longer. Serve over cooked rice. Serves 6.

Spanish Round Steak

1½ pounds round steak
¼ cup flour
1 teaspoon salt
2 teaspoons paprika
¼ teaspoon pepper
½ cup oil
2 cups sliced onions
1 one-pound can tomatoes, reserve juice

Combine flour and seasonings, and pound flour mixture into steak. Set aside flour. Heat oil in skillet and brown meat. Arrange in 1½-quart casserole dish. Add onions to skillet and sauté until golden brown, about 5 minutes. Pour onions and drained tomatoes over meat. Stir 1 tablespoon of reserved flour into skillet. Add reserved tomato juice, bring to a boil, stirring constantly. Pour over onions. Bake at 350° for 1 hour covered; then bake 1 hour uncovered. Serves 4. "I serve this with steamed rice, salad, and small whole mushrooms on the side. We like this very much for a company dish."

Swiss Steak

2 pounds round or Swiss steak
1/2 cup flour
3 tablespoons shortening
1 1/2 teaspoons salt
1/2 teaspoon pepper
1 clove garlic, crushed
1 medium-sized onion, sliced
1 teaspoon paprika
1 teaspoon onion salt
1 cup water

Cut steak into 6 pieces. Pound flour into each piece. Brown well in shortening over high heat. Season with salt and pepper. Add garlic and onion. Reduce heat to low and cook until onion slices are tender and brown. Remove from heat. Add paprika, onion salt, and water. Cover. Bake at 375° for about 2 hours or until meat is tender. Add additional water if necessary.

Marinated Chuck Roast

3 to 4 pounds boneless chuck roast
1/2 cup soy sauce
1/4 cup honey
1/2 teaspoon garlic powder

Combine soy sauce, honey, and garlic powder. Pour over roast and refrigerate for 12 hours. Drain meat and bring to room temperature. Place on a rack in a shallow pan. Bake at 425° to desired doneness. Cut in thin slices.

Savory Short Rib Dinner

3½ to 4 pounds beef short ribs
garlic salt
monosodium glutamate (Accent)
pepper
1 can (about 1¼ cups) condensed beef broth
whole carrots, pared
small to medium potatoes, pared
¼ cup all-purpose flour
salt and pepper

Sprinkle short ribs with garlic salt, monosodium glutamate, and pepper. Brown in a shallow pan in an extremely hot oven (500°) for about 15 minutes; pour off fat. Reduce oven temperature to 350°. Add beef broth to browned ribs; cover pan with lid or foil and cook for 1½ hours. Add carrots and potatoes; cover and cook 45 minutes to 1 hour longer or until meat and vegetables are tender. Pour off fat and meat juices. Skim off fat; measure ¼ cup into saucepan. Blend in flour; cook and stir until mixture is frothy. Add water to meat juices to make 2 cups. Stir into flour mixture; cook and stir until thickened. Season with salt and pepper to taste. Arrange meat and vegetables on platter; pass gravy. Serves 6.

To accompany short ribs: Mold a can of orange and grapefruit sections in lime gelatin, using fruit syrup for part of liquid; serve rye bread. For dessert, gingerbread topped with warm applesauce.

Crockpot Roast

2- to 3-pound arm or chuck roast
¼ cup flour
salt and pepper to taste
2 tablespoons cooking oil
½ cup beef broth
1½ cups water
1 package instant onion mushroom soup
4 medium potatoes (optional)
4 carrots (optional)

Cover roast with flour. Salt and pepper to taste and, using the cooking oil in a hot skillet, brown the roast. Remove, drain, and place in slow cooker. Cover with beef broth, water, and soup mixture. Peel potatoes and carrots and slice in half. Place in cooker. Cook on low heat 8 to 10 hours. To make gravy: Mix 2 tablespoons cornstarch with 1/4 cup cool water. Place in saucepan with 2 cups of juice from slow cooker. Bring to a boil and let simmer until it reaches desired thickness. Excellent when served on meat and potatoes.

Vegetable Pot Roast Au Jus

1 tablespoon meat drippings or salad oil
3-pound pot roast
1 1/2 teaspoons salt
dash cayenne pepper
dash pepper
1/2 green pepper
2 carrots
2 medium onions
1 clove garlic
3 tomatoes
2 stalks celery
few sprigs of parsley
2 small white turnips or parsnips

Heat drippings or salad oil in a Dutch oven or heavy skillet. Brown roast quickly on all sides. Sprinkle with salt, pepper, and cayenne pepper. Chop all vegetables in tiny pieces. Add to meat. Cook over very low heat, tightly covered, for 2 1/2 hours or until roast is tender when pierced with a fork. Stir vegetables occasionally, if desired, to keep from sticking to bottom of pan. Serve roast with unthickened vegetables—meat gravy spooned over light mashed potatoes. Serves 6.

Oven Barbecued Ribs

Sprinkle two slabs for 4, with salt, pepper, and garlic powder. Roast covered in 350° oven for 45 minutes. Drain and put ribs in shallow pan, cut into two rib sections, brush with barbecue sauce. Roast another 30 minutes, brushing with sauce every 10 minutes and turning ribs occasionally.

Roast Ribs of Pork Loin

Purchase rib half of a pork loin, about 6 pounds. Rub pork with salt and pepper. Place fat side up in a shallow roasting pan. Roast in a moderate oven, 350° for 30 to 35 minutes per pound or until meat thermometer inserted in center registers 185°. Glaze with sauce: 30 minutes before roast is done, drain drippings from roast. Spoon one-third of spicy barbecue sauce over meat. Roast 15 minutes and spoon on more sauce. Roast 15 minutes more. Decorate platter with crab apples, and serve remainder of sauce.

SPICY BARBECUE SAUCE

1 eight-ounce can tomato sauce
½ cup catsup
½ cup vinegar
½ cup brown sugar
1 teaspoon chili powder
¼ cup dark corn syrup
½ cup water
1 tablespoon cornstarch

Mix first 7 ingredients in a saucepan. Blend cornstarch with 2 table-spoons of mixture; stir into the rest. Cook over low heat until slightly thickened, stirring occasionally, about 15 minutes. This sauce will keep several days stored in a tightly covered jar in the refrigerator. This sauce is good over poultry and other meats. If doubled will make 2½ cups.

Butterfly Pork Chops

6 butterfly pork chops, 2″ thick
1 eight-ounce can tomato sauce
½ teaspoon onion salt
½ cup catsup
1 teaspoon Worchestershire sauce
1 teaspoon Liquid Smoke

Brown pork chops in skillet. Season with salt and pepper. Combine remaining ingredients and pour over chops. Bake at 350° for 1 hour, turning occasionally. Serves 6.

Sweet-and-sour Pork Chops

pork chops, 1" to 1¼" thick
¼ cup butter or margarine
1 cup brown sugar
¼ cup cornstarch
2 tablespoons soy sauce
1 tablespoon Worcestershire sauce
1 cup vinegar
3 cups pineapple juice
½ teaspoon salt
1 teaspoon Liquid Smoke (optional)
3 cups 7-Up

Cook sauce ingredients over low heat until clear and thickened, stirring constantly. If desired, add pineapple chunks, green pepper, thinly sliced onion, or tomato wedges the last 3 or 4 minutes. Prepare marinade by combining 1 cup of sauce (before adding fruit and vegetables) with 3 cups 7-Up. Pour marinade sauce over chops in large bowl, cover and chill several hours or overnight. Barbecue chops over medium-hot charcoal fire 10 to 12 minutes a side. Turn chops only once. They are done when center appears to be light gray color. Baste chops with sweet-n-sour sauce the last 4 or 5 minutes of broiling time. Heat remaining sauce and serve hot with chops.

Baked Pork Chops

4 to 6 lean pork chops, ½" thick
1 egg, beaten
salt
pepper
2 cups crushed cornflakes
6 tablespoons butter

Dip pork chops in egg seasoned with salt and pepper. Roll in cornflakes. Melt butter in baking dish, lay chops in dish. Dot with remainder of butter. Bake at 375° for 30 minutes, turning once during baking to brown both sides. Then bake at 350° for 1 hour. Serves 4 to 6.

Baked Lemon Pork Chops

4 loin pork chops, 1" thick
½ teaspoon salt
⅛ teaspoon pepper
1 cup flour
1½ teaspoons shortening
4 slices lemon
¼ cup catsup
½ cup water
1½ tablespoons brown sugar

Combine flour, salt, and pepper. Flour pork chops on both sides; brown in hot shortening. Set chops into roasting pan, placing lemon slices on top. Combine catsup, water, and brown sugar, and pour over pork chops. Cover pan. Bake at 325° for 60 minutes. Bake 30 minutes longer uncovered, or until tender.

Baked Stuffed Pork Chops

4 pork chops, 1½" thick
2 cups dry bread crumbs, ¼" cubes
½ cup finely chopped celery
⅓ cup minced onion
2 tablespoons parsley
½ teaspoon salt
¼ teaspoon pepper
¼ teaspoon poultry seasoning
2 tablespoons melted butter
¼ cup water

Flour pork chops and brown in skillet. Mix remaining ingredients in a bowl. Place in the bottom of a baking dish, cover with pork chops. Pour ½ cup water over chops. Bake at 325° for 1¼ hours or until done.

Barbecued Pork Chops

1/2 cup water

1/4 cup vinegar

2 tablespoons sugar

1 tablespoon prepared mustard

1 1/2 teaspoons salt

1/4 teaspoon pepper

1 slice lemon

1 medium onion, sliced

1/2 cup catsup

1 1/2 tablespoons Worcestershire sauce

2 teaspoons or more Liquid Smoke

4 or 6 rib pork chops, at least 1/2" thick

Mix water, vinegar, sugar, mustard, salt, pepper; add lemon and onion. Simmer 20 minutes; add catsup, Worcestershire sauce, and Liquid Smoke. Bring to boil. Put chops in shallow pan 11½" x 7½" x 1½". Pour sauce over. (Sauce may be made ahead and refrigerated.) Bake uncovered 350° for 1 hour and 15 minutes. If baked longer, cover with foil.

Stuffed Pork Chops

4 pork chops, 1½" thick

2 cups bread crumbs

4 tablespoons melted butter

1 small onion, minced

1 teaspoon Worcestershire sauce

salt and pepper to taste

Combine ingredients and stuff chops. Fasten with toothpicks and brown lightly. Cook in covered roaster with ½ cup water and 3 tablespoons tomato catsup for 45 minutes at 300°. Baste occasionally and add a little more water if needed.

Glazed Baked Pork Chops

1 cup apricot nectar

4 tablespoons Worcestershire sauce

½ tablespoon cornstarch

dash cinnamon

Bring to boil all ingredients. Brush over baked pork chops. Bake another 5 minutes. Makes 1¼ cups.

My Favorite Ham Loaf

½ cup brown sugar

2 tablespoons pineapple syrup

1⅛ cups spoon-sized pineapple cubes, drained

25 whole cloves

green pepper strips

1½ pounds ground ham

1 pound ground pork

¾ cup cracker crumbs

⅓ cup chopped onion

1 teaspoon dry mustard

2 beaten eggs

1 cup milk

Heat brown sugar and pineapple syrup, stirring until sugar is dissolved. Pour into greased, deep 6″ x 9½″ loaf pan. Arrange clove-studded pineapple cubes, clove side down, to form pineapple. Place green pepper strips shiny side down, to form leaves. Combine remaining ingredients; mix thoroughly. Press carefully but firmly over pineapple. Bake at 350° for 1¼ hours. Before serving, replace green pepper leaves with fresh strips. Serves 6 to 8. "May be made ahead of time in a bread loaf pan and baked before mealtime. Turn upside down after heating the loaf pan and bake like a roast. It will cut easily."

Upside-down Ham Loaf

3 tablespoons butter

3 slices pineapple, halved

1 pound lean smoked ham, ground

½ pound fresh lean pork, ground

¼ teaspoon pepper

2 eggs, beaten

¼ cup milk

2½ cups bread crumbs

5 tablespoons brown sugar

Melt butter in loaf pan and add sugar, stirring until dissolved. Add pineapple and sauté 5 minutes or until slightly browned. Mix meat with remaining ingredients. Spread in pan over pineapple sections and press down. Bake at 375° about 50 minutes. Turn out and serve with pineapple on top. Serves 8.

Ham Stroganoff

2 cups cool diced ham

2 tablespoons butter

½ cup chopped onion

⅓ cup sliced green pepper

1 four-ounce can sliced mushrooms

1 can cream of mushroom soup (10¾ ounce)

½ cup milk

½ cup sour cream

1 tablespoon Worcestershire sauce

Melt butter over low heat. Add onion and green pepper and brown lightly. Add drained mushrooms. Stir in soup, milk, sour cream, and Worcestershire sauce. Cook over low heat for 5 minutes. Add diced ham and cook over low heat for an additional 10 minutes. Serve over noodles. Serves 5.

Glazed Ham Loaf

1 pound ground ham
1 pound ground pork
½ cup fine bread crumbs (2 slices)
3 tablespoons finely chopped onion
1 egg, beaten
¾ cup milk
¼ teaspoon Liquid Smoke

BROWN SUGAR GLAZE

¾ cup brown sugar
1½ teaspoons dry mustard
¼ cup vinegar
¼ teaspoon Liquid Smoke

Combine loaf ingredients and mix well. Shape into an oval flat loaf in a glass baking dish. With a large knife, make three wide slashes at an angle across the top. Bake at 350° for 1 hour. Spoon off drippings and baste all of the brown sugar glaze over the loaf. Continue baking 30 minutes, basting often with the glaze.

Ham Loaf

1½ pounds ground ham
½ pound ground pork or beef
1 cup milk
1 cup cubed bread
1 tablespoon dry mustard
½ cup brown sugar
¼ cup vinegar
2 tablespoons water

Combine meat, bread, and milk; mix lightly. Form into loaf. Place in shallow baking pan. Combine remaining ingredients for sauce; pour over meat. Bake at 375° for 1½ hours, basting often with sauce in pan. Serves 8 to 10.

Ham Squares

¾ pound ground cooked ham

½ pound ground beef

¾ cup soft bread crumbs (about 1½ slices bread)

¾ cup milk

1 egg

2 tablespoons chopped onion

2 teaspoons snipped parsley

1 teaspoon dry mustard

½ teaspoon salt

dash freshly ground pepper

Combine all ingredients; mix thoroughly. Lightly pack into 10″ x 6″ x 1½″ baking dish. Bake, uncovered, at 325° for 1 hour. Spoon off drippings. Allow meat to stand a few minutes before cutting into squares. Serves 6.

CURRIED CREAM PEA SAUCE (for Ham Squares)

1 ten-ounce package frozen peas

2 tablespoons butter or margarine

1 tablespoon all-purpose flour

¼ teaspoon curry powder

¼ teaspoon salt

dash of pepper

1 cup milk

Cook frozen peas according to package directions; drain thoroughly. In saucepan melt butter or margarine, blend in flour and spices. Add milk, cook and stir until mixture thickens and bubbles. Cook 1 minute more and then add the cooked peas. Makes 2 cups sauce. Spoon sauce over squares. For a decorative touch, stud squares with peas.

Chow Mein

1 pound pork, cut in thin strips
3 tablespoons salad oil, hot
3 cups celery, sliced thin on the bias
1 cup onion slices
1 cup sliced fresh mushrooms or 1 small can, drained
2½ tablespoons cornstarch
¼ cup water
1 can condensed beef broth, undiluted
¼ cup soy sauce
1 tablespoon brown gravy sauce (optional)
1 one-pound can bean sprouts, drained
1 five-ounce can water chestnuts, drained and sliced
1 cup green peppers, cut in long strips
1 seven-ounce package snow peas, frozen
hot rice or fried noodles

In large skillet, cook pork in 1 tablespoon hot salad oil until done, about 10 minutes. Remove from skillet. Cook celery, onions, and mushrooms in 2 tablespoons salad oil until crisp-tender, 2 to 3 minutes, stirring often. Blend cornstarch and water; add beef broth, soy sauce, and brown gravy sauce, if desired. Stir into vegetables; add meat, bean sprouts, and water chestnuts. Heat and stir until thickened. Add green peppers and snow peas. Heat through. Important: Do not overcook. Serve very hot on rice or fried noodles. Serves 4 or 5.

Quick Chow Mein

1 pound groud beef
2 large onions, sliced
2 cups chopped celery
1 one-pound can bean sprouts

1 four-ounce can mushrooms
1½ cups water
4 tablespoons soy sauce
1 tablespoon Chinese-manufactured brown gravy sauce
3 tablespoons cornstarch
½ cup cold water
Chinese noodles

Brown meat in skillet. Drain off excess fat. Add all remaining ingredients except cornstarch, cold water, and noodles. Cover and cook over medium low heat about 20 minutes or until vegetables are tender. Thicken with cornstarch blended with cold water. Serve over noodles. Serves 6.

Hungarian Pork-n-Kraut Goulash

1½ tablespoons margarine
1 cup finely chopped onions
1 pound fresh pork, cut in small cubes
1 teaspoon paprika
1 sixteen-ounce can sauerkraut, well drained
¾ cup tomato juice
1 teaspoon salt
1 tablespoon sugar
1½ tablespoons flour
1 cup sour cream

In a large skillet, sauté onions in margarine until transparent. Add pork and paprika. Cook briefly until meat is very lightly browned. Stir in sauerkraut, tomato juice, and salt. Cover and cook over low heat for 1 hour. Add sugar, stirring to mix. Stir flour into sour cream and add to kraut mixture. Heat gently for a few minutes. Yields 4½ cups.

Eggplant and Sausage Casserole

1 pound pork sausage
salt to taste
pepper to taste
2 tablespoons salad oil
1 medium eggplant, washed
salt to taste (additional)
pepper to taste (additional)
⅓ cup flour
¼ cup olive oil
2 eight-ounce cans tomato sauce
½ to 1 teaspoon oregano
1 tablespoon Parmesan cheese
1 cup grated cheddar cheese

Shape sausage into thick patties. Season with salt and pepper. Heat salad oil in skillet and brown patties. Slice eggplant into thick slices (do not remove skin). Season with salt and pepper and coat with flour. Heat olive oil in skillet and brown eggplant. Place cooked eggplant slices in greased 1½- to 2-quart shallow baking dish. Top each with a sausage patty. Cover with tomato sauce. Sprinkle oregano and Parmesan cheese over all. Top with cheddar cheese. Bake at 300° for 35 minutes. Serves 6.

Sausage, Sauerkraut, and Tomato Casserole

1 No. 2 can sauerkraut
1 No. 2 can tomatoes
1 pound country-style sausage
1 tablespoon sugar

Put a layer of sauerkraut in the bottom of the casserole (fill it about one-third full of kraut). Put in a layer of tomatoes (until it is two-thirds full). Sprinkle 1 tablespoon of sugar over the tomatoes and cover with the sausage. Bake covered 325° to 350° for 30 minutes. Bake uncovered for the last 15 minutes of the 45-minute baking time. Serves 4. "Delicious as a one-dish dinner with baked potatoes, a salad, and a dessert."

Meat-n-Potato Pie

1 can cream of mushroom soup
1 pound ground beef
1/4 cup chopped onion
1 egg, slightly beaten
1/4 cup fine bread crumbs
2 tablespoons chopped parsley
1/4 teaspoon salt
dash pepper
2 cups mashed potatoes
1/4 cup grated cheddar cheese

Mix thoroughly 1/2 can soup, beef, onion, egg, crumbs, parsley, and seasonings. Press firmly into a 9″ pie pan or quiche pan. Bake at 350° for 25 minutes. Spoon off fat. Frost with potatoes. Top with remaining soup and cheese. Bake 10 minutes. Serves 6.

❧ ☙

Hamburger
and Noodles in Sour Cream

2 tablespoons fat
1 pound hamburger
1 cup onion
3 cups uncooked noodles
3 cups tomato juice
2 teaspoons celery salt
1 1/2 teaspoons salt
2 teaspoons Worcestershire sauce
1/4 teaspoon pepper
1 cup sour cream

Brown meat in onions and fat. Place *uncooked* noodles over meat. Mix remainder of ingredients (except sour cream), and pour over noodles. Cover and simmer for 30 minutes. Stir in sour cream, bring to a boil, and serve. Serves 6.

Chili Hamburger Pie

1½ pounds ground beef
⅓ cup chopped green pepper
½ cup chopped celery
¼ cup chopped onion
2 teaspoons salt
½ teaspoon pepper
3 teaspoons chili powder
1 sixteen-ounce can tomato sauce
pastry for 10-inch, 2 crust pie

Brown ground beef and drain off fat, leaving about 1 tablespoon for sautéing the pepper, celery, and onion. After sautéing, return meat to skillet and add salt, pepper, chili powder, and tomato sauce. Simmer 10 to 20 minutes or until mixture thickens. Cool. Turn mixture into pastry-lined pie pan and cover with top crust. Make slits in crust. Bake at 400° for 40 minutes or until browned. Cut in wedges and serve with vegetable sauce.

VEGETABLE SAUCE

4 tablespoons margarine
4 tablespoons flour
2 cups beef stock (or 4 bouillon cubes and 2 cups water)
1 one-pound can peas
1 cup cooked sliced carrots
2 teaspoons dried parsley
½ teaspoon garlic salt
pepper to taste

Melt butter in saucepan; blend in flour. Stir in stock. Cook, stirring until smooth and thick. Add remaining ingredients and heat. Serve over pie.

Sausage Soufflé

1½ pounds sausage
9 eggs, beaten
3 cups milk

4 slices bread, cubed

1½ cups grated sharp cheddar cheese

1½ teaspoons dry mustard

1 teaspoon salt

Brown sausage, drain. Combine all ingredients in greased 13" x 9" x 2" pan. Refrigerate overnight; bake uncovered at 350° for 1 hour.

❧ ❧

Stuffed Green Peppers

6 green peppers

1 pound ground beef

⅓ cup chopped onion

1 tablespoon oil

1 one-pound can stewed tomatoes

¾ cup precooked rice

2 tablespoons Worcestershire sauce

½ teaspoon salt, or to taste

pepper

1 cup grated sharp cheese

Cut tops off and core 6 peppers. Cook in boiling salted water 5 minutes. Drain well. Cook onion in oil until tender, add ground meat, tomatoes, rice, salt, pepper, and Worcestershire sauce. Mix well and simmer until rice is cooked, 5 minutes. Add cheese. Stuff peppers gently. Add 2 or 3 tablespoons of water to baking dish. Bake at 350° for 25 minutes.

TOMATO SAUCE

2 onions, sliced

3 tablespoons cooking oil

1 six-ounce can tomato paste

½ cup water

salt, pepper, and garlic salt to taste

3 tablespoons sour cream (optional)

Heat skillet, add 3 tablespoons oil and chopped onions (chopped pepper tops may also be added). Cook until soft and onions are transparent. Add tomato paste, water, and seasonings. Cook 2 or 3 minutes. Remove from heat and add sour cream.

Meatballs

2 cans tomato soup
1 can water
1 tablespoon chili powder
2 pounds hamburger
1/4 cup chopped onion
2 eggs, beaten
1/4 cup milk
1 cup oatmeal
1 teaspoon chili powder
salt and pepper

Combine tomato soup, water, and 1 tablespoon chili powder in a large baking dish. Heat oven to 350° and bake baking-dish mixture while mixing the meatballs. Combine hamburger, onion, eggs, milk, oatmeal, 1 teaspoon chili powder, salt, and pepper. Mix well and form into meatballs. Drop into the heated sauce and bake about 1 hour. Serves 8.

Lynn's* Meatball Stroganoff

1 cup cracker crumbs
1 teaspoon salt
dash of pepper, thyme, oregano
3/4 cup milk
2 eggs
1 pound ground beef
3/4 pound ground pork
2 tablespoons butter
1 beef bouillon cube
1/2 cup boiling water
1 1/3 cups sliced mushrooms
1 cup dairy sour cream

Combine crackers, seasonings, milk, eggs, and meat. Mix well. Form into balls 1½″ in diameter, chill. Brown slowly on all sides in hot fat. Combine bouillon cube and water. Add to meat. Bake at 325° in covered baking dish for 30 minutes. Add mushrooms, cook for 5 minutes. Add sour cream and heat to just boiling; serve. Serves 6.

Mrs. Lynn (Ralph) Neil, Nampa, Idaho.

Fiesta Meatballs
in Almond Sauce

1 beaten egg
½ cup water
1½ cups dry bread cubes (3 slices bread)
½ teaspoon salt
½ teaspoon dried oregano, crushed
½ teaspoon chili powder
¾ pound ground beef
¾ pound ground pork
½ cup raisins
2 tablespoons cooking oil
2 tablespoons finely chopped onion
1 clove garlic, minced
1½ cups chicken broth
½ cup tomato sauce
½ cup dry bread cubes (1 slice bread)
¼ cup slivered almonds, toasted
1 tablespoon snipped parsley
hot cooked rice

In mixing bowl, blend egg, water, 1½ cups bread cubes, salt, oregano, chili powder, and ⅛ teaspoon pepper. Add ground meats and raisins; mix well. Shape into 36, 1″ meatballs. In skillet, brown meatballs in hot oil, a few at a time. Drain off fat, reserving 1 tablespoon. Cook onion and garlic in reserved fat for 5 minutes. Add remaining ingredients except rice; bring to boil. Add meatballs; cover. Simmer 20 minutes. Serve over rice. Serves 6.

Norwegian Meatballs

1 onion, grated

⅓ cup butter, divided

2 pounds ground beef

1 pound ground pork

2 teaspoons salt

pepper to taste

¼ cup half-and-half

2 eggs

¼ teaspoon ground nutmeg

dash of ground allspice

4 tablespoons flour

2½ cups beef bouillon or water

Cook onion in 2 tablespoons melted butter for about 3 minutes. Combine with meats, salt, pepper, cream, eggs, and seasoning. Mix well with hands. Shape into firm balls about 1″ in diameter. Brown a few at a time in the rest of the butter. Shake frying pan to prevent sticking. Allow meatballs to brown all over. Remove from pan. Stir in flour and gradually stir in bouillon. Cook over low heat until thickened, stirring constantly. Pour brown sauce over meatballs. Serves 8.

Meatball Casserole

1 pound ground beef

¼ pound pork sausage

½ cup dry bread crumbs

⅓ cup evaporated milk

2 tablespoons chopped onion

1 teaspoon chili powder

⅛ teaspoon pepper

Combine all ingredients and shape by tablespoons into meatballs. Brown. Cover and cook 10 minutes over medium heat. Place in a 2½-quart casserole. Prepare sauce.

SAUCE

1 can cream of mushroom soup
1 can cream of celery soup
1 cup evaporated milk
½ cup water

Combine all ingredients. Heat until steaming and pour over meatballs. Top with unbaked biscuits and bake 20 to 25 minutes at 400°. Serves 6 to 8.

❧ ❧

Wilma's Swedish Meatballs with Parsley Spaghetti

1 cup dry bread crumbs
1 tablespoon instant minced onion
½ cup milk
1 egg
2 teaspoons salt
⅛ teaspoon pepper
½ teaspoon nutmeg
1 pound ground beef
¼ cup flour
1 tablespoon tomato paste
¼ teaspoon dill seed
2 cups water
1 cup sour cream

Mix together bread crumbs, onion, milk, egg, salt, pepper, nutmeg, and beef. Shape into balls and brown. Remove from pan and add flour. Stir well, then add tomato paste, dill seed, water, and meatballs. Cook for 30 minutes in covered pan. Cool 2 minutes, add sour cream. Cook until heated through. While meatballs are simmering for 20 minutes, cook 8 ounces of spaghetti. When tender, drain, and add ¼ cup butter, ¼ cup chopped parsley, and ¼ teaspoon garlic powder. Mix well. Pour meatballs and sauce over spaghetti. Serves 6.

Swedish Meatballs

³/₄ pound ground round

¹/₄ pound bulk sausage

1 egg

salt

pepper

³/₄ cup soft bread crumbs

1 onion

¹/₂ cup hot milk

Mix all together and drop by spoonfuls in hot fat and brown. Drain off fat and add 1 cup water, steam three-quarters of an hour.

Meatballs and Spaghetti Sauce

3 slices bread

³/₄ cup hot milk

1 egg, beaten

³/₄ pound ground chuck

¹/₄ pound lean pork

3 tablespoons chopped parsley

¹/₈ teaspoon sage

1 tablespoon onion powder

dash salt and pepper

Combine all ingredients and mix well. Form into balls the size of walnuts. Chill. Brown slowly in fat, add sauce, and cook 30 minutes. Serves 6.

SAUCE

³/₄ cup chopped onion

1 clove garlic

3 tablespoons fat

2 one-pound cans tomatoes

2 six-ounce cans tomato paste

1 cup water	
1¼ teaspoon oregano	
1 teaspoon salt	
½ teaspoon pepper	
1 bay leaf	
1 tablespoon sugar	

Cook onion and garlic in fat until tender. Add remaining ingredients, simmer covered 1 hour. Remove bay leaf.

Little Barbecue Loaves

1 cup cracker crumbs
1 egg
1½ pounds ground chuck
2 tablespoons minced onion
1½ teaspoons salt
4 ounces tomato sauce

Cook fat out of ground chuck, but do not brown meat. Fat is not used. With fork, slightly beat egg. Add next 4 ingredients. Then add cracker crumbs. Combine lightly but thoroughly. Shape into 4 individual oval loaves. Place in shallow baking dish. Bake at 350° for 40 minutes. Pour off most of the juices during this baking period. Prepare basting sauce to be ready for second baking period.

BASTING SAUCE

1 tablespoon cornstarch
2 tablespoons brown sugar
4 ounces tomato sauce
¾ cup beef broth
1 tablespoon vinegar
1 teaspoon prepared mustard
1 bouillon cube
¾ cup hot water

Combine cornstarch and brown sugar. Stir in next 4 ingredients and bouillon cube, dissolved in ¾ cup water. Cook, stirring constantly, until thickened. Pour over loaves, previously baked 40 minutes. Bake 30 minutes longer at 350°; basting often.

Lynn's Beef and Cheese Pie

1 pound ground beef
⅔ cup evaporated milk
¼ cup dry bread crumbs
1 teaspoon garlic salt
⅓ cup catsup
1 cup sliced mushrooms
1 cup shredded cheddar cheese
¼ teaspoon oregano
2 tablespoons grated Parmesan cheese

Combine meat, milk, bread crumbs, and garlic salt. Pat the mixture against sides and bottom of a 9″ pie pan. Spread catsup over meat mixture. Sprinkle with mushrooms, cheese, and oregano. Bake at 450° for 20 minutes.

Favorite Meat Loaf

1½ pounds ground beef
½ pound ground pork
½ cup diced onion
2 cups soft bread crumbs
2 eggs, beaten
½ cup canned tomatoes
½ cup finely diced celery
2½ teaspoons salt
¼ teaspoon pepper
1 teaspoon dry mustard
2 tablespoons horseradish

Combine all ingredients. Mix well. Put in 1-quart ring mold. Bake in 350° oven for 1 hour. Turn out on baking sheet, spread with mixture of ½ cup catsup, 1 tablespoon corn syrup, 1 teaspoon Worcestershire sauce. Return to oven and bake 15 minutes longer. Serve Mexican corn in center with spiced apples on side; trim with parsley. Serves 8.

Swedish Meat Loaf

1 pound ground beef

¼ pound ground pork

2 eggs

¾ cup milk

1 scant teaspoon ground sage

1 teaspoon sugar

1 teaspoon salt

¼ teaspoon pepper

½ cup bread crumbs

1 tablespoon finely chopped onion, sautéed in 1 tablespoon butter or margarine

Mix together. Mold into loaf, after warming your hands in hot water. Brown on both sides in a skillet in 2 tablespoons margarine. Cover and simmer for 1 to 1¼ hours. Heat 2 cups beef bouillon and baste every 15 minutes. Cream may be added to the liquid in the skillet to thicken it into gravy, if desired. Serves 4.

FISH & SEAFOOD

Seasoning with love...

*S*o, I have a big backyard! I can have the whole congregation over—225 for dinner, garden weddings with 400 guests.

My house is always open and almost every week of the year someone spends the night or company comes for a meal. Whether around the dinner table or outside in a barbecue, whether for refreshments or a time of fellowship, you can get acquainted better in a casual setting, and you can minister to them in a way you could never reach them in church.

How did it all start? My parents always had time for someone to come over to our house for dinner. My sisters and I were just kids when we learned table manners and hospitality skills around the dinner table with adult guests. Mom always had food in the "ice-box" for the minister, mission worker, and friends.

What a legacy to pass on to your kids!

—Dick Willis
Pasadena, Calif.

Oyster Surprise Appetizers

1 can small oysters (7¾ ounce), drained
½ pound lean ground beef
2 teaspoons Worcestershire sauce
½ teaspoon salt
¼ teaspoon pepper
⅛ teaspoon thyme
⅛ teaspoon marjoram
2 tablespoons salad oil or shortening

Cut oysters in 1″ pieces. Mix together thoroughly the ground beef, Worcestershire sauce, salt, pepper, thyme, and marjoram. Break off a small handful of the meat mixture, pat thinly in the palm of one hand, place an oyster piece on the meat, and roll the meat around it completely. Continue until all the oysters are encased in meat. Brown quickly in oil in a hot frying pan, turning to brown all sides. Skewer with toothpicks. Makes 14 appetizers.

Scalloped Oysters—1

1 pint small oysters
1½ cups cracker crumbs
½ cup butter, melted
¼ teaspoon salt
2 tablespoons parsley, chopped
¼ teaspoon paprika
¼ teaspoon celery salt
⅓ cup half-and-half
1 cup milk

Mix together crumbs, melted butter, salt, parsley, paprika, and celery salt. Sprinkle a layer of this mixture in a well-buttered baking dish. Cover with a layer of oysters. Repeat layers finishing with a layer of crumbs. Add half-and-half and milk. Bake at 350° for 30 minutes. Serves 6 as a side dish or 4 as a main dish.

Scalloped Oysters—2

2½ cups coarse cracker crumbs
1 pint oysters, drained (canned oysters may be used)
¼ cup oyster liquid
¾ cup cream
1 teaspoon Worcestershire sauce
¼ teaspoon salt
⅛ teaspoon pepper
⅓ cup butter

Put one-third of crumbs in well-buttered shallow 1-quart baking dish. Cover with ½ of oysters, repeat layer of crumbs and remaining oysters. Mix liquids and seasonings, pour over oysters. Cover with crumbs and dot with butter. Bake at 350° for 40 minutes. Serves 5.

Individual Salmon Molds

2 cups red salmon
2 eggs, beaten slightly
3 tablespoons melted butter
½ cup hot milk
¾ cup crushed cornflakes
½ teaspoon garlic salt
2 tablespoons grated onion
dash of pepper

Remove bones and skin. Flake and mix with eggs, melted butter, hot milk, and crushed cornflakes. Season with garlic salt, grated onion, and dash pepper. Mix and pack into four greased custard cups. Set in pan of hot water, bake at 375° for 30 minutes. Serve with cheese sauce.

CHEESE SAUCE

Melt 2 tablespoons butter, add 2 tablespoons flour, dash pepper, and dash of Tabasco. Pour in 1¼ cups milk gradually, stir. Add ½ cup grated sharp cheese, 1 canned pimiento (chopped), ½ clove garlic (crushed), and ½ teaspoon salt. Heat and stir until melted. "A good luncheon dish."

Summer Crab Aspic

2 cans (7½ ounce) king crab meat
1 envelope unflavored gelatin
¼ cup cold water
1¼ cups boiling water
1 three-ounce package lemon gelatin
2 cups tomato juice
2 tablespoons vinegar
1 teaspoon Worcestershire sauce
4 drops hot red pepper sauce
1½ teaspoons prepared horseradish
½ teaspoon salt
1 teaspoon grated onion
¾ cup chopped celery
⅔ cup chopped cucumber
¼ cup chopped green pepper
deviled eggs supreme (see page 120)
chive dressing

Drain canned crab. Soften unflavored gelatin in cold water. Add boiling water to lemon gelatin and softened gelatin, stirring until thoroughly dissolved. Add tomato juice, vinegar, Worcestershire sauce, hot red pepper sauce, horseradish, salt, and grated onion. Chill until mixture is consistency of unbeaten egg white. Pour small amount of gelatin mixture in oiled 1½- to 2-quart mold. Chill mold until almost set. Cut crab legs into chunks and place a few on top of chilled mold. Add crab, celery, cucumber, and green pepper to remaining gelatin mixture. Pour over crab layer in mold. Chill until firm. To serve, unmold salad on chilled platter. Garnish with parsley and deviled eggs. Serve with chive dressing. Serves 6 to 8.

CHIVE DRESSING

2 tablespoons freeze-dried or frozen chopped chives
1 medium avocado
1 tablespoon lemon juice
½ cup mayonnaise
½ cup dairy sour cream

¹/₄ teaspoon salt

dash garlic powder

Peel and seed avocado. Add lemon juice and mash or puree in blender until smooth. Add mayonnaise, sour cream, salt, and garlic powder. Blend well. Fold in chives, reserving 1 teaspoon for garnish. Chill. To serve, sprinkle reserved chives on top of dressing and serve with crab aspic. Makes about 1³/₄ cups.

❧ ☙   ˙

Seafood Delight

BISCUIT RING

2 cups quick biscuit mix

1 teaspoon salt

1 cup dairy sour cream

¹/₄ cup cooking oil

¹/₄ cup milk

2 tablespoons chopped chives

1 egg

Combine all ingredients in mixing bowl and mix until well blended. Spoon into greased 8″ ring mold. Bake at 450° for 18 to 20 minutes. Invert onto serving platter, spoon seafood sauce (below) into center. Garnish all with pimiento and serve immediately.

SEAFOOD SAUCE

³/₄ cup flour

1¹/₂ cups evaporated milk

1 four-ounce can sliced mushrooms, undrained

1 one-pound can green beans, drained

2 cans (12 ounces) tuna, drained and flaked

¹/₂ cup slivered almonds

1 teaspoon curry powder

1 teaspoon seasoning salt

Combine all ingredients except green beans in saucepan. Cook over medium heat or on thermostatic unit at 150°, stirring frequently until the mixture thickens, 5 or 7 minutes. Stir in green beans and heat thoroughly. Pour into center of hot biscuit ring. Serves 4 to 6.

Molded Fish Salad

1 tablespoon unflavored gelatin (1 envelope)
1/2 teaspoon salt
1/2 cup cold water
1 1/2 cups boiling water
2 tablespoons lemon juice
1 one-pound can salmon or 2 cans solid-pack tuna, drained and flaked

Combine gelatin and salt and cold water; let stand 5 minutes. Add gelatin to boiling water and stir until clear. Cool. Blend in lemon and salmon or tuna. Pour into fish mold or 9″ x 5″ x 3″ loaf pan that has been rinsed in cold water. Chill until set while preparing the cheese layer:

CHEESE LAYER

2 tablespoons unflavored gelatin (2 envelopes)
1 teaspoon sugar
1 teaspoon salt
1/2 cup cold milk
2 cups hot milk
1 cup cottage cheese
1/3 cup mayonnaise
1 tablespoon lemon juice
3/4 teaspoon grated onion
1/2 cup diced cucumber
3/4 cup diced celery

Combine gelatin, sugar, and salt. Soak in cold milk 5 minutes. Gradually add hot milk, stirring until gelatin is dissolved. Cool until thick and syrupy. Blend in cottage cheese and mayonnaise. Fold in remaining ingredients. Pour onto fish layer. Chill until firm. Unmold on crisp lettuce leaves. Garnish with sliced tomatoes and cucumbers. Serve with additional mayonnaise or sour cream dressing. Serves 10.

Salmon Mornay

1 one-pound can salmon
2 tablespoons butter
2 tablespoons flour
1/4 teaspoon salt
1/8 teaspoon paprika
1/8 teaspoon celery salt
1 teaspoon minced parsley
1/4 teaspoon minced onion
1 cup milk
1/3 cup grated cheese

Carefully unmold the can of salmon and place in buttered baking dish so as not to crumble. Cover and bake 10 minutes in a moderate oven to heat thoroughly. In saucepan melt butter and stir in flour. Add seasonings and milk. Cook until a creamy sauce forms. Pour sauce over the salmon. Sprinkle with cheese and bake 10 minutes in a moderate oven. Serve in the original baking dish.

Salmon Loaf

2 one-pound cans salmon, reserve liquid
1/4 cup finely minced onion
1/4 cup chopped parsley
1/4 cup lemon juice
1/2 cup coarse cracker crumbs
1/2 teaspoon salt
1/2 teaspoon pepper
1/2 teaspoon thyme
4 eggs
1/4 cup melted butter

Combine salmon, onion, parsley, lemon juice, and seasonings. Mix lightly. Add milk to reserved salmon liquid to make one cup. Add liquid, eggs, and butter to salmon. Mix lightly. Place in a greased glass loaf pan. Bake at 350° for 1 hour or until set. Serves 6. "Serve with sauce of peas in cream sauce."

Salmon Soufflé

2 egg yolks, well beaten
3 egg whites, beaten stiff
pinch salt
2 tablespoons butter, melted
2 tablespoons flour
1 cup milk, hot
1/2 teaspoon salt
1/2 teaspoon nutmeg
dash black pepper
1 one-pound can salmon

Prepare a 1-quart baking dish or four individual molds. Butter sides and bottom of dish or molds heavily. Then coat with bread crumbs or flour. Roll coating ingredient around, then shake out surplus. Refrigerate mold while preparing soufflé. Add pinch of salt to egg whites before beating them. Over moderate heat, stir 2 tablespoons flour into melted butter. Add hot milk and cook 2 minutes, stirring constantly. Sauce should be thick. Add sauce gradually to beaten egg yolks, stirring constantly. Add salt, nutmeg, and black pepper to sauce. Break salmon into large flakes and add to sauce. Stir in one-quarter of beaten egg whites until well mixed. Fold in remaining whites. Pour mixture into refrigerated mold. Place in preheated 400° oven. Turn heat down immediately to 375°. Bake 25 minutes. At this point, soufflé will have a creamy center. For a firmer texture, bake another 4 or 5 minutes. Serve immediately. Garnish with lemon slices, parsley, or mint sprigs.

Broiled Salmon Seattle Style

fresh salmon steaks, 1½" thick
2 tablespoons butter

Place salmon into a jelly roll pan. Sprinkle with salt, pepper, and paprika. Dot with butter. Sprinkle with lemon juice. Broil fish 6 to 8 inches from the source of heat for 7 minutes. Do not turn over.

Gourmet Salmon Pie

PIE CRUST

1 cup sifted flour
½ teaspoon salt
⅓ cup shortening
3 to 4 tablespoons cold water

To make pie crust sift together flour and salt. Cut in shortening until particles are the size of small peas. Sprinkle cold water over the mixture, a little at a time with a fork. Form into a ball. Flatten to about ½" thickness. Roll out on floured surface to a 9½" circle. Pat dough into an 8" pie pan. Flute edges. Fill with salmon filling. Bake at 425° for 20 to 25 minutes until golden brown. Top with cucumber sauce. Serve hot. Serves 4 to 6.

SALMON FILLING

2 hard-cooked eggs
1 one-pound can salmon, bone and skin removed
2 eggs
¼ cup melted butter
2 teaspoons minced parsley
¼ teaspoon salt
¼ teaspoon sweet basil

Slice eggs into the bottom of the pastry-lined pie pan. In bowl combine all remaining ingredients and mix well. Pour over eggs.

CUCUMBER SAUCE

⅓ cup cucumber, grated
1 tablespoon minced onion
¼ cup mayonnaise
2 teaspoons vinegar
½ cup dairy sour cream
2 teaspoons minced parsley
dash of salt and pepper to taste

Combine all ingredients.

Salmon Puffs

1 one-pound can red salmon, drained
¼ teaspoon salt
½ cup flour
⅓ teaspoon baking soda
½ cup buttermilk
2 eggs

Flake the salmon. Mix together the three dry ingredients. Combine buttermilk and eggs; add to dry ingredients and beat well. Stir that mixture into salmon. Drop the batter by spoonfuls into fat heated to 350°. Fry until golden. (Turn once.) Serve immediately with mushroom, egg, or pea sauce. Serves 6.

SAUCE

Make a white sauce by melting ½ stick butter or margarine, stirring in 2 to 3 tablespoons flour (stir until well blended) and adding 2 cups milk, salt and pepper to taste. Stir constantly until thickened, then add sliced mushrooms, chopped hard-boiled eggs, or peas. Yields 2½ cups sauce.

Salmon Loaf from Seattle

1 one-pound can salmon
1 cup soft bread crumbs
3 eggs
3 teaspoons lemon juice
½ teaspoon salt
¼ cup melted butter
⅓ cup liquid from salmon
2 teaspoons grated onion
1 three-ounce package cream cheese, room temperature

In a large bowl flake the salmon with a fork. Add well-beaten eggs. In another bowl combine bread crumbs, lemon juice, salt, butter, salmon liquid, and onions. Mix well. Cut cream cheese in small pieces and whip into bread mixture with a fork or blender. Add to salmon. Pour into a well-greased loaf pan so the loaf rounds up a little in the center. Bake 350° for 1 hour. Loaf should turn faintly golden on top. Turn out onto a heated platter and serve with a tomato and cheese sauce.

Salmon Loaf in a Blanket

1 one-pound salmon, pink or red
2 eggs, beaten
½ teaspoon salt
1 tablespoon minced onion
⅛ teaspoon pepper
1 cup fine dry bread crumbs
1 cup tomato juice
2 tablespoons melted shortening

Flake the salmon and remove the bones, mashing the fish with a fork. (You may use canned salmon.) Add the other ingredients and mix thoroughly. Press into a greased loaf pan and bake at 325° to 350° for 45 minutes. Cool slightly. Make a biscuit dough of 2 cups flour, 3 teaspoons baking powder, ½ teaspoon salt, 4 tablespoons shortening, and 1 cup milk. Turn out on a floured surface and roll into a large rectangle. Place the salmon loaf on the dough, upside down, and wrap securely. Place in greased pan and bake at 425° to 450° for 20 minutes. Serve on a platter bordered with pan-browned new potatoes, tiny bouquets of watercress, icicle radishes, and stuffed olives. Cut in ¾" slices to serve, and top with cheese sauce made by dissolving ½ cup grated cheese in 1½ cups seasoned medium white sauce. Serves 6 to 8. "This is an exceptional recipe."

❧ ❧

Tuna-n-Rice Soufflé

1 can condensed cream of mushroom soup
1 can tuna (6½ or 7 ounce), drained
1 cup cooked rice
¼ cup chopped pimiento
2 tablespoons chopped parsley
4 egg whites
4 egg yolks

Heat and stir the soup over low heat; add the next 4 ingredients and heat. Beat egg whites until stiff. Beat egg yolks until thick and lemon-colored; gradually stir in tuna mixture. Fold into egg whites. Pour into an ungreased 2-quart casserole. Bake at 350° for 30 to 35 minutes or until mixture is set in center. Serve at once with lemon wedges. Serves 6.

Tuna Rockefeller

1 can water-packed tuna (6½ ounce), drained
⅓ cup bread crumbs
1 ten-ounce package frozen chopped spinach, cooked and drained
1 tablespoon lemon juice
½ cup mayonnaise
1 cup Swiss cheese, grated
2 tablespoons grated Parmesan cheese
4 large mushroom caps
paprika

Combine tuna, crumbs, and spinach. Add lemon juice, mayonnaise, and Swiss cheese. Place equal amounts in 4 serving shells or individual baking dishes. Sprinkle with Parmesan cheese. Bake at 350° for 20 minutes. Top each serving with one buttered mushroom cap. Sprinkle with paprika and return to oven for 5 or 6 minutes. Serves 4.

Tuna Timbales

1 large can tuna
1 small onion, chopped fine
2 tablespoons salad oil
3 eggs, separated
1½ cups soft bread cubes
2 tablespoons lemon juice
1 teaspoon finely chopped parsley
½ teaspoon salt
⅛ teaspoon pepper
½ red pimiento, chopped

Lightly brown tuna and onion in salad oil. Cool and add beaten egg yolks, bread cubes, lemon juice, parsley, salt, and pepper. Cool and fold in stiffly beaten egg whites. Pour into greased ramekins or muffin tins, place in pan of hot water and bake 30 minutes at 350°, or until firm in center. Unmold and serve with combined white sauce and pimiento. Serves 8.

WHITE SAUCE

| 2 tablespoons butter |
| 2 tablespoons flour |
| 1 cup milk |
| 1/4 teaspoon salt (or to taste) |

Blend and cook to desired thickness and add pimiento for tuna timbale topping when served.

Creamed Tuna Royale

| 2 tablespoons butter or margarine |
| 1/4 cup chopped green pepper |
| 2 teaspoons minced onion |
| 1 three-ounce can sliced mushrooms, drained |
| 1/4 cup all-purpose flour |
| 1/4 teaspoon salt |
| dash pepper |
| 1/4 teaspoon paprika |
| 1 1/2 cups milk |
| 1 seven-ounce can (1 cup) tuna, drained |
| 1/4 cup chopped pimiento |
| 1 teaspoon Worcestershire sauce |
| 1 teaspoon lemon juice |
| 4 cups buttered, hot cooked rice |

Melt butter in skillet and cook green pepper, onions, and mushrooms until tender. Stir in flour and seasonings; slowly add milk, stirring constantly until smooth and thick. Add tuna and pimiento. Heat to simmering and cook about 10 minutes. Remove from heat and add Worcestershire sauce and lemon juice. Serve on beds of buttered, hot fluffy rice. Serves 6.

Tuna Loaf

| 3 cans white meat tuna, chunk-style, or 2 cans solid-pak albacore |
| 4 hard-cooked eggs, chopped |
| 1 cup chopped stuffed olives |
| 2 tablespoons minced onion |
| 1 cup finely chopped celery |
| 3 cups mayonnaise (not salad dressing) |
| 2 envelopes unflavored gelatin |
| ½ cup cold water |

Combine first 5 ingredients in a large mixing bowl. Sprinkle gelatin over cold water; place over pan of boiling water and stir until dissolved. Add gelatin to mayonnaise and combine with other ingredients. Pour into well-greased loaf pan or mold and refrigerate. The recipe makes 1 large loaf or mold. Several small molds can be used in place of a large one. Refrigerate until ready to use. Unmold and serve. It may be made 2 days before serving time. Serves 12 generously for a luncheon or 24 as a side dish at a buffet supper.

Tuna Pie with Cheese Crust

| ½ cup sliced green pepper |
| 2 slices onion |
| 3 tablespoons butter |
| 6 tablespoons flour |
| ½ teaspoon salt |
| 3 cups milk |
| 1 large can tuna fish, drained |
| 1 tablespoon lemon juice |

Melt butter, sauté green pepper and onion. Blend in flour. Stir until well blended. Add salt. Add milk slowly, stir constantly until thick and smooth. Add remaining ingredients. Pour into a large baking dish and cover with cheese crust.

CHEESE CRUST

1½ cups flour

3 tablespoons baking powder

½ teaspoon salt

3 tablespoons shortening

½ cup milk

¾ cup grated cheese

few grains cayenne pepper

2 pimientos, chopped

Sift together the first three ingredients; work in the shortening. Add the liquid and make a soft dough. Toss lightly on a floured board. Roll out into sheet 8″ x 12″. Sprinkle with grated cheese and pimiento. Roll like a jelly roll. With a sharp knife cut into 8 slices. Flatten slightly and lay on top of the creamed mixture. Bake at 450°-475° for about 25 to 30 minutes. Serves 8.

Baked Tuna Sandwiches

12 slices thin, white bread, crusts removed

6 slices American or cheddar cheese, mild

2 cans white chunk tuna, drained

½ teaspoon salt

6 eggs

3 cups milk

Grease an 8″ x 10″ pan, put 6 slices bread on bottom, tuna on top, mash up slightly, put cheese on each slice of bread. Add a buttered slice of bread, butter side up on top of cheese. Beat eggs, add milk, strain, pour over sandwiches, let stand 12 to 24 hours in refrigerator in covered pan. Remove from refrigerator 2 hours before baking. Bake at 350° for 20 minutes, then at 350° 40 minutes longer. Be sure to fit bread to pan to completely cover. Add pieces of bread if necessary to absorb milk and eggs. Diced ham or diced chicken is equally good. Try baking at 325° the full time uncovered. Serve one sandwich for each person. "Very good for a luncheon."

Baked Fish with Tomato Sauce

2 pounds fillet; such as sole, halibut, haddock, ocean catfish
1 small slice onion, chopped fine
salt
3 tablespoons butter, melted
2 tablespoons flour
1 tablespoon sugar
1 No. 303 can tomatoes
buttered bread crumbs or toasted almonds

Arrange fish in greased shallow baking dish or skillet. Sprinkle chopped onion over fish. Add salt to taste. In separate pan, blend flour into melted butter. Add sugar. Blend. When smooth, add tomatoes. Cook and stir mixture until it thickens. Pour hot sauce over fish. Bake in a preheated 425° oven for 20 minutes. During last few minutes of baking, sprinkle with bread crumbs or almonds. Serves 4 to 6.

Haddock Mornay

3 tablespoons butter or margarine
3 tablespoons flour
1½ cups milk
½ teaspoon prepared mustard
½ teaspoon salt
dash of cayenne pepper
¾ teaspoon Worcestershire sauce
¼ pound cheddar cheese, grated
1 one-pound package frozen haddock, thawed

Melt butter and stir in flour to make a smooth paste. Gradually add milk, stirring constantly, until thick and smooth. Add seasonings and cheese. Place fish in greased casserole and pour sauce over fish. Bake at 450° for 20 minutes. "It's a simple recipe and it can be used with any kind of fish."

Rolled Fillet of Sole

2 pounds flounder, gray or lemon sole fillets (fresh or frozen)

¹/₂ teaspoon salt

¹/₄ teaspoon freshly ground white pepper

1 stick (¹/₄ pound) sweet butter or margarine

¹/₂ cup finely chopped basil leaves

¹/₄ cup lemon juice

¹/₂ cup chicken broth

Thaw frozen fish. Drain well on paper towels. Sprinkle each fillet with salt and pepper. Cut butter into 8 equal pieces. Place a square of butter on each fillet. Add equal amounts of chopped basil and lemon juice to each and roll up, jelly-roll style. Place seam side down in a buttered baking dish. Pour chicken broth over all. Preheat oven to 375°. Baste with pan juices several times during baking. 324 calories per serving. Serves 8.

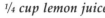

Tarragon Sauce for Fish

1 cup commercial sour cream

¹/₂ teaspoon dried tarragon leaves

1 teaspoon seasoned salt

¹/₈ teaspoon grated onion

¹/₂ teaspoon salt

Combine all the ingredients and mix thoroughly. Cover and chill at least 1 hour to blend flavors. Serve with broiled scallops, halibut, sole, or flounder. Makes 1 cup of sauce.

POULTRY ENTRÉES

Seasoning with love...

There must always be a beginning to the hospitable life! Unique to my ministry is the pleasure of looking back over the years and realizing that what I had learned from others, I have been able to pass along to college and seminary students who observed us as we entertained them in our home. They have carried the hospitality of love, simplicity, and beauty to their Kingdom work around the world.

Our guests have been one of the greatest joys of my life. During the past 52 years we have entertained people of many creeds, colors, and stations of life. They have given us more than we could ever give. Varied table settings and methods of entertainment have added to the enjoyment of "[doing] good to all people, especially to those who belong to the family of believers" (Gal. 6:10, NIV).

—Mabel Earle
Kansas City, Mo.

Chicken and Dumplings

3 fresh stewing hens

4 fresh chicken breasts

10 sprigs parsley

2 bay leaves

6 carrots, diced

6 stalks celery, sliced

½ cup chopped onion

Place the above ingredients in a large kettle of water. Stew chicken until the meat is tender; do not overcook. Remove from heat. Clean the *white* meat from the bones.

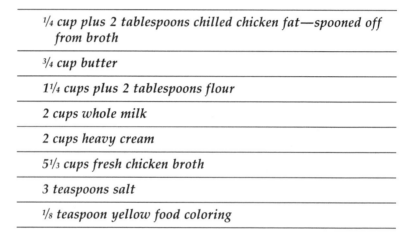

¼ cup plus 2 tablespoons chilled chicken fat—spooned off from broth

¾ cup butter

1¼ cups plus 2 tablespoons flour

2 cups whole milk

2 cups heavy cream

5⅓ cups fresh chicken broth

3 teaspoons salt

⅛ teaspoon yellow food coloring

Melt butter and chicken fat. Slowly add flour and salt. Blend well. Combine together milk, cream, and broth, then gradually add to the flour mixure. Cook over medium heat, stirring constantly, until the mixture becomes the consistency of a medium white sauce. Stir in food coloring to make mixture a very pale yellow. Add large pieces of white chicken meat to sauce. Pour into a soup tureen. Gently place egg dumplings on top. Garnish with fresh-snipped parsley.

EGG DUMPLINGS

1½ cups sifted flour

1 teaspoon salt

2 teaspoons baking powder

2 tablespoons shortening

1 egg

milk

Sift flour with baking powder and salt. Cut in shortening until fine as meal. Break egg in cup, slightly beat with a fork. Add milk to make ¾ cup liquid. Add all at once to flour mixure. Mix only to moisten the flour. Drop into hot chicken broth, only 1″ of liquid in bottom of pan. Use a tablespoon dipped into broth for each dumpling. Cover pan, cook slowly for 15 minutes. *Do not* lift lid to check while cooking. Makes 8 large dumplings.

Editor's note: The actual recipe was never written down, the above recipe is to the best of Richard and Patricia Benner's recollection.

Denver Buttermilk Fried Chicken

1 cup unsifted flour
2 teaspoons salt
½ teaspoon paprika
¼ teaspoon pepper
1 cup buttermilk
1 teaspoon baking powder
2 fryers (2½ pounds each), cut

Make seasoned flour: combine flour, salt, paprika, and pepper in clean paper bag. In bowl combine buttermilk with baking powder, set aside. Wipe chicken with damp towel. Dip in buttermilk mixture, then shake a few pieces at a time in the flour. Refrigerate, covered, for 2 or 3 hours. In skillet add salad oil, about ½″ deep, heat to 340°. Add chicken pieces, cook uncovered, turning to brown evenly until tender, about 30 minutes.

My Best Fried Chicken

"Shake or roll the chicken in salt and peppered flour. Let set to dry for 10 minutes, then flour again and place into the pan. The cooking oil should be a good ½″ deep, at least. It shouldn't be smoking hot but 'hot enough.' Brown pieces on all sides, then turn the heat down and keep on cooking until the chicken tests tender. Don't cover the pan or you will lose all the crispness. Everything depends on having the shortening deep enough, the right temperature, and you do have to stand over it to keep turning pieces until the chicken is done. This is an old Missouri recipe. Really good! My best."

Oven Fried Chicken—1

1 three-pound chicken, cut into quarters
1 egg
½ cup flour
2 teaspoons salt
2 teaspoons paprika
½ cup butter

Mix together flour, salt, and paprika. Beat egg, then dip chicken into egg. Coat chicken with flour. Melt butter in a shallow baking pan. Roll chicken pieces in butter. Place skin side down in a single layer. Bake at 350° for 40 minutes. Turn chicken over. Bake another 35 minutes. Serves 4.

Oven Fried Chicken—2

Clean chicken and soak in milk overnight. Season flour with salt and pepper. Roll chicken in flour, dip into milk, and roll again in flour. Place into lightly buttered baking dish, skin side down. Brush with melted butter. Bake at 350° for 25 minutes, turn chicken, and bake another 20 minutes or until tender.

Janet's
Oven Fried Chicken Parmesan

1 cup crushed packed herb stuffing
⅔ cup grated Parmesan cheese
¼ cup chopped parsley
¼ teaspoon garlic
1 three-pound chicken, cut up
½ cup butter, melted

Mix together crumbs, cheese, parsley, and garlic. Dip chicken in butter, roll in crumb mixture. Place chicken in a jelly-roll pan, skin side up so they do not touch. Sprinkle with remaining butter or crumbs. Bake at 375° for 45 minutes or until tender. Serves 4.

Wilma's Scalloped Chicken

1 medium-sized cooked chicken or 1 quart of cooked diced chicken

1 cup soft bread crumbs

2 cups cooked, drained rice

1/4 cup diced pimiento

4 beaten eggs

1 teaspoon salt

1 teaspoon pepper

1/4 cup melted butter or chicken fat

3 cups milk or chicken stock

yellow food coloring

Mix in order named and pour in a greased ring or casserole. Bake in slow oven 325° for 1 1/4 hours. Let stand 10 minutes, then turn out on a deep platter. If baked in ring mold, fill center with mushroom sauce, or put in a dish in center. If baked in casserole, pour sauce over when served.

MUSHROOM SAUCE

4 tablespoons fat

5 tablespoons flour

2 cups chicken stock

salt and pepper

1 tablespoon chopped parsley

1 teaspoon lemon juice

1/2 pound cooked mushrooms

2 egg yolks, beaten

1/4 cup thick cream

Melt fat, add flour, add chicken stock and seasonings. Stir and cook until thick. Add mushrooms and beaten egg yolks mixed with cream. Cook, gently stirring, until egg yolks are cooked. Serves 8 to 10.

Easy Chicken Divan

2 ten-ounce packages frozen broccoli or 2 bunches fresh broccoli
2 cups sliced cooked chicken or 3 chicken breasts, cooked and boned
2 cans condensed cream of chicken soup
1 cup mayonnaise or salad dressing
1 teaspoon lemon juice
1/2 teaspoon curry powder
1/2 cup shredded sharp processed American cheese
1/2 cup soft bread crumbs
1 tablespoon butter or margarine, melted

Cook broccoli in boiling salted water until tender; drain. Arrange broccoli in greased 11½" x 7½" x 1½" baking dish. Place chicken on top. Combine soup, mayonnaise, lemon juice, and curry powder; pour over chicken. Sprinkle with cheese. Combine bread crumbs and butter; sprinkle over all. Bake at 350° for 25 to 30 minutes or until thoroughly heated. Trim with pimiento strips. Serves 6 to 8.

Party Chicken Breasts

4 chicken breasts
1/4 cup flour
1/2 teaspoon salt
1/2 teaspoon pepper
1/4 teaspoon paprika
1 recipe stuffing
1/2 cup butter

Split breasts just enough to fold. Combine flour, seasonings in paper bag, add chicken and shake. Fill cavity of each piece with stuffing. Mix 2 cups dry bread cubes, 1 tablespoon chopped onion, ½ teaspoon salt, ¼ teaspoon poultry or sage seasoning, and pepper. Add 2 tablespoons butter and ¼ cup hot water, toss gently. Hold stuffing in by skewering opening with toothpicks. Dip chicken in melted butter, place in baking dish. Put any remaining butter over the top. Bake at 325° for 45 minutes, turn and bake 45 minutes longer or until tender. Sprinkle with chopped parsley, serve with mushroom sauce.

MUSHROOM SAUCE

1/2 *pound fresh mushrooms cut in half, or canned mushrooms*
1/4 *cup minced onions*
2 *tablespoons butter*
2 *tablespoons flour*
1/2 *cup heavy cream*
1/2 *cup sour cream*
1/2 *teaspoon salt*
1/4 *teaspoon pepper*

Cook mushrooms and onions in butter until tender but not brown. Cover and cook 10 minutes over low heat. Push mushrooms aside and stir flour into butter. Add heavy cream, sour cream, and seasonings. Heat slowly, almost to boiling point, stirring constantly. Pour around chicken and serve. Makes 1½ cups sauce.

Oven Fried
Chicken with Stuffing

3½ *to 4 pounds chicken, cut up*
flour, seasoned with salt and pepper
1/2 *cup shortening*
6 *cups dry bread crumbs*
1/2 *cup sliced celery*
2 *tablespoons chopped onion*
3/4 *teaspoon salt*
1¼ *teaspoons poultry seasoning*
1/3 *cup melted butter*
1 *can cream of chicken soup*
2 *tablespoons flour*
1½ *cups water*

Dip chicken into seasoned flour, brown in melted shortening. Combine bread, celery, onions, seasonings, butter, and half of undiluted soup. Place chicken around the edge of a greased casserole dish and stuffing mixture in the center. Blend flour, 3 tablespoons drippings, remaining soup, and water. Pour over chicken and stuffing. Cover. Bake at 300° for 2 hours. Serves 6. "Very good for Sunday dinner."

Stuffed Chicken Breasts

8 small whole chicken breasts, boned
salt and pepper to taste
1/2 pound lean ground round steak
1/4 cup soy sauce or to taste
1 can water chestnuts, thinly sliced
2 slices soft white bread
1/3 cup milk
1 egg
1/4 teaspoon dried tarragon
1/4 teaspoon dried rosemary
honey
sesame seeds

Cook the ground meat for a few minutes until it loses the red color. Add soy sauce, salt, pepper, and water chestnuts. Add the bread that has been soaked in the mixture of milk, egg, and seasonings. Mix well.

Place chicken breasts skin side down on a plate and put 1/8 of the stuffing mixture in the center of each breast. Bring the sides of the chicken toward the center, then draw up the top and bottom to form sort of a ball. Place breasts, skin side up, in a shallow pan, allowing them to touch to keep in shape. Bake for 1 hour at 350°, spooning off the juice as it forms. Save juice. About 15 minutes before the chicken is done, glaze each breast with teaspoon of honey and sprinkle the whole thing with sesame seeds. Thicken the juice with a little flour to make a sauce.

Chicken Almond Party Bake

3 to 4 cups cooked bite-size chicken pieces
3 tablespoons butter
3 tablespoons flour
2 cups chicken stock
1/2 cup button mushrooms
2 teaspoons grated onion

¼ cup diced pimiento

½ teaspoon Accent

½ teaspoon salt

¼ cup blanched, slivered almonds

Melt butter, blend in flour. Add stock gradually; cook over medium heat, stirring constantly until thickened. Stir in mushrooms, onion, pimiento, and seasonings. Add chicken and almonds. Pour into a 12″ x 8″ baking pan. Top with almond biscuits (below) while hot. Bake at 425° for 20 to 25 minutes, until biscuits are golden brown. Serves 6 to 8.

ALMOND BISCUITS

2 cups flour

4 teaspoons baking powder

½ teaspoon salt

⅓ cup ground blanched almonds

¼ cup shortening

¾ cup milk

⅛ teaspoon almond extract

Sift together flour, baking powder, and salt. Add almonds. Cut in shortening. Add milk and almond extract. Knead lightly about 10 strokes on well-floured board. Roll out to ¼″ thick and cut into circles. Place on hot chicken mixture.

Chicken Crunch

½ cup chicken broth or milk

3 cups cooked chicken, cubed

¼ cup chopped onion

⅓ cup slivered almonds

2 cans mushroom soup, undiluted

1 cup diced celery

1 can water chestnuts, drained, sliced thin

1 three-ounce can chow mein noodles

Blend all ingredients. Pour them into greased casserole. Bake at 325° for 40 minutes. Serves 6.

À La King on Noodles

¼ cup butter or margarine
¼ cup enriched flour
1½ cups milk
½ cup light cream
salt and pepper
2 cups diced chicken
½ cup chopped mushrooms
2 tablespoons chopped pimiento
2 egg yolks, slightly beaten
1 tablespoon lemon juice

Melt butter; add flour; blend. Gradually add milk and cream; cook over low heat until smooth and thick, stirring constantly. Add seasonings, chicken, mushrooms, and pimiento. Heat through. Add small amount hot mixture to egg yolks; add to remaining hot mixture. Cook 2 minutes. Add lemon juice. Serve over noodle squares.

NOODLE SQUARES

Cook 1 six-ounce package thin noodles in boiling, salted water until tender. Drain. Rinse with cold water. Add 1 tablespoon butter or margarine, ½ teaspoon salt, 3 slightly beaten eggs, and ⅓ cup light cream. Pour into greased 8″ square pan. Bake at 350° until firm, about 40 minutes. Cut into squares. Serves 6.

Chicken Loaf

1 four-pound hen or 2 fryers, cooked and diced
2 cups fresh bread crumbs
1½ teaspoons salt
1½ cups milk
1½ cups broth
4 eggs, well-beaten
1 cup cooked rice
⅛ cup chopped pimiento

Combine ingredients and bake in greased 9″ x 13″ pan 1 hour at 325°. Serve with sauce. Serves 16.

SAUCE

¼ *cup margarine*
½ *cup fried mushrooms*
¼ *cup cream*
2 *tablespoons chopped parsley*
5 *tablespoons flour*
⅛ *teaspoon paprika*
1 *pint chicken broth*

Melt margarine. Add flour and stir until smooth. Stir in broth. Add the cream. Cook over low fire until thickened. Add remaining ingredients. Serve over hot chicken loaf.

Creamy Chicken and Rice Casserole

1 *cup wild rice*
½ *cup chopped onion*
½ *cup butter*
¼ *cup flour*
1 *six-ounce can broiled, sliced mushrooms, reserve liquid*
1 *to* 1½ *cups chicken broth*
1½ *cups light cream*
3 *cups diced cooked chicken*
¼ *cup diced pimiento*
1½ *teaspoons salt*
2 *tablespoons pepper*
½ *cup blanched, slivered almonds*

Prepare wild rice according to package directions. Sauté onion in butter. Stir in flour, remove from heat. Drain mushrooms, add enough chicken broth to mushroom liquid to measure 1½ cups. Gradually add to flour. Slowly blend in cream, cook and stir until mixture thickens. Add rice, mushrooms, chicken, pimiento, parsley, salt, and pepper. Place in a 2-quart casserole. Bake at 350° for 25 to 30 minutes. Serves 8.

Chicken Casserole

4 tablespoons butter
5 tablespoons flour
1 cup chicken stock
1½ cups evaporated milk
1 teaspoon salt
3 cups cooked rice
1½ cups cooked chicken
¾ cup sliced mushrooms
¼ cup chopped pimiento
⅓ cup chopped green peppers
½ cup blanched, slivered almonds

Melt butter, add flour and blend. Slowly add stock and milk. Cook, stirring constantly. Add salt. Alternate layers of rice, chicken, vegetables, and sauce in a baking dish. Top with almonds. Bake at 350° for 30 minutes. Garnish with pineapple slices, apricots, and watercress. Serves 8 to 10.

Chicken and Rice Casserole

1 cup cooked chicken, diced
1½ cups cooked rice
1 cup cooked sliced celery
½ cup chopped almonds or cashews
3 hard-cooked eggs, sliced
1 can cream of chicken soup
½ teaspoon salt
¼ teaspoon pepper
1 tablespoon lemon juice
¾ cup mayonnaise
¼ cup chicken stock

Combine rice, chicken, celery, onion, nuts, soup, seasonings, lemon juice, mayonnaise, and chicken stock. Fold in eggs, turn into a greased casserole dish. Bake at 450° for 15 minutes or until bubbly.

Turkey Plantation

1/2 cup minced onion

1 cup diced celery

5 tablespoons butter

6 tablespoons flour

3 cups milk

1 can mushroom soup

1 small can pimientos, drained and chopped

4 cups cooked turkey cut in small pieces

crushed cornflakes

salt and pepper

Cook onion and celery in butter very slowly, until soft. Add flour to make a smooth paste. Add milk, soup, turkey, pimientos, and seasoning to taste. Pour into buttered baking dish and cover with cornflakes. Bake at 375° for 45 to 60 minutes. Serves 8.

Hot Turkey Salad

5 cups turkey meat

4 cups diced celery

1 cup mayonnaise

1 can cream of chicken soup

2 cups slivered almonds

1/2 cup diced onion

1 teaspoon salt

1/2 teaspoon pepper

1 cup chopped green pepper

3 cups crushed potato chips

1 1/2 cups grated American cheese

Mix all ingredients except cheese and potato chips. Put in 9" x 13" casserole. Cover with potato chips mixed with cheese. Bake at 375° for 45 minutes. Garnish with paprika and parsley. Serves 12.

Chicken with Dressing Casserole

3- to 4-pound stewing chicken, cut up
1 stalk celery
1 onion, sliced
2 teaspoons salt
3 peppercorns
¼ cup minced onion
⅓ cup butter
6 cups dry bread crumbs
½ teaspoon sage
½ teaspoon salt
⅛ teaspoon pepper
¾ cup flour
1 teaspoon salt
4 egg yolks, beaten

Place the first five ingredients in a large saucepan and cover with water. Cover pan and simmer two hours. Remove chicken, reserve broth. Bone chicken and place in a baking dish. Sauté onion in butter. Combine onion, bread, sage, salt, and pepper. Sprinkle over chicken. Stir flour into ½ cup fat, slowly add salt and broth. Cook until thickened. Gradually add sauce to egg yolks, cook 1 minute. Pour over casserole. Bake at 375° for 35 minutes or until custard is set and golden brown on top. Serves 8.

Turkey Tetrazzini

½ pound spaghetti
5 tablespoons margarine
½ cup flour
1 teaspoon salt
4 cups milk
¾ pound sharp cheddar cheese, grated
1 four-ounce can mushroom pieces
1 four-ounce jar pimiento, sliced and drained

1 medium green pepper, chopped

4 tablespoons grated onion

1/4 teaspoon paprika

1/2 teaspoon black pepper

1/4 teaspoon curry powder

4 cups turkey meat, cut in large pieces

Cook spaghetti in broth, if possible. (To make broth, cover turkey bones with water and boil 2 hours. Strain.) Drain spaghetti. Make a sauce by melting margarine and adding flour, salt, and milk. Cook, stirring constantly, until thick. Add cheese, mushrooms, pimiento, green pepper, onion, and seasonings. Add turkey meat and spaghetti. Pour into shallow, buttered pan. Bake at 350° for 1 hour. Serves 12.

❧ ❧

EGGS & CHEESE

Seasoning with love...

---

*O*ne time I discovered a tasty and economical dish that I used so many times that we had to caution the children not to say, "Are we having **this** again?!!"

With three children and tight finances, our beginning days as host and hostess required total simplicity. It took me a while to realize it wasn't the gourmet dishes or beautiful appointments that created the atmosphere of friendship we desired to share. Indeed, many times when my inviting got carried away, the children sat on boxes with blankets thrown over them!

Years have gone by. We've come up in the world! Our life has included extensive travel, and we've run across so many people who have reminded us that we entertained them at some point in the distant past. They don't talk about what we had to eat, and the silverware pattern is the farthest thing from their minds. What they say is, "You made us feel so at home!"

—Lois Hicks
Edmonds, Wash.

Quiche Lorraine—1

1 unbaked pie crust (10")
4 eggs
2 cups light cream
dash sugar
dash nutmeg
dash cayenne pepper
¾ teaspoon salt
½ teaspoon pepper
1 cup grated Swiss cheese
10 slices bacon, cooked and crumbled

Preheat oven to 450°. Mix eggs, cream, and seasonings. Butter the bottom of pie crust, and sprinkle with bacon and cheese. Pour egg mixture carefully into pie crust. Reduce oven temperature to 400° immediately. Bake for 12 minutes at 400°, then reduce heat to 325° and bake 25 to 30 minutes. Serves 8.

Quiche Lorraine—2

1 unbaked pie crust (9")
½ pound sliced bacon
1½ cups grated natural Swiss cheese (6 ounces)
3 eggs
1½ cups light cream
¾ teaspoon salt
dash nutmeg
dash cayenne pepper
dash black pepper

Preheat oven to 375°. Fry bacon until it is crisp; drain on paper towels. Crumble into bits, and sprinkle over bottom of the unbaked pie shell. Sprinkle grated cheese over bacon. In medium bowl, with rotary beater, beat eggs with cream, salt, nutmeg, cayenne pepper, and black pepper until mixture is well combined, but not frothy. Place pie shell on middle shelf in oven. Pour egg mixture into pie shell. Bake 35 to 40 minutes, or until the top is golden and center is firm when it is gently pressed with a fingertip. Let cool on a wire rack for 10 minutes before serving. Nice for lunch or supper with a green salad and with fruit for dessert. Serves 6. "Delicious served warm in small wedges as an hors d'oeuvre."

Quiche Lorraine with Swiss Cheese

1 unbaked pie shell (9")
9 slices bacon or 1 cup diced baked ham
3 eggs (large)
1½ cups whole milk, evaporated milk, or half-and-half
1 teaspoon Worcestershire sauce
¾ teaspoon salt
1 cup (¼ pound) grated Swiss cheese
1½ cups canned French fried onions or 1 medium raw onion

Cube bacon and fry until crisp; drain. If raw onion is used, dice and cook until limp in 1 tablespoon of bacon fat. Beat or blend together the eggs, milk, and seasonings. Sprinkle the grated cheese, onions, and bacon or ham into the pie shell; cover with the egg mixture. Bake at 375° for about 40 minutes or until the tip of a silver knife inserted into the custard comes out clean. "This is nice served with asparagus and sliced or broiled tomatoes."

Egg and Cheese Puffs

4 eggs
1 tablespoon chopped onion
½ cup flour
½ teaspoon salt
1 teaspoon baking powder
½ pound sharp cheese
⅓ cup lard substitute

Beat eggs, combine with onion, flour, salt, and baking powder. Add cheese (cut up), drop tablespoon of mixture in hot grease. Makes 12 puffs.

Sunday Special

2 tablespoons butter or margarine
2 tablespoons finely chopped fresh mushrooms
1/8 teaspoon salt
dash pepper
1/2 cup dairy sour cream
1/8 teaspoon Worcestershire sauce
1/4 teaspoon dry mustard
1/4 cup shredded cheddar cheese
6 poached eggs
3 English muffins, split, toasted, and buttered

Melt butter in saucepan, add chopped mushrooms, and brown lightly. Stir in salt, pepper, sour cream, Worcestershire sauce, mustard, and cheese, and stir over low heat until cheese melts. Prepare 6 poached eggs and place them on 6 muffin halves. Top with warm creole sauce and serve immediately. Serves 6.

Individual Cheese Casseroles

6 slices toast, cubed
1 eight-ounce package processed sharp cheddar cheese, shredded
3/4 cup sliced stuffed olives
4 eggs
3 cups milk
1 teaspoon salt
1/4 teaspoon pepper
1 teaspoon prepared mustard

About 1 hour before serving: Divide half of toast cubes between 6 one-cup individual casseroles. Top each with layer of half of shredded cheese, then half of sliced olives. Repeat.

Start heating oven to 350°. Beat eggs with milk, salt, pepper, and mustard.

Pour an equal amount of egg mixture into each casserole. Then bake 40 minutes or until puffed up and browned. Serves 6 luncheon main-dish servings.

Saturday Omelet

2 tablespoons margarine
1/4 cup enriched flour
1/2 teaspoon salt
pepper
1 cup milk
4 egg yolks, well beaten
4 egg whites, beaten stiff
2 tablespoons fat

Melt margarine; add flour and seasonings; blend. Add milk gradually; cook until thick and smooth, stirring constantly. Fold in egg yolks; fold in egg whites. Heat 2 tablespoons fat in 10″ skillet (sides should not be greased); pour in egg mixture. Cover and cook over low heat until mixture puffs, about 10 to 12 minutes. Uncover and finish cooking in broiler, about 1 minute. Fold over. Serve on warm platter with creole sauce. Serves 6.

CREOLE SAUCE *(Make in advance)*

Melt 2 tablespoons fat; add 3 tablespoons chopped onions, 1/4 cup chopped olives, and 1/4 cup chopped green pepper. Cook until green pepper is soft. Add 2 tablespoons enriched flour, 1/4 teaspoon salt, dash of pepper, 1 teaspoon sugar, and 2 cups canned tomatoes. Simmer until thick and flavor-blended, about 45 minutes.

Eggs Newport

1 can cream of mushroom soup, undiluted
1/2 cup mayonnaise
6 hard-cooked eggs, sliced
1/2 cup milk
1 teaspoon chopped chives
8 slices bacon, crisply cooked
English muffins, toasted

Blend the mushroom soup with the mayonnaise. Gradually add the milk, stirring until well blended. Add chives. Layer egg slices and mayonnaise sauce in a 1-quart baking dish. Bake at 350° for 20 minutes or until heated through. Remove from oven and sprinkle the crumbled bacon over the top. Return to the oven about 5 minutes. Serve on toasted English muffins. Serves 4.

Bubbly Eggs

¼ cup margarine or butter
¼ cup flour
¼ teaspoon salt
⅛ teaspoon pepper
1¼ teaspoons dry mustard
2 cups milk
1 cup (4 ounces) grated processed American cheese
1 cup cooked cubed ham
2½-ounce jar (¼ cup) sliced mushrooms, drained
6 hard-cooked eggs, sliced
1 tablespoon margarine or butter
1½ cups fortified high protein cereal

Melt ¼ cup margarine in medium-size saucepan over low heat; stir in flour and seasonings. Remove from heat. Add milk gradually, stirring until smooth. Return to medium heat and cook until bubbly and thickened, stirring constantly. Add cheese; mix until blended. Remove from heat. Portion ham, mushrooms, and eggs evenly into 6 ten-ounce well-buttered casserole dishes. Pour approximately ½ cup sauce over each portion. Place dishes on baking sheet. Bake at 350° for 20 minutes or until thoroughly heated and bubbly. About 10 minutes before serving, melt 1 tablespoon margarine in medium-size fry pan. Add cereal; stir to coat. Remove casseroles from oven. Sprinkle 2 rounded tablespoons of warm cereal in a ring around the top edge of each just before serving. Serves 6.

Cheese and Egg Puffs

6 eggs
¾ cup all-purpose flour
1½ teaspoon baking powder
½ teaspoon salt
½ teaspoon celery salt
1½ cups (6 ounces) shredded cheddar cheese
butter

Beat eggs at high speed of mixer until thick, about 10 minutes. Combine flour, baking powder, salt, and celery salt. Gradually add flour mixture to eggs, beating at lowest speed until dry ingredients are moist. Fold in cheese. Using about ½ cup for each puff, pour batter onto lightly buttered preheated griddle. Turn when brown and bake other side. Top with Spanish sauce. Serve 3 egg puffs each. Serves 4.

SPANISH SAUCE

¾ *cup chopped green pepper*
¾ *cup chopped onion*
¼ *cup (½ stick) butter*
2 *teaspoons all-purpose flour*
1 *fifteen-ounce can tomato sauce*
1 *four-ounce can mushroom stems and pieces, drained*
2 *teaspoons sugar*

Sauté green peppers and onion in butter until tender. Stir in flour, add tomato sauce, mushrooms, and sugar. Cook over low heat, stirring constantly until thickened. Keep warm.

Cheese Soufflé

2 *tablespoons butter*
2 *tablespoons flour*
½ *teaspoon salt*
dash cayenne pepper
¾ *cup milk*
½ *pound cheddar cheese, thinly sliced or shredded*
4 *eggs, separated*

Make a sauce by melting butter in the top half of a double boiler over boiling water. Add unsifted flour, salt, and cayenne pepper gradually, stirring constantly until smooth. Gradually blend in milk; stirring until sauce is thick and smooth. Add cheese, stirring until it is melted. Remove from heat. Add beaten egg yolks. Mix well. Let mixture cool slightly, then slowly fold into stiffly beaten egg whites. Pour into an ungreased 1½-quart soufflé dish or casserole. Draw a line with a spoon 1″ inside the rim of the dish to give soufflé a "top hat" effect. Bake at 300° for 55 to 60 minutes. Serve at once. The slow baking time is essential to the success of the soufflé.

Rainbow Eggs

1 ripe avocado, peeled, seeded, and mashed (¹/₂ cup)
¹/₂ cup dairy sour cream
1 tablespoon lemon juice
1 teaspoon sugar
¹/₄ teaspoon salt
¹/₄ teaspoon garlic powder
dash bottled hot pepper sauce
1 tomato, peeled, seeded, and chopped
4 eggs
¹/₄ cup milk
¹/₂ teaspoon salt
dash pepper
2 tablespoons butter or margarine
¹/₄ cup chopped onion
4 slices buttered toast
4 slices tomato

In a small mixing bowl, combine mashed avocado with dairy sour cream, lemon juice, sugar, the ¹/₄ teaspoon salt, garlic powder, and bottled hot pepper sauce. Fold the chopped tomato into the avocado mixture; set aside. In another bowl, beat eggs, milk, the ¹/₂ teaspoon salt, and pepper. In an 8″ skillet, melt butter or margarine; cook onion until tender but not brown. Add egg mixture to cooked onion in skillet and scramble until eggs are just set but still shiny. To serve, spread about 1 tablespoon of the reserved avocado mixture over each slice of buttered toast. Top each serving with ¹/₄ of the scrambled eggs, one slice of tomato, and about ¹/₄ cup avocado. Serves 2 to 4.

Stuffed Cheese Wafers

¹/₄ pound sharp cheddar cheese, grated
¹/₄ pound butter
¹/₂ to ³/₄ cup flour, sifted
1 teaspoon paprika
stuffed olives

Mix together cheese, butter, flour, and paprika. Pinch off a small amount of dough. Flatten in palm of floured hand. Shape dough around small stuffed olive. Place on tray and freeze. Store in plastic bag after frozen until ready to use. To bake, place frozen cheese-covered olives on an ungreased cookie sheet 1″ apart. Bake 12 to 15 minutes at 400°. Remove and place on paper towel. Serve hot. Yields 25 to 30.

Baked Cheese Grits

6 cups boiling water
1½ cups grits
3 teaspoons seasoning salt
1 pound grated sharp cheddar cheese
4 eggs, beaten
1 cup butter
1 teaspoon paprika
dash Tabasco sauce

Cook boiling water, grits, and seasoning salt together for five minutes. Remove from heat, add all remaining ingredients. Pour into a buttered 9″ x 13″ casserole dish. Bake at 350° for one hour. Serves 8 to 10.

Olive Appetizers

¼ pound (1 cup) grated mild cheddar cheese
¼ cup soft butter
½ cup flour
⅛ teaspoon salt
⅛ teaspoon cayenne pepper
½ teaspoon paprika
24 small stuffed olives

Mix together cheese, butter, flour, salt, cayenne pepper, and paprika. Form into small balls around olives. Refrigerate to chill. Bake 12 minutes at 400°. Serve warm. May be frozen and reheated before serving.

Deviled Eggs Supreme

| 6 hard-cooked eggs |
| 2 tablespoons freeze-dried chives |
| 2 tablespoons blue cheese, crumbled |
| 1½ teaspoons prepared mustard |
| ¼ teaspoon salt |
| dash pepper |
| 3 tablespoons mayonnaise |
| paprika |

Cut eggs in half crosswise, using a fluted vegetable cutter, if desired. Cut a thin slice from rounded ends so eggs will stand. Carefully remove yolks and mash with fork until very fine. Add 1 tablespoon chives, blue cheese, mustard, salt, pepper, and mayonnaise. Mix thoroughly. Refill egg whites with yolk mixture. Sprinkle with paprika and remaining 1 tablespoon chives.

Breakfast on a Bun

| 1 cup oatmeal |
| 1 cup buttermilk |
| 5 tablespoons melted butter |
| ¼ cup dark brown sugar |
| 1 cup sifted all-purpose flour |
| ½ teaspoon baking soda |
| ½ teaspoon baking powder |
| ½ teaspoon salt |
| 3 cooked small, country-style sausages, cut into ¼" slices |
| 5 eggs |

Soak oatmeal in buttermilk for 15 minutes. Add 4 tablespoons butter and brown sugar; blend thoroughly. Combine flour, baking soda, baking powder, and salt together. Add to oatmeal mixture. Butter 5 six-ounce custard cups, using remaining 1 tablespoon butter. Fill custard cups one-third full with oatmeal mixture. Add sausage slices in a circle design. Break one egg over sausage in each cup. Cover with remaining oatmeal mixture. Bake for 20 to 25 minutes at 350°. Serves 5.

Swiss Ham Puff

2 cups cooked ham, ground (about 1 pound—turkey or
   chicken may be used)

2 cups grated Swiss cheese, about ½ pound

½ cup mayonnaise

1 teaspoon prepared mustard

12 slices white bread, toasted

butter

6 eggs

2½ cups milk

dash onion salt or seasoning salt

parsley

Combine ham and cheese in a medium-sized bowl. Blend in mayonnaise, mustard, and seasonings. Trim thin crusts from toast, butter lightly. Make sandwiches. Cut sandwiches diagonally into quarters. Stand points up in a buttered 13" x 9" x 2" baking dish. Beat eggs slightly with milk. Pour over sandwich points. Cover and chill at least 4 hours or overnight. Bake at 325° for 35 minutes or just until custard sets. Garnish with parsley. To serve, cut between sandwiches, lift onto serving plate with large spatula. Serve hot.

Egg Cups Piquant

⅓ cup mayonnaise

¼ teaspoon salt

⅛ teaspoon pepper

1 teaspoon Worcestershire sauce

¼ cup milk

1 cup grated American cheese

6 eggs

Combine first 4 ingredients. Add milk gradually, stirring until smooth. Add cheese. Cook over low heat, stirring constantly until cheese has melted and mixture is thick and smooth, about 5 minutes. Put 2 tablespoons of mixture in bottom of 6 custard cups. Break an egg into each cup, then add another 2 tablespoons mixture in each. Place in shallow pan, 1" hot water surrounding. Bake at 350° for 30 to 35 minutes.

Baked Eggs with Cheese Sauce

2 tablespoons butter

2 tablespoons flour

¼ teaspoon salt

½ teaspoon prepared mustard

1 cup milk

¼ pound processed American cheese, grated

¼ teaspoon Tabasco sauce

8 eggs

Melt butter. Blend in flour and seasonings. Gradually add milk and cook, stirring constantly until mixture thickens and comes to a boil. Remove from heat. Add grated cheese, stirring occasionally until cheese is melted. Pour 2 tablespoons of sauce into each of 4 individual buttered baking dishes. Break 2 eggs into each dish and top with remaining sauce. Bake at 350° until eggs are set (about 12 minutes).

Eggs Benedict

½ stick butter or margarine

3 tablespoons flour

3 tablespoons minced onion

1 cup milk

1 can cream of celery soup, undiluted

1 can cream of mushroom soup, undiluted

¾ cup processed American cheese, cut up

10 hard-boiled eggs, quartered

1 small can sliced mushrooms, drained

Make a paste by melting butter and stirring in flour until smooth. Add minced onion and stir. Add milk, continue stirring, and when mixture begins to thicken, add both soups, mushrooms, and cheese. When mixture is thoroughly heated and thickened, add eggs. Serve over melba toast, rusk buns, or Chinese noodles.

Black Olive Cheese Ball

1 eight-ounce package cream cheese, softened

1 stick margarine

2 ounces blue cheese

1 small can chopped black olives, drained

Worcestershire sauce to taste

garlic salt to taste

Mix all ingredients and roll into a ball. Chill. Serve with corn chips.

Blue Cheese Ball

6 ounces cream cheese

2 ounces blue cheese

1 tablespoon chopped onion

$1/8$ teaspoon pepper

mayonnaise

$1/2$ cup finely chopped nuts

Blend the cheeses together. Add onion, pepper, and just enough mayonnaise to hold the mixture together. Form into a ball and roll ball in nuts. Chill. Serve with crackers.

Hot Cheese Balls

1 cup flour

1 cup sharp cheddar cheese, grated

$3/4$ stick margarine

$1/2$ teaspoon salt

dash cayenne pepper

20 small stuffed olives

Mix together flour, cheese, margarine, salt, and pepper. Shape mixture into small walnut-size balls, each around an olive. Sprinkle balls with paprika. Bake on a cookie sheet at 350° for 10 minutes. Easy to freeze. Yields 20 balls.

Olive Cheese Ball

1 eight-ounce package softened cream cheese

4 ounces crumbled blue cheese

1/4 cup soft margarine

2/3 cup drained chopped stuffed olives

1/3 cup chopped pecans

Blend cheese and margarine together. Add olives and stir well. Form mixture into a ball and roll the ball in the pecans. Chill. Serve with crackers. Makes 2½ cups.

RICE & PASTAS
Seasoning with love…

A *man's spaghetti speciality led me to the Lord! The wife of a young pastor in our small community invited my husband, little girl, and me over for a spaghetti dinner, after which we would attend a special service at the church. In a simple, lovely setting we enjoyed a dinner that the pastor and evangelist had prepared.*

That was over 35 years ago. The outcome of that evening changed the direction of my life. As the invitation was given that evening, I found myself opening my heart's door and inviting Jesus to reside.

The hospitality and acceptance shown to me by people who hardly knew me was a demonstration of the love of Christ. My husband and I picked up the hospitality habit. We work as a team, and the blessings are too innumerable to count.

—Patricia Norton
Grosse Ile, Mich.

Green Rice Casserole

3 cups cooked rice
1 cup finely chopped fresh parsley
¼ cup chopped green pepper
¼ cup finely chopped onion
½ cup (2 ounces) grated cheddar cheese
1 teaspoon salt
¼ teaspoon pepper
¼ teaspoon seasoned salt
¼ teaspoon Accent
1 tablespoon lemon juice
1 teaspoon grated lemon peel
1 clove garlic, minced
¼ cup cooking oil
2 eggs, beaten
1 can evaporated milk (14½ ounce)
paprika

Combine cooked rice, parsley, green pepper, onion, and cheese. Stir in remaining ingredients. Sprinkle with paprika. Bake in shallow baking dish 10″ x 6″ x 1½″ at 350° for 35 to 45 minutes until like a soft custard. Remove from oven and let stand 5 minutes before serving. Serves 8 to 10.

Green Rice

3 cups rice, cooked
1 cup rice, uncooked
1½ cups sharp cheddar cheese, grated
¾ cup butter, melted
5 tablespoons onion, minced
1½ cups parsley, chopped
4 egg yolks, beaten
4 egg whites, stiffly beaten
1½ tablespoons Worcestershire sauce

1½ teaspoons paprika
2 teaspoons salt
½ cup milk

Combine all ingredients except egg whites. Blend thoroughly. Fold in egg whites. Bake in a greased baking dish at 350° for 30 minutes. Serves 6 to 8.

My Favorite Macaroni and Cheese

1 cup broken macaroni
1½ tablespoons butter
2 tablespoons flour
½ teaspoon salt
1½ cups milk
2½ cups grated sharp cheese
1 cup buttered soft bread crumbs

Cook macaroni, drain and rinse. Melt butter, add flour, add salt and pepper. Add milk and cook until thick. Add 2 cups cheese to hot sauce, stir until blended. Mix with macaroni. Sprinkle a layer of crumbs in a greased 1-quart dish. Add macaroni mixture. Top with remaining ½ cup cheese and crumbs mixed together. Bake at 400° for 20 minutes. Serves 4.

Spinach Ring

3 cups cooked spinach, drained
½ cup bread crumbs
1 teaspoon onion juice
1 tablespoon chopped celery
¼ teaspoon salt
¼ teaspoon pepper
2 tablespoons butter
3 eggs, beaten

Mix ingredients and pour into buttered ring mold. Set in pan of hot water and bake 30 minutes in 250° oven. Unmold and fill center with creamed cauliflower. Border dish with buttered carrots.

Cheddar Rice Casserole

1 cup long grain rice
1/4 cup butter
2 tablespoons chopped onion
1 ten-ounce package frozen chopped spinach, thawed and drained
1 tablespoon Worcestershire sauce
1/2 teaspoon thyme
1/2 teaspoon marjoram
4 eggs, slightly beaten
1 cup milk
2 1/2 cups shredded sharp cheddar cheese
1/8 teaspoon salt
1/8 teaspoon pepper

Cook rice. Melt butter in frying pan, add onion and sauté till limp. Combine cooked rice, onion mixture, well-drained spinach, Worcestershire sauce, marjoram, thyme, eggs, milk, 2 cups cheese, salt, and pepper. Put in a shallow 2-quart casserole, sprinkle remaining cheese on top. Bake uncovered at 250° for 30 to 40 minutes or until center is set. Serves 6 to 8.

Chicken Rice Ring
with Mushroom Sauce

1 cup diced, cooked chicken
2 cups cooked rice
1 cup dry bread crumbs
1 teaspoon salt
1/2 teaspoon paprika
4 eggs, well beaten
1/4 cup chopped pimiento
1/4 cup butter or margarine, melted
2 1/2 cups milk or chicken stock, or half-and-half

Combine ingredients in order given. Use ½ teaspoon salt if chicken stock is used instead of milk. Turn into a greased 1½-quart ring mold. Bake at 325° for 1 hour. Let stand for 15 minutes before unmolding onto a warm platter. Serve with mushroom sauce. Serves 6.

MUSHROOM SAUCE

½ *pound mushrooms, sliced*
¼ *cup butter or margarine*
¼ *cup flour*
¼ *teaspoon salt*
2 *cups chicken stock*
2 *egg yolks, slightly beaten*
¼ *cup light cream*
1 *teaspoon lemon juice*
1 *teaspoon finely chopped parsley*

Sauté mushrooms in 2 tablespoons of the butter until lightly browned. In another pan melt remaining 2 tablespoons butter. Stir in flour and salt. Add chicken stock and cook, stirring constantly, over low heat, until mixture comes to a boil and thickens. Combine egg yolks and cream. Stir into hot sauce. Cook a few minutes longer. Remove from heat. Stir in lemon juice, parsley, and sautéed mushrooms. Reheat if necessary.

Tuna and Noodle Casserole

3 *tablespoons butter*
3 *tablespoons flour*
2 *cups milk*
1 *cup flaked tuna*
1 *cup sliced mushrooms*
½ *teaspoon salt*
¼ *teaspoon pepper*
1 *cup grated cheese*
1 *four-ounce package noodles, cooked*

Melt butter, add flour and milk. Add to this cream sauce the flaked tuna, mushrooms, and cooked noodles. Put in casserole and add grated cheese on top. Bake 20 to 25 minutes in moderate oven. Serves 6.

Sicilian Supper

1 pound ground beef

1/2 cup chopped onion

1 six-ounce can tomato paste

3/4 cup water

1 1/2 teaspoons salt

1/4 teaspoon pepper

3/4 cup milk

1 eight-ounce package cream cheese, cubed

1/2 cup grated Parmesan cheese

1/2 teaspoon garlic salt

1/2 cup chopped green pepper

2 cups egg noodles, cooked

Brown meat. Add onion; cook until tender. Add tomato paste, water, salt, and pepper; simmer 5 minutes. Heat milk and cream cheese; blend well. Stir in 1/4 cup Parmesan cheese, garlic salt, green pepper, and noodles. In a 1 1/2- or 2-quart casserole, alternate rows of noodles and meat sauce. Bake at 350° for 20 minutes. Sprinkle on remaining cheese. Serves 6.

Chicken Loaf

4-pound hen or 2 fryers, cooked and diced

2 cups fresh bread crumbs

1 1/2 teaspoons salt

1 1/2 cups milk

1 1/2 cups broth

4 eggs, well beaten

1 cup cooked rice

1/8 cup chopped pimiento

Combine ingredients and bake in greased 9" x 13" pan at 325° for 1 hour. Serve with sauce. Serves 16.

SAUCE

¼ cup margarine
½ cup fried mushrooms
¼ cup cream
2 tablespoons chopped parsley
5 tablespoons flour
⅛ teaspoon paprika
1 pint chicken broth

Melt margarine. Add flour and stir until smooth. Stir in broth. Add the cream. Cook over low fire until thickened. Add remaining ingredients. Serve hot over chicken loaf.

Ham-Stuffed Manicotti with Cheese Sauce

8 manicotti shells (4 ounces)
¼ cup chopped onion
2 tablespoons cooking oil
3 cups ground cooked ham (8 ounces)
1 six-ounce can chopped mushrooms, drained (1 cup)
3 tablespoons grated Parmesan cheese
¼ cup chopped green pepper
3 tablespoons butter or margarine
3 tablespoons all-purpose flour
2 cups milk
4 ounces (1 cup) shredded processed Swiss cheese

Cook manicotti in boiling salted water for 15 to 20 minutes or just until tender; drain. Rinse with cold water; drain. In a small skillet, cook onion in hot oil until tender. Add ham and mushrooms; cool. Stir in Parmesan; set aside. In small saucepan, cook green pepper in the butter or margarine until tender; blend in flour. Add all milk at once. Cook and stir until thickened and bubbly. Stir in Swiss cheese until melted. Mix ¼ cup of the cheese sauce with ham and mushroom mixture. Fill each tube with about ⅓ cup ham filling. Arrange tubes in greased 11¾″ x 7½″ x 1¾″ baking dish. Pour remaining cheese sauce over stuffed manicotti. Sprinkle with paprika. Bake, covered, at 350° for 30 minutes or until heated through. Serves 4.

Ham and Rice Casserole

2 cups instant rice
2 cups water
2 tablespoons minced onions
1 ten-ounce package frozen peas
4 cups diced ham
1 can cheddar cheese soup
1 cup milk
1 cup cheese crackers, rolled
3 tablespoons melted butter

Grease a 9″ x 13″ dish or two 8″ x 8″ pans. Cook rice in water according to directions. Layer rice, peas, and ham in dish. Blend soup, milk, and onions. Pour liquid mixture over layered ingredients. Make topping of cracker crumbs and butter. Bake at 350° for 35 minutes. May be frozen for later use. Serves 8.

Chinese Casserole

2 pounds bulk sausage
1 medium onion, diced
½ green pepper, diced
1½ cups celery, diced
1 eight-ounce can water chestnuts, sliced
½ cup long grain and wild rice mixture
2 packages chicken noodle soup mixture
¾ cup almonds, slivered
4 cups cold water
1 three-ounce can sliced mushrooms

Brown sausage and drain on paper towels. Sauté onion, celery, and green pepper in a small amount of the sausage fat. Add remaining ingredients. Mix well. Ladle into a 9″ x 13″ baking dish, cover and bake at 325° for 40 minutes. Remove cover and bake 20 minutes longer. Serves 8.

Sour Cream Noodle Bake

1 eight-ounce package medium egg noodles

2 tablespoons butter or margarine

1¼ pounds ground chuck

1 eight-ounce can tomato sauce

1 teaspoon salt

¼ teaspoon garlic salt

⅛ teaspoon pepper

1 cup cottage cheese

1 cup dairy sour cream

½ cup chopped green onions

1 cup coarsely shredded cheddar cheese

Cook noodles according to package directions; rinse and drain. Melt butter in skillet; add meat and stir over moderate heat until meat loses its pink color. Add tomato sauce, salt, garlic salt, and pepper, cover and simmer 5 minutes. Fold together noodles, cottage cheese, sour cream, and onions; spoon half the mixture into the bottom of a 2½-quart casserole. Cover with half the meat mixture. Repeat layers once again. Sprinkle shredded cheese over top. Bake at 350° for 25 to 30 minutes or until mixture is thoroughly heated and cheese is melted. Serves 6.

Broccoli Green Rice

1 seven-ounce box instant white rice

1 pound American cheese

1 package frozen chopped broccoli

2 eggs

⅔ cup milk

½ cup cooking oil

clove garlic, chopped, or equivalent in dehydrated garlic

medium white onion, chopped

1 can cream of mushroom soup

Cook rice according to directions on package. Cut cheese into 1½″ cubes. Cook broccoli several minutes. Place all ingredients into large mixing bowl and stir until mixed. Pour into 2-quart dish and bake 1½ hours at 325°. Serves 8 to 10. "Very good."

Company Casserole—1

8 ounces medium noodles

1 pound ground beef

3 tablespoons butter or margarine

2 eight-ounce cans tomato sauce

1 cup cottage cheese

1 eight-ounce package cream cheese

$1/2$ cup sour cream

$1/2$ cup green onions, chopped

1 tablespoon green pepper, chopped

2 tablespoons melted butter or margarine

Cook noodles, rinse and drain. Brown meat in 3 tablespoons butter. Stir in tomato sauce. Combine cottage cheese, cream cheese, sour cream, onions, and peppers and beat. Spread half of the noodles in a 2-quart greased casserole or baking dish. Build layers of cheese, meat, noodles, until all is used or casserole is filled. Pour 2 tablespoons melted butter over top and bake at 350° for 30 minutes. Generously serves 6 to 8.

Company Casserole—2

$1/2$ pound noodles (4 cups)

1 tablespoon butter or margarine

1 pound ground chuck

2 eight-ounce cans tomato sauce

1 cup cottage cheese

1 eight-ounce package soft cream cheese

$1/4$ cup commercial sour cream

$1/3$ cup snipped green onion tops

1 tablespoon minced green pepper

2 tablespoons melted butter or margarine

Cook noodles as label directs; drain. Meanwhile, melt 1 tablespoon hot butter in skillet, sauté ground chuck until browned. Stir in tomato sauce. Remove from heat. Combine cottage cheese, cream cheese, sour cream, onion tops, and green pepper. In 2-quart casserole spread half of noodles. Cover with cheese mixture; then cover with the rest of noodles. Pour on melted butter, then meat mixture. Refrigerate. About 1 hour before serving, preheat oven to 375°. Bake casserole 45 minutes, or until heated through. Serves 6.

Manicotti with Meat Sauce

1 pound ground beef
2 cups water
2 six-ounce cans tomato paste
½ cup chopped onion
1 three-ounce can sliced mushrooms, drained
2 tablespoons snipped parsley
2 teaspoons dried oregano, crushed
1½ teaspoons salt
1 teaspoon sugar
1 large clove garlic, minced
3 cups ricotta or cream-style cottage cheese, drained
½ cup grated Parmesan cheese
2 eggs, slightly beaten
¼ cup snipped parsley
½ teaspoon salt
8 manicotti shells (4 ounces)

In a large saucepan, brown meat; drain off excess fat. Add water, tomato paste, onion, mushrooms, the 2 tablespoons parsley, oregano, the 1½ teaspoons salt, sugar, and garlic. Simmer uncovered for 30 minutes, stirring occasionally. Meanwhile, combine ricotta, Parmesan cheese, eggs, the ¼ cup parsley, the ½ teaspoon salt. Cook manicotti shells in boiling water just until tender, about 20 minutes; drain. Using a small spoon, stuff each shell with ⅓ to ½ cup cheese mixture. Put half the tomato meat sauce into a 14½" x 8" x 1¾" baking dish. Arrange stuffed shells in a row. Drizzle with remaining sauce. Bake at 350° for 30 to 40 minutes. Let stand 10 minutes before serving. Pass Parmesan cheese. Serves 4 to 6. "Good for lunch."

Janet's Supreme Beef Casserole

1¼ pounds ground chuck
1 teaspoon shortening
1 sixteen-ounce can tomatoes
1 eight-ounce can tomato sauce
2 teaspoons salt
2 teaspoons sugar
2 garlic cloves, minced
1 five-ounce package medium-wide egg noodles
1 cup sour cream
1 three-ounce package cream cheese
6 green onions, chopped with tops
1 cup grated cheese

Melt shortening in skillet; add beef, breaking into pieces with fork, and cook until light brown. Drain off fat. Stir into meat the tomatoes and tomato sauce, adding salt, sugar, and garlic. Simmer 5 to 10 minutes. Meanwhile, cook the noodles; drain well, and with a fork blend in the sour cream, cream cheese, and onions. In lightly greased 2- or 3-quart casserole, pour small amount of meat sauce, cover with layer of noodles and cheese; repeat layers, topping with meat sauce. Bake at 350° for 35 minutes.

VEGETABLES AND FRUIT

Seasoning with love...

*W*ith *a mother like mine, I almost* **had** *to turn out to be a hostess. Mother kept a calendar record of guests, and even in her 75th year of life, she entertained over 500 guests in her home, and loved it. I was the oldest of seven children. I have beautiful memories of helping to entertain (even if I* **did** *have to do the dishes).*

The example and training I have received in my home stood me in good stead because I married a preacher. After the pastorate, he was for 30 years a district superintendent of our church, with heavy responsibilities. Our home became Grand Central Station. Was I glad I had learned the secrets of my mother's ease at entertaining! Believe me, all that dishwashing experience came in handy. If I had my life to live over, I'd plunge in again, entertaining missionaries, pastors, foreign students, and anyone else the Lord brought along.

—Madlyn Hance
Bethany, Okla.

Hot Spiced Cherries

| 1 No. 2 can cherries, drained |
| 1½ tablespoons cornstarch |
| ¼ cup sugar |
| juice from cherries plus enough water to make 1 cup |
| ⅛ teaspoon cinnamon |
| ⅛ teaspoon nutmeg |
| ¼ teaspoon red food coloring |

Combine sugar, cornstarch, and spices. Add to cherries and liquid. Add red coloring and cook over medium heat, stirring constantly until thickened.

Orange Compote

| 4 seeded oranges |
| ¼ cup sugar |
| 1 cup orange juice |
| 1 teaspoon orange rind, grated |

Peel oranges and slice ⅛″ thick across the sections. Arrange slices in deep dish. Cook sugar, orange juice, and rind until sugar has dissolved and liquid comes to a boil. Cool and pour over orange slices and serve with sugar cookies. "A perfect way to end a heavy meal."

Party Fruit Delight

| 1 No. 2½ can pears, drained and quartered |
| 1 No. 2½ can peaches, drained and quartered |
| 1 No. 2 can pineapple chunks, drained |
| 2 cups white seedless grapes |
| 2 cups miniature flavored marshmallows |
| 1 large can frozen orange juice, undiluted |

Mix drained fruit. Fold in marshmallows. Add frozen orange juice and let mixture stand in refrigerator 2 to 3 hours or overnight. Serves 8.

Spicy Filled Peaches

16 peach halves (a 29-ounce can yields about 10 halves)

¹/₄ cup vinegar

4 whole cloves

cinnamon sticks

¹/₃ cup chopped almonds

¹/₃ cup chopped raisins

¹/₃ cup chopped shredded coconut

6 candied cherries, diced

Drain syrup from peaches and boil ¹/₂ can syrup with vinegar, cloves, and 2″ piece of cinnamon stick about 5 minutes. (There will be about ¹/₃ cup liquid.) Mix almonds, raisins, coconut, cherries, and ¹/₄ cup cooked liquid, and let stand about 10 minutes. Pour remaining liquid over peach halves. Put 2 peach halves together with spoonful of nut mixture in center and put a cinnamon stick through all. Chill until serving time. Arrange around turkey and garnish with parsley. Serves 8.

Peaches Glamour

6 canned cling peaches

¹/₄ cup brown sugar

1 tablespoon butter

¹/₄ cup ground gingersnaps

¹/₂ teaspoon grated lemon rind

1 tablespoon syrup from peaches

sour cream

cinnamon

Drain peaches, and place cup side up, in a shallow baking dish. Combine sugar, butter, gingersnaps, lemon rind, and syrup in a small bowl, and press with a fork until thoroughly blended. Fill peaches with mixture. Bake at 350° for 25 minutes. When cooked, place a small dollop of sour cream in the center of each and sprinkle with cinnamon. (Or serve sour cream separately.)

Curried Fruit

1 one-pound can pear halves
1 one-pound can pineapple chunks
1 one-pound can peach halves
1 one-pound can apricot halves
$\frac{1}{3}$ cup butter or margarine
2 teaspoons curry powder
$\frac{3}{4}$ cup brown sugar
8 to 10 maraschino cherries

Drain fruit and put in a shallow baking dish. Melt the butter and add the curry powder and brown sugar. Pour over the fruit and bake at 375° for 1 hour.

Hot Stuffed Avocados

3 avocados
1 tablespoon vinegar
garlic
2 tablespoons butter, melted
2 tablespoons flour
1 cup light cream
$\frac{1}{2}$ teaspoon Worcestershire sauce
$1\frac{1}{4}$ teaspoons salt
dash pepper
1 tablespoon grated onion
$\frac{1}{4}$ teaspoon celery salt
2 cups cooked crab meat or lobster
dash cayenne pepper
$\frac{1}{3}$ cup grated cheddar cheese

Cut avocados in half. Remove pits. Put vinegar and a slice of garlic in each half. Let stand 30 minutes. Melt butter. Blend in flour. Add light cream and cook, stirring until thickened. Add Worcestershire sauce, salt, dash of pepper, onion, celery salt, and 2 cups cooked crab meat or lobster, and a dash of cayenne pepper. Heat. Pour vinegar and garlic from avocados. Peel. Fill with creamed mixture. Sprinkle with grated cheddar cheese. Place in baking pan with ¼" water in bottom of pan. Bake 15 minutes at 350° until cheese melts. Serves 6.

Ginger Apple Rings

4 tablespoons butter
4 tablespoons honey
½ teaspoon ground ginger
¼ teaspoon cinnamon
2 tablespoons lemon juice, freshly squeezed
4 medium apples, unpeeled

In medium skillet melt butter. Add honey, ginger, cinnamon, and lemon juice. Cook for 3 to 5 minutes. Wash, core, and slice apples in ½" slices or rings. Add to honey and butter for 4 to 5 minutes, turning twice. Makes 16 rings.

Hot Spiced Fruit

1 sixteen-ounce can pear halves
1 can pineapple spears (1 pound, 4 ounces)
1 sixteen-ounce can peach halves
1 can figs (1 pound, 1 ounce)
1 tablespoon brown sugar
¼ cup butter
1 teaspoon curry powder
1 teaspoon ground cinnamon
½ teaspoon ground nutmeg

Drain, then dry fruit; place in 10" x 6" x 2" baking dish. Center pears and pineapple, with peaches and figs at either end. Sprinkle with sugar, dot with butter, freezer wrap and freeze. Remove from freezer 1 hour before serving; then, start heating oven to 325°. Unwrap dish of frozen fruit; sprinkle with curry, cinnamon, and nutmeg. Bake 50 minutes. Serve warm from baking dish with ham, lamb, or poultry. Serves 12.

Ritzy Rhubarb

1 can pineapple chunks (1 pound, 4 ounce)
2 cups rhubarb, cut into 1" pieces
1/2 cup sugar
1/2 teaspoon nutmeg
sour cream

Pour pineapple and syrup into 8" square glass baking dish. Add rhubarb. Sprinkle with sugar and nutmeg. Cover with aluminum foil and bake at 350° for 30 to 35 minutes or until rhubarb is tender. Chill. Serve topped with sour cream. Serves 6.

Pears and Spice

1 can pears (29 ounce), drained
1/4 teaspoon cinnamon
1/8 teaspoon garlic salt
1/4 teaspoon seasoned salt
1/2 cup raisins
1/4 teaspoon ginger
1/4 cup currant or grape jelly

Place pears rounded side up in a saucepan. Combine remaining ingredients, blend well and pour on pears. Heat slowly for 2 minutes. Turn pears hollow side up and fill with raisins. Simmer until thoroughly heated.

Glazed Apple Slices

3 apples
2 tablespoons butter
1/4 cup brown sugar
1/4 cup water

Slice tart red apples, removing core. Place butter and brown sugar in skillet, heat slowly till butter melts, stirring constantly. Stir in water, heat to boiling. Add apple slices. Simmer until apples are tender, turning occasionally to glaze. Serves 4. "Good to serve with baked stuffed pork chops or any pork dish."

Janet's Lima Bean Casserole

2 slices bacon

2 tablespoons flour

1 sixteen-ounce can stewed tomatoes

2 tablespoons instant minced onion

2 tablespoons dark corn syrup

1 tablespoon molasses

1/4 teaspoon chili powder

1 teaspoon salt

2 ten-ounce packages frozen lima beans, thawed

1/3 cup shredded cheddar cheese

Cook bacon in skillet until lightly browned. Add flour, tomatoes, and onion. Cook over moderate heat until thick. Stir in corn syrup, molasses, chili powder, and salt. Add lima beans. Pour into a 1 1/2-quart casserole, cover and bake at 375° for 50 minutes. Uncover and add cheese, bake 15 minutes longer. Serves 6 or 8.

Beans

1 fifteen-ounce can dried limas, drain

1 one-pound can green beans, drain

1 one-pound can red kidney beans, do not drain

1 one-pound 11-ounce can New England style baked beans, do not drain

4 large onions, cut in rings

3/4 cup brown sugar

1 teaspoon dry mustard

1/2 teaspoon garlic powder

1 teaspoon salt

1/2 cup cider vinegar

8 slices bacon

Cut up bacon and brown; remove bacon and cook onions in bacon grease. Add seasonings and vinegar. Cook slowly 20 minutes. Add beans and bacon. Bake uncovered in 3-quart casserole 1 hour at 350°. The beans can be frozen. Serves 10 to 12.

Baked Beans

2 cups pinto beans
1 good-sized ham hock
water
2/3 cup diced green pepper
1 large onion, diced
2/3 cup diced celery
2/3 to 1 cup dark brown sugar
2 tablespoons vinegar
4 tablespoons catsup
1 teaspoon salt
1 eight-ounce can tomato sauce

Soak beans overnight. Drain and wash with cold water. Trim ham hock of excess fat. Cover beans and ham hock well with water and cook over low heat 3 to 4 hours. When beans are tender, add the following: green pepper, onion, celery, brown sugar, vinegar, catsup, salt, and tomato sauce. Cut ham from bone and remove any additional excess fat. Add ham to beans. Pour into a 2-quart casserole and bake 4 hours. Bake the first 30 minutes at 400° and the remainder at 300°.

Broccoli Supreme

2 tablespoons butter, melted
2 tablespoons all-purpose flour
1 three-ounce package cream cheese, softened
1/4 cup crumbled blue cheese
1 cup milk
2 ten-ounce packages frozen chopped broccoli, cooked and drained
1/3 cup crackers, crushed

In a large saucepan blend butter, flour, and cheese. Add milk; cook, stirring until mixture boils. Stir in cooked broccoli. Place in a 1-quart casserole; top with cracker crumbs. (This may be made up in the morning to serve at night, but do not add crumbs until just before baking.) Bake at 350° for 30 minutes. Serves 8 to 10.

Broccoli Rice Bake

½ cup chopped celery

½ cup chopped onion

½ cup butter

1 can condensed cream of mushroom soup

½ cup water

1 eight-ounce jar pasteurized processed Cheese-Whiz

1 ten-ounce package frozen chopped broccoli, thawed and drained

1 seven-ounce package precooked rice

Sauté celery and onion in melted butter until tender. Combine soup, water, and cheese spread in saucepan with vegetables. Heat until cheese melts, add broccoli. Cook rice according to package directions. Combine with hot cheese mixture, put in 2-quart casserole, or in two casseroles. Bake at 350° for 45 minutes for large size, less for smaller ones. Can be made ahead, also frozen. Serves 6 to 8.

Broccoli Casserole

¼ cup finely chopped onion

6 tablespoons butter

2 tablespoons flour

½ cup water

1 eight-ounce jar processed cheese

2 ten-ounce packages frozen chopped broccoli

3 eggs

½ cup crushed cracker crumbs

Sauté onions in 4 tablespoons butter. Add flour, slowly add the water. Cook over low heat until thickened and the sauce comes to a boil. Blend in cheese. Combine with broccoli and eggs. Mix slowly. Pour into a 1½-quart baking dish. Cover with crumbs, dot with remaining butter. Bake at 325° for 30 minutes. Serves 8.

Skillet Cabbage

1 tablespoon salad oil
3 cups finely shredded cabbage
1 cup chopped celery
1 small green pepper, chopped
1 small onion, chopped
1/2 teaspoon salt
dash pepper

About 20 minutes before serving: In a 10" skillet over medium-low heat, in hot oil, stir all ingredients until well mixed. Cover pan and cook 5 minutes, stirring occasionally. Serve immediately. Vegetables will be crisp. Serves 4.

Carrot Casserole—1

2 pounds carrots
4 tablespoons chopped onion
14 soda crackers, crushed
cheese sauce
buttered cracker crumbs

Cook carrots in boiling salted water until tender. Mash carrots; add onion and crackers. Blend in cheese sauce (recipe below). Pour mixture into casserole and top with buttered cracker crumbs. Bake at 350° for 30 to 40 minutes.

CHEESE SAUCE

2 tablespoons butter
2 tablespoons flour
1/2 teaspoon salt
1/4 teaspoon pepper
1 1/4 cups milk
1 cup diced processed cheese spread

Melt butter; add seasoning and flour. Stir in milk gradually. When mixture thickens, blend in diced cheese.

Carrot Casserole—2

2 cups cooked carrots
1 cup cracker crumbs
1/2 pound American cheese, grated
3/4 cup chopped onion
1/2 cup stuffed olives, sliced
3/4 cup cream or milk
bread crumbs and butter pats for topping

Cut cooked carrots in 3/8″ thick slices. Mix ingredients together. Add a few bread crumbs and pats of butter to top. Bake at 350° for 30 minutes in 1½-quart casserole. May be mixed ahead of time, except for milk. Add milk just before baking.

Corn and Carrot Casserole

2 tablespoons butter
2 tablespoons flour
1 cup scalded milk
1 teaspoon salt
1/8 teaspoon pepper
3/4 teaspoon paprika
2 beaten eggs
1½ cups shredded carrots
1¾ cups cream-style corn
1/3 cup chopped green pepper
2 tablespoons chopped onion

Melt butter, add flour, blend. Gradually add milk, cook over low heat until thick. Stir constantly. Add seasonings. Stir a little hot sauce into eggs, add egg mixture to sauce. Stir in vegetables. Bake at 350° in a greased 1½-quart casserole for 50 to 55 minutes or until done. Serves 5 or 6.

Creamed Celery and Almonds

2¹/₂ cups celery, ¹/₄″ slices
¹/₄ cup toasted almonds
2 tablespoons flour
2 tablespoons butter
1 cup milk
1 cup soft bread crumbs

Blend together celery and almonds. In a saucepan melt butter, add flour. Gradually add the milk. Heat, stirring constantly until thickened. Add to the celery and ¹/₂ cup crumbs. Season with salt and pepper. Top with remaining crumbs. Bake at 350° in buttered casserole for 15 to 20 minutes.

Curried Baked Cauliflower

1 large head cauliflower
¹/₂ teaspoon salt
1 can condensed cream of chicken soup
1 cup grated cheddar cheese
¹/₃ cup mayonnaise
1 teaspoon curry powder
¹/₄ cup dried bread crumbs
2 tablespoons butter, melted

Break cauliflower into flowerets and cook 10 minutes in large, covered saucepan in 1″ boiling salted water over medium-low heat. Drain well. Next, in a 2-quart casserole, stir together undiluted soup, cheese, mayonnaise, and curry powder; add cauliflower; mix well. Toss bread crumbs in melted butter; sprinkle on top. Bake at 350° for 30 minutes or until casserole is hot and bubbly. Serves 8 to 10.

Celery Regal

6 cups celery, cut diagonally
salt

1 can condensed cream of chicken soup
1 can water chestnuts (8½ ounce), drained and sliced
½ cup toasted slivered almonds
2 tablespoons butter
buttered bread crumbs

Cook celery in slightly salted water until crunchy tender. Drain well. Combine cream of chicken soup and sliced water chestnuts with celery. Sauté the slivered almonds in butter. Pour the celery mixture into a buttered casserole and top with buttered bread crumbs, then sprinkle with the almonds. Bake at 350° for 35 to 40 minutes. Serves 4 to 6.

Perfect Scalloped Corn

2½ cups cream-style corn
¾ cup milk
1 egg, well beaten
¾ teaspoon salt
⅛ teaspoon pepper
1 cup cracker crumbs
¼ cup minced onion
3 tablespoons chopped pimiento
2 tablespoons butter, melted
½ cup cracker crumbs

Heat corn and milk, stir into egg gradually. Add seasonings, 1 cup cracker crumbs, onion, and pimiento. Mix well. Pour into a 1-quart greased baking dish. Blend together butter and remainder of crumbs. Sprinkle over corn. Bake at 350° for 30 minutes. Serves 6.

Eggplant Mixed Broil

Peel eggplant, slice crosswise ½″ thick. Brush slices with melted butter on both sides. Broil lightly, until tender. Top each with thick slices of tomatoes, salt and pepper to season. Sprinkle with generous amounts of grated cheddar cheese and cooked crumbled bacon. Broil until cheese melts. Serve immediately.

Stuffed Carrots

2 pounds large-sized carrots, halved and cooked until tender
3 cups instant rice, prepared as directed on box for 6 servings
8 slices bacon, cut fine
2 stalks celery, chopped fine
1 green pepper, chopped fine
melted butter

Cook carrots in boiling, salted water. Fry the bacon. Remove from skillet. Add the cooked rice, green pepper, and celery to the bacon grease and cook slowly until tender. Scoop out the center of the cooked carrots and add to the rest of the mixture. Stuff the carrots, pour melted butter over the top, and bake at 350° for a few minutes or until hot. Serves 6 to 8.

Eggplant Soufflé

1 medium eggplant
2 tablespoons butter
2 tablespoons flour
1 cup milk
1 cup grated cheese
2 eggs
¾ cup soft bread crumbs
¼ cup catsup
salt and pepper to taste
¼ cup grated onion

Peel, dice, and boil eggplant in salted water until tender. Drain and mash. Melt butter, add flour and blend. When smooth, add milk and stir until thickened. Add eggplant, cheese, bread crumbs, and seasonings. Separate eggs. Beat yolks and add to eggplant mixture. Beat whites until stiff and gently fold into eggplant mixture. Bake in greased soufflé dish at 350° for 45 minutes or until knife inserted into center comes out clean. Serve at once.

Stuffed Mushrooms—1

| 16 large mushrooms |
| 1/2 onion, chopped fine |
| 2 tablespoons butter |
| 1/2 cup fine bread crumbs |
| 1 tablespoon chopped fresh parsley |
| 1 tablespoon cream |

Remove mushroom stems, mince fine. Sauté onions in butter. Add crumbs, parsley, mushroom stems; cook 1 minute. Add cream, mix well. Fill raw mushrooms, dot with butter. Bake at 400° for 7 to 10 minutes. "Very good with steak."

Stuffed Mushrooms—2

| 12 large, fresh mushrooms |
| 6 teaspoons finely chopped onion |
| 6 white soda crackers, crushed |
| 3 tablespoons finely chopped parsley |
| 3 tablespoons melted butter |
| cream |

Wash mushrooms, remove cap from stem. Turn caps upside down on paper towel. Cut off dead part of stems and finely chop remainder of stems in a bowl, mix the chopped stems, chopped onion, parsley, crackers, and melted butter. Add enough cream to make a thick paste or dressing. Stuff the mushroom caps with mixture. Sprinkle with paprika and place in a baking dish stuffed side up. Pour cream into pan around mushrooms to about 1/4" depth. Bake uncovered at 350° for 20 to 25 minutes. Baste twice during cooking time. Serves 4.

French Fried Mushrooms

Dip large, clean mushrooms into flour, then into beaten eggs and bread crumbs. Let stand at least 15 minutes. Fry in deep fat.

Mushroom Casserole

1 pound fresh mushrooms
4 tablespoons butter
8 slices white bread
1/2 cup chopped onion
1/2 cup chopped celery
1/2 cup chopped green pepper
1/2 cup mayonnaise
3/4 teaspoon salt
1/4 teaspoon pepper
2 eggs, slightly beaten
1 1/2 cups milk
1 can cream of mushroom soup
1/2 cup grated cheddar cheese

Wash mushrooms and slice coarsely. Sauté in 2 tablespoons butter until most of the liquid is absorbed. Butter bread slices, cut 3 slices into 1" squares and place in buttered casserole or soufflé dish. Sauté onion, celery, and green pepper in remaining 2 tablespoons of butter; then mix with mayonnaise, salt, and pepper. Layer mushrooms over bread cubes. Next, place sautéed vegetable mixture over mushrooms. Make another layer of 3 slices of cubed bread. Combine eggs and milk, and pour over casserole. Refrigerate at least 1 hour. Spread undiluted soup over mixture. Top with remaining bread cubes. Bake uncovered at 350° for 40 to 50 minutes. Sprinkle with cheese and bake 10 minutes longer. Serves 8.

Mushroom Instant

1 pound mushrooms
1/4 pound crackers
1 cup cream
1 teaspoon salt
paprika
pepper
butter

Crush crackers. Add sliced, raw mushrooms. Pour melted butter over the combination and add cream. Dot with butter, sprinkle with paprika, and bake in casserole at 350° for 45 to 60 minutes.

Company Stuffed Onions

4 large or 6 medium white onions
1 cup fresh bread crumbs
⅔ cup chopped walnuts
2 tablespoons minced parsley
dash pepper
¼ cup melted butter
1 egg, beaten
1 can condensed cream of mushroom soup
½ cup water

Peel onions; cook until partially tender (about 20 minutes) in large amount of salted water. When partially tender, drain and cool. Slice ends from onions; remove centers and place onions in shallow baking pan. (Use centers later as creamed vegetable.) Combine remaining ingredients except soup and water; fill onions. Blend soup and water; pour around onions, not over. Bake at 375° for 30 minutes, or until onions are tender. Serves 4 to 6.

Onion-Broccoli Cups

12 large yellow onions
2 bunches broccoli (about 1½ pounds each)
1 teaspoon salt
4 tablespoons butter or margarine (½ stick)
2 tablespoons lemon juice

Trim and peel onions; cut a thin slice from each to make tops even. Stand onions in a large frying pan; add boiling water to depth of about 1″; heat to boiling; cover. Simmer 10 minutes. Lift onions carefully from water with a slotted spoon; cool until easy to handle, then remove center from each to make a cup. Empty frying pan; return onion cups to pan. Trim flowerets from broccoli; wash well. Stand 3 or 4 in each onion cup. Sprinkle with salt; add boiling water to a depth of 1″. Heat to boiling; cover. Cook 15 minutes, or until tender. Arrange on a serving platter. Melt butter or margarine in a small saucepan, stir in lemon juice. Drizzle over vegetables. Makes 12.

Stuffed Onions

8 large Bermuda onions
1½ pounds bulk sausage
1½ cups chopped celery
1½ cups soft bread crumbs (3 slices)
8 tablespoons chopped parsley
¼ cup melted butter or margarine

Peel onions; cut ½" off tops. Parboil in boiling salted water for 10 minutes; drain. Remove centers of onions, leaving a shell ¼" thick. (Use centers to season vegetables or soup at another meal.) Sauté sausage and celery until sausage is lightly browned; drain off fat. Combine sausage, celery, bread crumbs, and parsley; fill onions. Place onions in shallow, 2-quart casserole; brush with melted butter or margarine. Pour remaining butter or margarine around onions in casserole. Bake, uncovered, at 425° for 20 to 25 minutes or until onions are tender and filling is browned. Baste with drippings during baking. Serve with mushroom sauce (see below). Garnish with parsley and pimiento, if desired. Serves 8.

MUSHROOM SAUCE

Sauté ½ pound sliced mushrooms in ½ cup butter or margarine for 5 minutes or until tender. Place ½ cup flour in skillet. Cook over medium heat, stirring constantly, until flour is lightly browned; reserve. Melt ¼ cup butter or margarine in saucepan; blend in browned flour. Remove from heat. Gradually blend in 2 cups light cream or half-and-half. Add mushrooms. Cook over low heat, stirring constantly, until sauce bubbles and thickens. Simmer 3 minutes, stirring occasionally. Makes about 2½ cups.

Baked Stuffed Onions

4 medium-sized white onions
1 can cream of mushroom soup
1 package frozen peas
fine cracker crumbs
2 tablespoons butter

Cut off ½" slice from tops of peeled onions. Cover with water, add 1 teaspoon salt. Boil without a cover for 30 to 40 minutes or until tender. Cool. Use paring knife to remove center portions, leaving just outer layers to form a cup. Use some of center portion to cover up small hole in bottom of each onion cup. Combine mushroom soup and frozen peas. Fill onion cups with mixture and cover tops with cracker crumbs. Dot with butter. Grated cheese and paprika may be added. Place in shallow pan, bake at 400° for 20 minutes or until filling is hot.

Stuffed Onions with Nuts

4 large or 6 medium white onions
1 cup fresh bread crumbs
²/₃ cup chopped walnuts
2 tablespoons minced parsley
dash pepper
¹/₄ cup melted butter
1 egg, beaten
1 can cream of mushroom soup
¹/₂ cup water

Peel onions, cook until partially tender (20 minutes) in large amount of salted water. Drain and cool. Slice ends and remove center from onions and place in shallow pan. Mix remaining ingredients. Fill onions. Bake at 375° for 30 minutes, or until tender.

Herbed Onion Slices

3 tablespoons butter or margarine
1 tablespoon brown sugar
¹/₂ teaspoon salt
dash pepper
2 large mild onions, cut into ¹/₂″ slices
¹/₄ cup finely chopped celery
2 tablespoons finely snipped parsley
¹/₄ teaspoon dried oregano, crushed

In large skillet, melt butter or margarine; add brown sugar, salt, and pepper. Place onion slices in a single layer in butter mixture. Cover and cook slowly for 10 minutes on one side. Turn slices; sprinkle with celery, parsley, and oregano. Cook, uncovered, 10 minutes more. Serves 6.

Peas-n-Cheese Onion Cups

6 large onions
4 tablespoons butter
2 tablespoons flour
1 cup heavy cream
¼ cup grated Monterey Jack or Swiss cheese
1 egg yolk
1 package baby peas
¼ cup walnuts, chopped

Parboil onions 15 to 20 minutes. Drain, remove centers. Place in casserole with 2 tablespoons butter, bake at 350° until golden brown, brushing occasionally with melted butter. Melt remaining butter in saucepan and add flour and blend well. Slowly stir in cream. Add cheese. When sauce thickens, stir in egg yolk. Cook peas as directed on the package. Drain. Mix with nuts. Spoon peas and nuts into onion centers. Pour sauce over all. Serves 6.

Refrigerator Mashed Potatoes

5 pounds potatoes (9 large ones)
2 three-ounce packages cream cheese
1 cup dairy sour cream
2 teaspoons onion salt
1 teaspoon salt
¼ teaspoon pepper
2 tablespoons butter or margarine

Peel and dice potatoes. Boil in salted water until tender. Drain. Mash until smooth. Add remaining ingredients and beat until light and fluffy. Cool. Cover and place in refrigerator. The potatoes may be used any time within 2 weeks. To use, place desired amount in greased casserole, dot with butter and bake at 350° for 30 minutes. Makes 8 cups. Serves 12. If you use full amount, heat in a 2-quart casserole and dot with 2 tablespoons butter.

Party Onions

2 pounds small or medium white onions, quartered

5 tablespoons butter or margarine

3 tablespoons all-purpose flour

1 cup water

1 tablespoon brown sugar

1 teaspoon salt

1 teaspoon Worcestershire sauce

dash pepper

1/4 teaspoon paprika

2 tablespoons slivered almonds, toasted

Cook onions, covered, in small amount of boiling salted water until tender, 25 to 30 minutes. Drain well. Arrange in 1-quart casserole. In saucepan, melt butter or margarine; blend in flour. Stir in water, brown sugar, salt, Worcestershire sauce, and pepper. Cook until mixture thickens slightly and bubbles. Pour over onions in casserole. Sprinkle with paprika. Cover and bake at 375° for 20 minutes. Just before serving, sprinkle with toasted almonds. Serves 5 or 6.

Gourmet Potatoes

6 medium-size potatoes

1/4 cup butter

2 cups grated cheddar cheese

1 1/2 cups sour cream

1/2 cup chopped onion

1 teaspoon salt

1/4 teaspoon pepper

paprika

Boil potatoes until almost done. Cool, peel, and shred. Mix the remaining ingredients, except the paprika, with the shredded potatoes. Turn into a buttered baking dish. Top with more cheese, if desired. Dot with butter, sprinkle with paprika. Bake uncovered 30 minutes at 350°. Serves 6 to 8.

Cheesed Onion Bake

6 cups onions, thinly sliced
¼ cup butter
¼ cup flour
1¾ cups milk
½ teaspoon salt
2 cups grated sharp cheddar cheese

Place onion rings in ungreased 1½-quart casserole dish. Melt butter in a saucepan, add flour, slowly add milk. Cool until sauce is thickened. Add salt and cheese. Pour over onions. Bake at 350° for 1 hour or until onions are tender. Serves 6.

Crusty Potatoes

½ cup melted butter
4 baking potatoes, cut into ½″ slices
¾ cup crushed cornflakes
1½ cups grated sharp cheddar cheese
1 teaspoon salt
1½ teaspoon paprika

Melt butter onto a jelly-roll pan. Roll potatoes in butter. Mix together remaining ingredients and place on top of potatoes. Bake at 375° for 30 minutes. Do not turn.

Inside-out Potatoes

1 large potato for each person. Wash and pierce once to allow steam to escape. Rub skins with butter. Bake at 400° for 45 minutes to 1 hour. Turn once or twice. Cut lengthwise, scoop out potatoes, saving skins. Mash potatoes with milk and butter. (About 1 cup milk and 4 tablespoons butter for 8 potatoes.) Add 4 tablespoons grated sharp cheese for each potato. Salt and white pepper to taste. Put in shells, brush with melted butter. Place under broiler until brown on top, or bake in oven at 350° for 25 minutes.

Candied Sweet Potatoes

4 to 6 sweet potatoes

3 tablespoons butter

1 tablespoon lemon juice

½ teaspoon grated lemon peel

¾ cup dark corn syrup

¼ cup brown sugar

Cook pared, halved potatoes in salted boiling water for 15 minutes in covered skillet. Use ¼ cup water for 4 to 6 potatoes. Do not drain unless liquid exceeds ¼ cup. Dot with butter. Make syrup by combining lemon juice and grated lemon peel to dark corn syrup mixed with firmly packed brown sugar. Pour over potatoes. Cook uncovered 15 minutes over low heat. Spoon syrup over potatoes frequently during second cooking and turn them once. Handle gently. When potatoes are glazed, remove from heat at once. Overcooking makes them mushy.

Orange-Sweet Potato Cups

6 large sweet potatoes or yams (about 3¾ pounds)

boiling water

6 large navel oranges

¼ cup white vinegar

1 can crushed pineapple (13½ ounce), undrained

¼ cup butter or margarine, melted

1½ teaspoons salt

¼ teaspoon cinnamon

⅛ teaspoon nutmeg

jellied whole-cranberry sauce

parsley sprigs

Scrub potatoes. Cover with boiling water in large saucepan; cook covered 30 to 35 minutes, or until tender. Drain well. Halve oranges crosswise; scoop out orange pulp, keeping shells intact. (Reserve orange pulp for another use.) Place orange shells in large bowl; cover with hot water; add vinegar. Let stand 5 minutes; drain. Peel potatoes; mash with potato masher. Blend in pineapple, butter, salt, and spices. Fill orange shells with potato mixture, mounding high. Place on cookie sheet; bake at 300° for 20 minutes. Serve hot. Garnish tops with cranberry sauce and a parsley sprig. Serves 12.

Raisin-Filled Sweet Potatoes

1 eighteen-ounce can sweet potatoes
2 tablespoons butter or margarine, softened
1 egg
1/2 teaspoon salt
dash ground cinnamon
dash ground ginger
2 tablespoons butter or margarine, melted
1/4 cup sugar
2 teaspoons cornstarch
1 teaspoon grated orange peel
1/2 cup orange juice
1/2 cup raisins

Beat together sweet potatoes, the first 2 tablespoons butter or margarine, the egg, salt, cinnamon, and ginger. Spoon into 6 mounds on greased baking sheet. Hollow out centers with spoon. Brush with the melted butter. Bake at 350° for 15 to 20 minutes. Next, combine sugar, cornstarch, and peel. Stir in juice. Add raisins. Cook and stir until thickened and bubbly. To serve, spoon into sweet potato shells. Serves 6.

Sweet Potato Rolls

2 1/4 cups canned sweet potatoes, drained and mashed
1/2 teaspoon salt
dash pepper
2 tablespoons soft butter
1/3 cup warm honey
1 cup chopped walnuts

Combine sweet potatoes, salt, pepper, and butter. Mix well, then form into balls. Refrigerate 2 hours. Coat balls with honey, roll in walnuts. Refrigerate another 2 hours. Bake at 350° for 20 minutes. Serve with ham or poultry. Serves 6.

Sweet Potato-Cashew Bake

 1/3 cup packed brown sugar

 1/3 cup broken cashews

 1/2 teaspoon salt

 1/4 teaspoon ground ginger

 4 medium sweet potatoes, cooked and sliced (about 3 cups)

 1 cup drained and diced canned peaches

 2 tablespoons butter or margarine

In small mixing bowl, blend together the packed brown sugar, broken cashews, the salt, and the ground ginger. In 1½-quart casserole, arrange in alternate layers, half of the sliced sweet potatoes, half of the diced peaches, and half of the brown sugar mixture. Repeat layers. Dot with butter or margarine. Bake covered at 350° for about 30 minutes. Uncover and continue baking an additional 10 minutes. Garnish with additional peach slices, if desired. Serves 6.

Hot Spinach Molds

 2 ten-ounce packages frozen chopped spinach

 3 tablespoons butter

 6 eggs, beaten

 1 1/3 cups milk

 2 medium onions, chopped fine and sautéed

 1 1/4 teaspoons salt

 1/4 teaspoon pepper

 1 tablespoon white vinegar

 1/4 teaspoon dried savory

 8 tomato slices

Cook spinach according to package directions; drain very well. Combine spinach, melted butter, eggs, milk, onions, salt, pepper, vinegar, and savory. Start heating oven to 350°. Butter 8 or 9 six-ounce custard cups. Divide mixture evenly among custard cups. Place cups in shallow roasting pan in 1″ of hot water. Bake 35 to 40 minutes or until custard is set. Sprinkle tomato slices with salt and pepper. Loosen each spinach mold and unmold on tomato slice.

Baked Spinach-Topped Tomatoes

¼ cup butter or margarine
1 medium onion, minced
1 large garlic clove, minced
2 ten-ounce packages frozen chopped spinach
1 cup dried bread crumbs
2 eggs, beaten
2 teaspoons salt
4 large tomatoes, each cut in half

In 10″ skillet over medium heat, cook onion and garlic in hot butter or margarine until onion is tender; about 5 minutes. Add spinach and cook 8 minutes or until tender, separating spinach with spoon and stirring occasionally. Remove from heat; stir in bread crumbs, eggs, and salt; set aside. Place tomato halves, cut-side up, in 9″ x 13″ baking dish. (If needed, cut a thin slice from bottom of each tomato half so it stands upright.) Mound a scant ½ cup spinach mixture onto each tomato half. Cover and refrigerate. About 45 minutes before serving, uncover and bake tomatoes at 350° for 35 minutes or until heated through. Serves 8.

Spinach Soufflé Roll

4 tablespoons butter
½ cup flour
½ teaspoon salt
⅛ teaspoon white pepper
2 cups milk
5 egg yolks
5 egg whites
spinach filling

Grease a 15½″ x 10½″ x 2″ jelly-roll baking pan. Line with waxed paper and grease again. Dust lightly with flour. In saucepan, melt the butter; then blend in flour, salt, and pepper. Add milk all at once, and cook and stir until thickened and bubbly. Remove the white sauce from the heat. Beat egg yolks until thick and lemon-colored.

Gradually add the white sauce to the beaten egg yolks, stirring constantly. Cool slightly. Beat egg whites into stiff peaks, then fold into cooled sauce. Pour into and spread evenly over prepared jelly-roll pan. Bake at 400° for 25 to 30 minutes, or until puffed and brown. When done, turn out immediately onto a clean towel. Spread with spinach filling and roll up jelly-roll style, beginning with long edge, by lifting edge of towel. Transfer to serving plate, seam side down. Garnish with paprika and fresh parsley sprigs. To serve, slice like a jelly roll into 8 portions, each about 1¼″ thick.

SPINACH FILLING

2 tablespoons butter
1 tablespoon finely chopped shallots
½ cup chopped mushrooms
1 ten-ounce package frozen chopped spinach, cooked and well drained
1 tablespoon Dijon-style mustard
¼ teaspoon ground nutmeg

In a skillet, melt butter; add shallots and cook until tender. Add mushrooms and cook 3 minutes. Add spinach, mustard, and nutmeg. Heat through, stirring occasionally. Season with salt and pepper, if desired.

Spinach Timbales

2 ten-ounce packages chopped spinach, cooked and drained
¼ cup melted butter
salt and pepper to taste
few grains of nutmeg
1 tablespoon prepared horseradish
2 eggs
1 cup milk

Combine spinach, butter, salt, pepper, nutmeg, and horseradish. Beat eggs; add milk. Combine with spinach mixture. Pack into greased individual custard cups. Place in pan of water and bake at 350° for 1 hour or until inserted knife comes out clean. Unmold on platter. Cover with hollandaise sauce. Serves 4.

Savory Chopped Spinach

1 ten-ounce package frozen chopped spinach
1 three-ounce package cream cheese, softened
3 slices bacon
¹/₂ cup sour cream
1 tablespoon dried minced onion
1 tablespoon horseradish
salt to taste

Cook spinach according to package directions. Drain thoroughly. Add cream cheese and stir until blended. Cook bacon until crisp. Drain on paper toweling. Crumble. In a greased 1½-pint casserole, combine spinach mixture with bacon and remaining ingredients. Bake at 350° for 20 to 30 minutes or until thoroughly heated.

Cheese-Crowned Baked Tomatoes

4 large tomatoes
salt and pepper
1 cup (¹/₄ pound) grated American cheese
2 egg yolks
4 tablespoons heavy cream
¹/₄ teaspoon curry powder
¹/₂ to ³/₄ cup crushed cracker crumbs
3 tablespoons butter

Cut tomatoes in half. Turn upside down and squeeze very gently so that some of the seeds and liquid come out. Place in shallow casserole or baking pan, cut sides up; sprinkle with salt and pepper. Blend together cheese, egg yolks, cream, curry powder, and ⅛ teaspoon salt. Place about 2 tablespoons of this mixture on each tomato half, pressing down into the center with back of spoon. Sprinkle cracker crumbs over top; dot crumbs with butter. Bake tomatoes at 350° for 15 to 20 minutes. Good served with buttered broccoli and parsley potatoes. Serves 4.

Crusty Tomato Scallop

2½ cups tomatoes
1 cup dry bread cubes
1 tablespoon minced onion
¼ cup butter
1 tablespoon flour
1 teaspoon salt
¼ teaspoon pepper
1 tablespoon sugar
1 teaspoon dry mustard
2 slices buttered bread

Combine tomatoes, bread cubes, onion. Melt butter, add flour, seasonings, and mustard. Add tomato mixture and pour into greased 1-quart baking dish. Cut bread slices in cubes, sprinkle over tomatoes. Bake at 400° for 45 minutes. Serves 6.

Broiled Tomatoes
with Dill Sour Cream Sauce

½ cup sour cream
¼ cup mayonnaise
2 tablespoons finely chopped onion
1 teaspoon dried dill or snipped fresh dill
dash salt
3 large firm tomatoes
salt and pepper
butter or margarine

Mix sour cream, mayonnaise, onion, dill, and salt. Set aside. Cut tomatoes in half crosswise and core. Season cut surface with salt and pepper. Dot with butter or margarine. Broil cut-side up 3″ from heat for about 5 minutes or until heated through. Spoon sauce over broiled tomatoes. Sauce can be used as dressing. Serves 6.

Stuffed Zucchini Casserole

6 large zucchini
1 can Italian plum tomatoes (1 pound, 13 ounce)
3 ounces tomato paste
1 egg, slightly beaten
½ cup soft bread crumbs
⅓ cup chopped onion
⅓ cup chopped green pepper
1 tablespoon pure vegetable oil
¾ pound ground chuck or round steak
¾ teaspoon salt
dash pepper
½ teaspoon oregano, crumbled
½ teaspoon basil, crumbled
1 clove garlic, mashed
1 teaspoon salt
dash pepper
½ cup sliced, pitted ripe olives
½ cup thinly sliced onion
⅓ cup grated Parmesan cheese

Wash zucchini; remove and discard ends. Cut thick slice lengthwise from top of each zucchini; scoop out seeds, leaving shell ⅛″ to ¼″ thick. Chop, slice, and remove seed portion; reserve. Parboil zucchini in boiling salted water 5 minutes or until almost tender. Drain well, upside down on paper towels. Combine tomatoes and tomato paste in bowl; break up tomatoes with fork. Mix 3 tablespoons tomato mixture, egg, and bread crumbs. Sauté chopped onion and green pepper in oil in skillet 3 minutes. Add ground beef; cook until meat is browned, breaking up with fork as it cooks. Add ¾ teaspoon salt, dash of pepper, and bread-crumb mixture. Fill zucchini with mixture. Place in greased, shallow 2½-quart casserole. Combine remaining tomato mixture, reserved chopped zucchini, oregano, basil, garlic, 1 teaspoon salt, dash of pepper, ripe olives, and sliced onion. Pour around zucchini. Sprinkle with Parmesan cheese. Cover; bake at 350° for 30 minutes. Uncover; bake 10 minutes or until cheese is browned. Serves 6.

Ribbon Vegetables

1 pound potatoes, peeled and grated

2 tablespoons butter

4 ounces sour cream

4 ounces Swiss cheese, grated

4 ounces cheddar cheese, grated

1 teaspoon salt

¼ teaspoon pepper

⅓ cup chopped onion

1 cup milk

2 cups milk

2 tablespoons cornstarch

1 twelve-ounce package frozen broccoli or asparagus, green beans, or spinach

Stir together potatoes, butter, sour cream, cheese, seasoning, onion, and 1 cup milk. Simmer 2 cups milk and cornstarch and add to potato mixture. Cook, drain, and chop broccoli or other vegetable. Spread half of the potato mixture into greased casserole dish 10 to 12 inches long. Spread green vegetable on top and cover with remaining potato mixture. Bake 1 hour at 350° covered. Bake 15 minutes longer uncovered.

Sesame Cheese Tomatoes

2 large tomatoes

½ cup shredded cheddar cheese

1 tablespoon butter, melted

1½ tablespoons sesame seeds

2 tablespoons soft bread crumbs

Cut tomatoes in half horizontally. Place in shallow baking pan, cut side up. Salt and pepper. In a mixing bowl, blend together cheese, butter, sesame seeds, and bread crumbs. Broil tomatoes *5 minutes*. Top each with about 1½ tablespoons cheese mixture and return to broiler about 2 or 3 minutes. Serves 4.

Stuffed Tomatoes

10 tomatoes

2 eight-ounce packages cream cheese

¼ pound Roquefort cheese

cauliflower

2 tablespoons sweet cream

1 tablespoon Worcestershire sauce

parsley for garnish

Cut tomatoes in eighths, starting at the top but cutting only halfway through the tomato. Cut membranes and squeeze out juice. Combine cream cheese and Roquefort and let soften. Grate cauliflower and mix with cheeses. Add cream and Worcestershire sauce. Stuff tomatoes with mixture and garnish with parsley.

Marinated Vegetables Vinaigrette

1 teaspoon salt

½ teaspoon freshly ground pepper

¼ teaspoon paprika

⅛ teaspoon red pepper

4 tablespoons vinegar

½ cup olive oil

2 tablespoons pimiento, chopped fine

2 tablespoons capers

3 tablespoons sweet pickle relish

3 tablespoons chopped parsley

3 tablespoons chopped green onions with tops

watercress or parsley

Cold cooked asparagus spears and baby carrots, vertical-pack green beans, artichoke hearts, Brussels sprouts or cauliflower. In blender, mix thoroughly salt, pepper, paprika, red pepper, vinegar, and olive oil. Add remaining ingredients except greens. Pour over vegetables and marinate at least 24 hours. Serve on beds of watercress or parsley. Serves 8.

Scalloped Tomatoes

3 cups canned tomatoes, drained and chopped or fresh, peeled tomatoes

1 small onion, chopped

3 tablespoons bacon grease

dash garlic salt

3 thick slices of dry bread, cut in large cubes

1/4 cup brown sugar

1 teaspoon salt

pepper to taste

1 teaspoon sweet basil

Sauté onion and bread cubes in bacon grease, cooking slowly. Add sugar and spices to the drained tomatoes. Layer the tomatoes and bread cubes in a buttered baking dish. Bake at 350° covered for 40 minutes. Serves 6.

Maxine's* Vegetable Casserole

2 boxes frozen chopped broccoli

1 box frozen baby lima beans

1 can water chestnuts

1 can mushroom soup

1/3 cup canned sliced mushrooms

1 pint dairy sour cream

1/2 package dry onion soup mix

2 cups crushed Rice Krispies

2 tablespoons butter

Cook broccoli and lima beans together until just heated. Add water chestnuts. Place into a 1½-quart baking dish. Combine soup, sour cream, and onion soup mix. Pour over beans/broccoli mixture. Mix together Rice Krispies and butter. Sprinkle on top of casserole. Bake at 350° for 30 minutes.

*Mrs. Maxine (Dr. Howard) Hamlin, Leawood, Kans.

Vegetables and Cashews

2 tablespoons salad oil
1 medium onion, sliced ¼" thick
2 cups sliced mushrooms
2 cups diagonally sliced celery
2 red or green peppers, cut into chunks
1 five-ounce can water chestnuts, drained
½ cup chicken broth
2 tablespoons cornstarch
1¼ teaspoons salt
2 tablespoons water
2 tablespoons soy sauce
1 sixteen-ounce can bean sprouts, well drained
2 cups cashews

Heat oil in a large skillet. Add onion, mushrooms, celery, peppers, and water chestnuts; cook over high heat, stirring quickly and frequently (stir-fry), until vegetables are well coated. Add chicken broth; cover and cook 10 minutes. Meanwhile, combine cornstarch, salt, water, and soy sauce until smooth. Stir into vegetable mixture. Cook, stirring quickly until mixture boils and thickens. Stir in bean sprouts and cashews. Cook until heated through. Serves 8.

QUICK BREADS

Seasoning with love...

*O*ur *"great room" allows our home to be a "house/church"
where groups can gather in an unpretentious, comfortable, and at times even sacred atmosphere to break bread and
even to worship. Every Tuesday morning we unlock the front
door, set the coffeepot perking, quick-sweep the kitchen rug, give
the furniture a last-minute polish, and bring in the folding
chairs for a group of women who meet and study God's Word.*

*Each week it is much the same: the sun streaming in
through birch branches at the window, a fire crackling on the
hearth, the scent of spice and coffee mixed, the pleasant din of
conversation, and then the quiet; the quiet that invites and recognizes the very presence of God. And every time—there is affirmation.*

*No other effort in "open heart, open home" brings greater
satisfaction or anticipation, for contained within the motive are
giving, redemption, healing, comfort, reconciliation, hope, and
peace.*

—Jeanne Millhuff
Olathe, Kans.

Hot Biscuits

2 cups sifted flour
4 teaspoons baking powder
1 teaspoon salt
1 tablespoon sugar
6 tablespoons shortening
²/₃ to ³/₄ cup milk

Sift together the dry ingredients. Cut in shortening to make fine crumbs. Add milk, mixing with a fork. Knead on board 16 times, roll to ½″ thick, cut with a 1½″ cutter. Coat both sides with butter. Put on buttered baking pans. Bake at 425° to 450° for 12 to 15 minutes. Yields 12 to 14 biscuits.

Upside-down Biscuits

¼ cup butter or margarine
½ cup brown sugar, firmly packed
2 tablespoons water
½ cup pecan halves
2 cups sifted flour
1 teaspoon baking soda
½ teaspoon salt
2 tablespoons granulated sugar
⅓ cup shortening
¼ cup white (distilled) vinegar
6 tablespoons milk

Combine butter or margarine, brown sugar, and water in saucepan. Heat, stirring constantly until sugar melts. Do not boil. Pour a scant tablespoon of this syrup into each of the 2½″ muffin cups. Arrange pecans over the syrup. Sift flour, baking soda, salt, and granulated sugar together. Cut in shortening. Combine vinegar and milk (or you may use ²/₃ cup of buttermilk instead of vinegar and milk); add to dry ingredients. Stir with fork until flour is dampened. Knead 1-4 minutes on lightly floured board. Roll or pat out about ½″ thick. Cut with floured 2″ cutter. Place a biscuit in each muffin cup. Bake at 400° about 15 minutes or until lightly browned. Serve hot. Makes 16 biscuits.

Apple-Date Muffins

1 cup whole bran cereal
³/₄ cup milk
1 egg
¹/₄ cup soft shortening
1 cup sifted flour
2¹/₂ teaspoons baking powder
¹/₂ teaspoon salt
¹/₂ teaspoon cinnamon
¹/₄ teaspoon nutmeg
¹/₄ cup sugar
¹/₂ cup finely chopped raw apple
¹/₂ cup finely cut dates

Combine whole bran cereal and milk; let stand until most of moisture is taken up. Add egg and shortening; beat well. Sift together flour, baking powder, salt, spices, and sugar; mix with chopped apple and dates. Add to first mixture, stirring only until combined. Fill greased muffin pans two-thirds full. Bake at 400° about 25 minutes. Serve immediately. Makes 12 muffins, 2¹/₂" in diameter.

Cheese Biscuits

¹/₄ pound butter
1 sixteen-ounce package cheddar cheese
2 cups flour
¹/₂ teaspoon salt
4 level teaspoons baking powder
4 tablespoons shortening
milk

Melt butter and cheese. Make a smooth paste and allow to cool while preparing biscuit dough. Sift together the flour, salt, and baking powder. Cut shortening into flour mixture until it resembles coarse meal. Add enough milk to make soft dough. Roll out about ¹/₄" thick, spread with melted butter, then the cheese mixture. Roll as for jelly roll, cut ¹/₂" slices and place on buttered cookie sheet. Place cut side up and two across pan, but crowd them together lengthwise because they spread. Bake at 375° for 15 to 20 minutes.

Caramel-Nut Oatmeal Muffins

⅓ cup brown sugar
2 tablespoons butter, softened
36 nut halves
1 cup sifted flour
¼ cup sugar
1 tablespoon baking powder
½ teaspoon salt
¼ cup shortening
1 cup 3-minute oats
1 egg, beaten
1 cup milk

Blend brown sugar and butter. Pat evenly in 12 greased muffin cups. Arrange nut halves in each. Sift together dry ingredients. Cut in shortening until mixture is like coarse cornmeal. Blend in oats. Lightly stir in egg and milk. Carefully spoon into muffin cups, filling two-thirds full. Bake at 425° for 20 minutes. Remove from pans immediately, tipping upside down so the caramel runs down the sides. Makes 12 muffins.

My Best Refrigerator Bran Muffins

2½ cups sifted flour
2½ teaspoons baking soda
1 teaspoon salt
1 cup boiling water
1 cup whole bran cereal
1 cup sugar
½ cup shortening
2 eggs, beaten
1 pint buttermilk
2 cups whole bran buds
½ cup raisins

Sift flour, soda, salt. Pour boiling water over whole bran cereal. Set aside. Cream sugar and shortening until light, add eggs, beat well. Add buttermilk, bran buds, and soaked whole bran cereal. Add sifted dry ingredients. Mix well, add raisins. Store in tightly covered container in refrigerator. Will keep up to 6 weeks. Fill greased muffin pans two-thirds full. Bake at 400° for 15 or 20 minutes. Makes 2½ dozen.

Down-South Stuffing Balls

5 cups crumbled corn bread
5 cups day-old white bread crumbs
½ cup butter or margarine
¾ cup minced onion
½ cup minced green peppers
½ cup minced celery
1 chicken bouillon cube
⅔ cup hot water
½ pound fresh pork sausage links, cut up
¼ teaspoon salt
⅛ teaspoon pepper
½ teaspoon poultry seasoning
2 eggs, beaten
¾ cup chopped pecans
½ cup snipped parsley

Day before: Make corn bread from mix or your own recipe. When cool, crumble 5 cups. Also prepare white bread crumbs.

Morning: In hot butter in skillet, sauté onion, green peppers, and celery until tender. Next dissolve bouillon cube in hot water. Place all bread crumbs in large bowl; then sprinkle with bouillon. Add sautéed vegetables. Sauté sausages until browned; add to crumb mixture along with drippings, salt, pepper, poultry seasonings, eggs, pecans, parsley; toss lightly. Turn stuffing mixture into 9 greased six-ounce ovenproof pottery or custard cups. Bake, uncovered with turkey at 325° during last 45 to 55 minutes, or until lightly browned. Makes 9.

Mother Keith's Corn Muffins

½ cup flour
2 teaspoons baking powder
1 teaspoon salt
1 tablespoon sugar
1 cup cornmeal
1 egg
½ cup buttermilk
½ teaspoon baking soda
¼ cup melted butter

Sift flour with baking powder, salt, sugar, and cornmeal. In another bowl mix egg, buttermilk, baking soda, and butter. Blend all ingredients together. Bake at 400° for 20 minutes. "From her mother's 100-year-old recipe."

My Favorite Corn Bread Dressing

3 cups dry bread cubes
5 cups coarsely crumbled corn bread
1 to 2 teaspoons sage
1 teaspoon salt
1 teaspoon pepper
1 cup chopped celery
½ cup finely chopped onion
½ cup butter
2 eggs, beaten
½ to 1 cup chicken broth

Mix together bread cubes, corn bread, and seasonings. Sauté celery and onion in butter until tender but not brown. Lightly toss onions, celery, and eggs into bread mixture. Add broth to moisten. Makes 6 cups or enough for 2 five-pound roasting chickens. Nuts may be added to dressing for variety.

Banana Bran Muffins

| 1½ cups sifted flour |
| 1 cup bran flakes |
| 2 teaspoons baking powder |
| ½ teaspoon salt |
| 2 tablespoons brown sugar |
| ½ cup mashed bananas |
| 1 egg, beaten |
| 1 cup cold milk |
| ¼ cup melted butter |

Sift dry ingredients. Add the liquid ingredients all at once. Stir just to moisten the dry ingredients; the batter should be lumpy and rough. Fill greased muffin tins only two-thirds full. Bake at 400° for 20 to 25 minutes. Serve hot with plenty of butter. Makes 12 muffins.

Cinnamon Bran Muffins

| 3 cups whole bran cereal |
| 1 cup boiling water |
| 2½ cups flour |
| ¾ cup sugar |
| 2½ teaspoons baking soda |
| 1½ teaspoons cinnamon |
| ½ teaspoon salt |
| 2 eggs |
| 2 cups buttermilk |
| ½ cup oil |
| ½ cup currants or raisins |

In bowl stir cereal with water to moisten, set aside, cool. Sift together flour, sugar, baking soda, cinnamon, and salt. Set aside. Stir eggs, buttermilk, oil, and currants into cereal mixture until well blended. Stir in flour mixture until well mixed. Bake or store for future. Before using, stir to distribute currants or raisins. Fill greased 2½" muffin pan two-thirds to three-quarters full. Bake at 425° for 20 minutes or until done. Makes 24 to 30 muffins. "I keep these muffins in an airtight container in the refrigerator for about two weeks."

Carrot Bread

1 cup sugar
¾ cup salad oil
2 eggs
1½ cups sifted flour
¼ teaspoon salt
1 teaspoon cinnamon
1 teaspoon baking soda
1 teaspoon baking powder
1 cup grated carrots
½ cup chopped walnuts

Cream sugar, oil, and eggs. Add flour, salt, cinnamon, soda, and baking powder sifted together, mix. Add carrots and nuts, stir. Bake in greased loaf pan at 375° for 55 minutes, for a large loaf. Smaller loaves bake at 350° for 25 minutes.

Apricot-Date Bread

¾ cup milk
1 egg, beaten
1 tablespoon grated orange rind
1 tablespoon melted shortening
1 cup flour, sifted
2 teaspoons baking powder
¼ teaspoon baking soda
½ teaspoon salt
½ cup sugar
½ cup unsifted whole wheat flour
½ cup finely chopped apricots
½ cup finely chopped dates

Mix together milk, egg, orange rind, and shortening. Add and stir in flour that has been sifted with baking powder, soda, salt, and sugar. Add whole wheat flour. Mix. Fold in apricots and dates. Pour into greased loaf pan. Bake at 350° for 40 to 45 minutes. Next day slice and serve spread with cream cheese.

Iowa Corn Bread

⅔ cup cornmeal
1⅓ cups sifted flour
4 teaspoons baking powder
2 tablespoons sugar
½ teaspoon salt
1 egg
1 cup milk
4 tablespoons melted shortening or oil

Beat egg slightly, add milk. Sift dry ingredients, add to egg mixture, mix well and add shortening or oil. Do not overbeat, just until mixed. Bake in greased pans, muffin pans, or cornsticks at 425° for 15 to 20 minutes. Makes 12 sticks or muffins.

Apricot-Nut Bread

1½ cups dried apricots, washed, drained and cut into strips
¾ cup sugar
2¾ cups flour
4 teaspoons baking powder
½ teaspoon salt
½ teaspoon baking soda
1 egg, beaten
1 cup buttermilk
3 tablespoons cooking oil
½ cup chopped walnuts

Set aside 1 tablespoon flour. Sift together dry ingredients. Mix together egg and oil with buttermilk. Add to dry ingredients. Stir only until well mixed. Mix remaining flour with apricots, add walnuts. Fold into batter. Pour into a greased and floured loaf pan. Bake at 350° for 50 to 60 minutes. Cool on wire rack. "This bread slices better the second day. It is very good spread with cream cheese and served with fruit salad."

Orange Bread—1

1 tablespoon butter
1 cup sugar
1 egg
3 cups flour
3½ teaspoons baking powder
¼ teaspoon salt
1 cup milk
1 cup orange preparation
1 teaspoon vanilla or lemon extract

Cream butter and sugar, add egg. Add sifted dry ingredients to egg mixture alternately with milk. Add orange preparation and extract. Pour into three small loaf pans. Bake at 350° for 45 minutes.

ORANGE PREPARATION

4 small oranges or 3 large ones
sugar

Grind rind of oranges, cover with cold water and bring to boil. Drain. Repeat 3 more times. After last draining add 1 cup sugar for each cup boiled rind. Simmer slowly uncovered until mixture is thick and syrupy but not dry. Watch carefully at this point. Will thicken when cold. Keeps indefinitely in refrigerator. Can be used as topping for ice cream or in cookies that call for grated orange or in buttercream icing.

Orange Bread—2

rinds of 2 large oranges
1½ cups sugar
½ cup water
1 teaspoon salt
3 cups sifted flour
3 teaspoons baking powder
1 cup milk
1 egg

Take the rind of 2 large oranges and scrape off as much of the white membrane as possible. Cut rind into tiny pieces. In a saucepan, mix together sugar and water; add rind and simmer 15 to 20 minutes until rind is clear. Add salt and let cool. Mix flour, baking powder, milk, and egg; slowly add rind syrup. Mix well and put in greased loaf pan. Let stand 15 minutes. Bake at 375° for 45 minutes. Makes 1 loaf.

Sour Cream Coffee Cake

½ cup butter
1 cup sugar
2 eggs
2 cups sifted flour
1 teaspoon baking soda
1 teaspoon baking powder
½ teaspoon salt
1 cup sour cream
1 teaspoon vanilla

Cream butter and sugar, add eggs, 1 at a time. Sift dry ingredients. Add to butter mixture alternately with sour cream, beginning and ending with flour. Add vanilla. Pour half of mixture into a buttered 13″ x 9″ x 2″ pan.

NUT TOPPING

⅓ cup brown sugar
¼ cup granulated sugar
1 teaspoon cinnamon
1 cup chopped pecans

Pour remaining batter over nut topping. Sprinkle with remaining topping mixture. Bake at 325° for 25 minutes. "This cake may be frozen and reheated. It's delicious."

Good,

Favorite Orange Rolls

¼ cup butter
½ cup orange juice
½ cup sugar
2 teaspoons orange rind
2 cups flour
3 teaspoons baking powder
½ teaspoon salt
3 tablespoons shortening
¾ cup milk
¼ cup sugar
½ teaspoon cinnamon

Cook butter, orange juice, sugar, and orange rind for 2 minutes, then place in bottom of muffin pans. Sift dry ingredients, cut in shortening, add milk. Roll out in rectangular shape and sprinkle sugar and cinnamon over dough. Roll up and cut 1″ thick and place on top of liquid in muffin pans. Bake at 400° about 12 or 15 minutes.

Orange Roll-ups

2 cups sifted flour
3 teaspoons baking powder
1 teaspoon salt
2 tablespoons sugar
¼ cup shortening
1 egg, beaten
½ cup milk
2 tablespoons melted butter
1 tablespoon orange peel
¼ cup sugar

Sift flour, baking powder, salt, and sugar; cut in shortening. Beat egg, add milk, add to dry ingredients. Roll to 10″ x 6″ rectangle. Brush with melted butter. Mix orange peel and ¼ cup sugar, sprinkle on dough. Roll like jelly roll, cut in 1″ slices. Arrange cut-side down in a circle in greased 9″ x 1½″ round pan. Bake at 425° for 15 to 20 minutes. Serves 10.

Best Doughnuts

| 2 tablespoons shortening |
| 1 cup sugar |
| 2 eggs, well beaten |
| 3/4 cup milk |
| 3¼ cups flour |
| ½ teaspoon mace |
| 5 teaspoons baking powder |
| ¼ teaspoon cinnamon |
| ½ teaspoon nutmeg |
| 1 teaspoon salt |

Cream shortening and sugar. Beat eggs and milk together, then add to creamed sugar mixture. Sift remaining ingredients together, add to sugar mixture. Chill batter. Roll ½″ thick, cut with cutter; let stand for 15 minutes. Fry in deep fat at 325° to 365°. Cook until brown and then turn immediately and finish browning. Roll in sugar. Makes 3 dozen.

Potato Doughnuts

| 1 cup sugar |
| 1 cup milk |
| 1 cup mashed potatoes |
| 2 eggs |
| 2 tablespoons shortening |
| 4 teaspoons baking powder |
| 2 teaspoons vanilla |
| ¼ teaspoon salt |
| 4 to 5 cups flour |
| sugar for shaking doughnuts |

Beat eggs until light. Add milk and cooked mashed potatoes, sugar, and shortening. Beat well. Add remaining ingredients, including flour, to make a soft dough, stirring with spoon. Roll out dough to about ⅓″ thickness. Cut with doughnut cutter or biscuit cutter. With biscuit cutter, make small doughnut hole with thimble. Fry in deep fat at 375°. Shake doughnuts in bag of sugar to coat. Makes about 3 dozen.

Best Gingerbread

½ cup sugar
1 egg
¼ cup light molasses
1 cup flour
1 teaspoon soda
¼ teaspoon cinnamon
¼ teaspoon ginger
¼ teaspoon nutmeg
¼ teaspoon salt
½ cup melted butter
½ cup hot water

Mix sugar, egg, and molasses; sift flour, soda, and spices. Mix together and add ¼ cup melted butter and hot water. Bake in greased and floured 8″ x 8″ pan, at 350° about 20 minutes. When done, while still in pan, pour the remaining ¼ cup melted butter over gingerbread. Serve warm. "This will appear too thin, but do not add any more flour. So simple, but so good."

My Best Coffee Cake

1 cup brown sugar
¾ cup granulated sugar
2½ cups flour
1 teaspoon nutmeg
1 teaspoon salt
2 teaspoons cinnamon
1 teaspoon baking soda
1 egg
1 cup buttermilk
¾ cup cooking oil
½ cup chopped nuts

Mix together all dry ingredients except cinnamon and soda. Add oil and mix. Take out one-quarter of this mixture for topping and add cinnamon, 1 more tablespoon oil, and walnuts for the topping. To cake mixture add egg, buttermilk, and soda, blend well. Pour into an 11" x 7" x 1½" pan. Sprinkle topping on top of batter. Bake at 350° for 35 minutes.

Egg Dumplings

1½ cups sifted flour
1 teaspoon salt
2 teaspoons baking powder
1 egg
2 tablespoons shortening
milk

Sift flour with baking powder and salt. Cut in shortening fine as meal. Break egg in cup, slightly beat with a fork. Add milk to make ¾ cup liquid. Add all at once to flour mixture. Mix *only* to moisten the flour. Drop into hot broth (only 1½" of liquid in bottom of pan). Use a tablespoon dipped into broth. Use about 1 tablespoon of dumpling mixture for each. Cook 15 minutes. *Do not* lift lid to check while cooking. *Cook gently.* Makes 8 large dumplings.

Three-Minute Dumplings

1 egg, beaten lightly
scant ½ cooled chicken broth
1½ cups sifted flour
2 teaspoons baking powder
½ teaspoon salt

Sift dry ingredients. Beat egg and add chicken broth. Add to dry ingredients. Drop batter the size of walnuts into boiling liquid. Cover and cook 1½ minutes, turn carefully with fork and cook 1½ minutes longer. "This recipe is 40 years old."

Fluffy Tom Thumb Pancakes

1 egg
¾ cup plus 2 tablespoons milk
2 tablespoons melted shortening or oil
1 cup flour
½ teaspoon salt
2 tablespoons sugar
2 tablespoons baking powder

Combine egg, milk, shortening. Add sifted dry ingredients. Beat smooth with egg beater. Bake on an ungreased frying pan.

YEAST BREADS

Seasoning with love...

*T*hrough friendship, many doors are opened for opportunities to demonstrate the love of God. A home-cooked meal or a cup of coffee together can help greatly to lift the spirits and provide encouragement. I know, for I have been on the receiving end myself, three times moving to large cities where I knew no one.

In earlier years, finances were very limited, dishes didn't match, and there weren't enough chairs, but no one ever seemed to mind. I think they all knew they were there because I loved them, and they all came. Even my teacher friends went without their cigarettes and drinks to come to my coffee hours. And they looked for my goodies that I often took to school.

Many cakes, plates of cookies, and baskets of food have left my kitchen to cheer lonely, hurting hearts—or to keep up l'esprit de corps at work. So you don't have to invite people in to be hospitable. You can take food—seasoned with love—*out*.

—Mabel P. Adamson
Kansas City, Mo.

Oatmeal Bread

2 cups boiling water
1 cup regular or quick oatmeal
1 tablespoon salt
1 tablespoon shortening
2 packages dry yeast
½ cup lukewarm water
½ cup white syrup
5 or 6 cups flour (1 cup whole wheat or unprocessed bran can be used)

Mix boiling water, oatmeal, salt, and shortening; let stand until luke-warm. Mix yeast with lukewarm water and syrup. Add cooled oat-meal mixture and enough flour to make a stiff dough. Knead on board enough flour to make dough elastic, at least 10 minutes. Put in bowl and rise until double in bulk, about 1 hour. Shape in 2 loaves and let rise to top of bread pans, about 45 minutes. Brush with water and sprinkle with oatmeal before baking, or brush with butter and add oatmeal after baking. Use 2 pans that are the same size. Bake at 325° for 45 minutes.

Prune-Nut Bread

3 cups whole wheat flour
½ cup whole bran cereal (buds)
2 packages dry yeast
1 tablespoon salt
2½ cups water
1 cup nonfat dry milk powder
¼ cup cooking oil
¼ cup honey
1 egg
2 cups chopped walnuts
3½ cups sifted flour
2 cups finely snipped prunes

In large bowl combine 2½ cups whole wheat flour, bran, yeast, and salt. Heat together water, milk powder, oil, and honey until warm (115° to 120°), stirring constantly. Add to yeast in bowl. Add egg. Beat at low speed in electric mixer ½ minute, scraping sides constantly. Beat 3 minutes at high speed. By hand stir in rest of whole wheat flour, nuts, and enough of the all-purpose flour to make a moderately stiff dough. Knead on lightly floured board until smooth and elastic, 8 to 10 minutes. Divide dough in half (dough does not need to rise at this point), roll each half to a 12″ x 9″ rectangle, sprinkle each with half of prunes. Roll up jelly-roll fashion, starting at short end. Seal ends. Place in greased loaf pan. Cover and rise in warm place until double, 40 to 45 minutes. Bake at 350° for 40 to 45 minutes or until done. Remove from pans. Makes 2 loaves.

"I use unpitted prunes since they are softer. Cut with kitchen shears. Cut nuts by hand, not too fine or too coarse. If too fine, they make the bread heavy. I like to just heat or warm a slice for breakfast; it toasts well."

∽৯ ৶∾

Three-Hour Rolls

1½ cups scalded milk
2 tablespoons sugar
1 teaspoon salt
⅓ cup shortening
2 yeast cakes or active dry yeast
1 egg, beaten
4½ cups flour

Put milk in a large bowl, add sugar, salt, and shortening. Cool to lukewarm. Dissolve yeast cakes in a little lukewarm water, add to milk. Add beaten eggs. Add sifted flour, to stiffen. Cover and set in warm place. Let dough rise to twice its original bulk; take out and knead lightly. Shape in rolls, cover and let rise to almost twice their size. Keep rolls small. May be made in bow knots or cut with doughnut cutter and twisted into figure eight, brushed with beaten egg with chopped, blanched almonds sprinkled over the top. Bake at 425° for 12 to 15 minutes.

NUT TOPPING

Shape rolls in balls or other shapes, then have ready 1½ cups chopped, blanched almonds that have been crisped in oven but not browned. Beat 2 eggs, dip rolls in egg, then in chopped almonds. When risen to twice the bulk, bake in usual way.

Light Rolls with Eggs

1 cup mashed potatoes

1 cake yeast, dissolved in ½ cup lukewarm water

1 cup milk, scalded and cooled

⅔ cup shortening

½ cup sugar

1½ teaspoons salt

2 eggs, beaten

6 cups flour

Pour scalded milk over shortening in greased bowl. Add mashed potatoes, sugar, salt, and eggs. Add 3 cups flour. Blend well. Add yeast. Stir in rest of flour. Knead dough on bread board for 10 minutes. Grease bowl again. Return dough to bowl. Let rise 1 hour. Roll out. Cut with biscuit cutter. Dip rolls in melted shortening. Let rise 1 hour until double in size. Bake at 450° for 15 to 20 minutes.

Raisin Bread

1 package dry yeast

¼ cup warm water

1 cup seedless raisins

¼ cup soft butter

¼ cup sugar

1 teaspoon salt

½ cup buttermilk or scalded milk

3¼ to 3½ cups flour

2 eggs, beaten

Soften dry yeast in warm water, combine next 4 ingredients, add hot milk, stir to dissolve sugar. Cool to lukewarm. Add 1 cup flour, mix well. Add yeast and eggs, beat well. Stir in remaining flour, mix well. Turn out on floured surface, cover. Let rest 10 minutes. Knead until smooth (8 to 10 minutes). Place in greased bowl, turning once to grease surface. Cover, let rise until double, 1½ to 2 hours, in warm place. Punch down, cover, let rest 10 minutes. Shape in 1 large loaf or 3 smaller loaves. Cover and let rise until double, 45 to 60 minutes. Bake at 375° for 25 minutes. Place foil over top the last 10 minutes. Remove and cool, glaze with icing if desired.

GLAZE

1 cup powdered sugar

2 tablespoons melted butter

1 tablespoon lemon juice

Mix well. Put on cool bread.

Swedish Rye Bread Supreme

¼ cup brown sugar, firmly packed

¼ cup molasses

1 tablespoon salt

2 tablespoons shortening

1½ cups boiling water

1 package active dry yeast

¼ cup lukewarm water (110° to 115°)

2½ cups rye flour

1 tablespoon caraway seeds (or omit and use 1 tablespoon orange rind or peel)

3½ to 4 cups sifted flour

6 buds cardamom seeds, crushed

brush with melted butter

Combine brown sugar, molasses, salt, and shortening in large bowl, add boiling water and stir until sugar is dissolved. Cool to lukewarm. Sprinkle yeast on lukewarm water, stir to dissolve. Stir rye flour into brown sugar-molasses mixture, beat well, stir in yeast and seeds or orange rind. Beat by hand. Add enough flour a little at a time to make smooth soft dough. Knead about 10 minutes. Place in greased bowl, turn over, cover, let rise in warm place 1½ to 2 hours. Punch down, divide in half, cover, let rise in warm place for 1½ to 2 hours. Bake at 375° for 25 to 30 minutes. Cover with aluminum foil the last 15 minutes. Remove from pans, brush with melted butter.

"I prefer the round loaves, placed on a greased cookie sheet, sprinkled with cornmeal."

Cheese Bread Ring

2³/₄ to 3 cups all-purpose flour

2 tablespoons sugar

1 package active dry yeast

³/₄ teaspoon salt

1 cup milk

2 tablespoons butter

1¹/₂ cup (6 ounces) shredded sharp cheddar cheese

Thoroughly combine 1½ cups flour, sugar, undissolved yeast, and salt in a large bowl. Heat together milk and butter until very warm (120° to 130°). Gradually add to dry ingredients and beat 2 minutes at medium speed of mixer, scraping bowl occasionally. Add ½ cup flour and cheese. Beat 2 minutes at high speed, scraping bowl occasionally. Stir in enough additional flour to make a stiff dough. Turn out on a lightly floured surface; knead until smooth and elastic, 5 to 8 minutes. Place in a buttered bowl, turning to butter top. Cover; let rise in warm place until doubled, about 1 hour. Punch dough down. Turn out on a lightly floured surface and shape to form a 20-inch rope. Place seam down in a buttered 6½-cup ring mold, pinching ends together. Cover; let rise in warm place until nearly doubled in bulk, 35 to 40 minutes. Bake in preheated oven at 350° for 25 to 30 minutes. Makes 1 loaf.

Quick Cinnamon Rolls

5¹/₂ cups flour

¹/₄ cup sugar

1 teaspoon salt

1 teaspoon grated lemon peel

1 cup (2 sticks) margarine

¹/₂ cup warm water

2 packages dry yeast

1 cup warm milk

2 eggs, beaten

additional sugar

1 teaspoon cinnamon

frosting

Combine flour, sugar, salt, and lemon peel. Cut in margarine with pastry blender until mixture resembles coarse meal. Measure warm water in small bowl. Sprinkle in yeast; stir until dissolved. Add warm milk, eggs, and dissolved yeast to flour mixture. Beat until thoroughly blended. Cover the bowl with plastic. Let it stand for 20 minutes. Punch dough down. Divide the dough in half and turn out onto a heavily floured board. Roll half into a rectangle, 18″ x 8″. Brush with melted margarine. Sprinkle with ½ cup sugar and 1 teaspoon cinnamon. Roll up into an 18″ roll. Cut into 21, 1½″ rolls. Place, cut-side up, in a greased 9″ cake pan. Repeat with remaining dough. Cover loosely with plastic. Refrigerate 2 to 24 hours. When ready to bake, remove from refrigerator. Uncover the dough carefully. Let stand 10 minutes at room temperature. Bake at 350° about 30 minutes, or until done. Drizzle with frosting made by mixing 1 cup powdered sugar, a few drops of vanilla, and 2 teaspoons milk. Makes 2 dozen rolls.

Mashed Potato Rolls

1 medium potato
2 packages quick-acting dry yeast
3 to 4 cups flour
2 teaspoons salt
¾ cup sugar
2 eggs, beaten
½ cup liquid vegetable shortening
4 to 5 cups flour
melted butter

Boil potato in enough water to have 2 cups liquid when done. Mash potato and then add to 2 cups potato water. Cool to lukewarm. Add yeast, 3 to 4 cups flour, salt, eggs, sugar, and shortening. (The less flour used, the softer the rolls will be.) With electric mixer, beat batter until smooth. Let rise until double in bulk. Punch down, add 4 to 5 cups more flour. (Keep dough soft as possible to handle.) Let rise again until double in bulk. To make rolls, roll out ball of dough on lightly floured board. Roll into a circle 12 inches in diameter, brush lightly with melted butter. Cut into pie-shaped pieces, roll up, starting at wide end. Place on greased baking sheet; let rise again until doubled. Bake at 375° for 15 minutes, or until golden brown. Brush with melted butter after removing from oven. Makes 4 to 5 dozen.

Favorite Icebox Rolls

1/2 cup sugar
1/3 cup shortening
2 1/2 teaspoons salt
2 cups boiling water
1 package dry yeast
2 eggs, beaten
6 to 7 cups flour
1/3 cup butter

Combine sugar, salt, and shortening in mixing bowl. Add boiling water and cool. Crumble yeast cake or dry yeast in a cup with 1 tablespoon sugar and 1/4 cup of warm water. Stand a few minutes. Put beaten eggs and yeast mixture in mixing bowl with other mixture. Stir in flour until dough is stiff enough to put out on a board and knead. Knead for 10 minutes. Put in greased bowl, let rise until double in bulk, 2 1/2 or 3 hours. Work down and store in refrigerator covered. Cut off one-quarter or one-half of dough, roll in 8" x 15" rectangle, spread with butter, roll beginning with long side, cut 1" slices, place in greased muffin pans, after giving the underside a poke with finger, so they will rise high in center. Dough can be kept in the refrigerator for 3 or 4 days. Bake at 400° for 20 minutes. Makes 40 rolls. "This makes excellent Caramel-Pecan rolls, too."

SYRUP FOR CARAMEL-PECAN ROLLS

3/4 cup brown sugar
1/3 cup white corn syrup
1/4 cup butter
1/3 cup pecans
1/3 cup granulated sugar
1/2 teaspoon cinnamon

Mix together brown sugar, corn syrup, and butter. Cook for 1 minute, put in 7" x 11" x 2" pan or 8" x 8" x 2" pan, add pecans. Roll dough as before, spread with butter, sprinkle with granulated sugar and cinnamon mixed together, cut 1" thick, put cut-side down in syrup. Let rise 2 1/2 or 3 hours if taken from refrigerator. Bake at 375° for 20 minutes. Turn upside down and leave pan on top for 5 minutes.

FROSTINGS AND CAKES

Seasoning with love...

There is an indescribable feeling that I experience as I pre-pare for guests, a feeling I have at no other time. It's the thought that my guests are sharing for a few moments one of the most significant parts of my life—my home. I love to prepare the food and arrange the table, but my most important goal is for my guests to leave with just a pocketful of the kind of love that is within the walls of our home.

—Brenda Dunlop
Broken Arrow, Okla.

Recently a young couple new to our area and needing an apartment were introduced in the evening service. After church a friend and I decided to invite them to lunch. As we listened to their needs, we made suggestions. When we parted, they had good prospects for an apartment and the wife had a possible job!

What better way to encourage one another than across a table of tasty food!

—Mary F. Stevens
Arcadia, Calif.

Chocolate Cake

2 cups sugar
2 cups flour
1 stick margarine
5 tablespoons cocoa
½ cup shortening
1 cup water
2 eggs
½ cup buttermilk
1 teaspoon baking soda
1 teaspoon vanilla

Thoroughly mix sugar and flour in large mixing bowl. Place margarine, cocoa, shortening, and water in saucepan and bring to boil. Pour over dry ingredients. Beat a few seconds to mix well. Add vanilla, eggs, and buttermilk in which soda has been dissolved. Mix well. Pour in greased jelly-roll pan, 11″ x 16″ x 1½″. Bake at 400° for 12 minutes. You may bake in a 15½″ x 10½″ x 1″ pan at 400° for 25 minutes.

When the sheet cake has been in oven 5 minutes, start the frosting, using the same saucepan.

ICING

1 stick margarine
5 tablespoons cocoa
⅓ cup sweet milk
1 box powdered sugar
½ cup nuts
1 teaspoon vanilla

Combine margarine, cocoa, and milk. Bring to boil. Add powdered sugar just before removing from heat. Blend well and add nuts and vanilla. Beat about 1 minute. Pour frosting on warm cake immediately after removing from oven. Cut in squares and serve from pan. Serves 12 to 24.

Pineapple Upside-down Cake

½ cup shortening
1 cup sugar
2 eggs, beaten
2 cups flour
2 teaspoons baking powder
¼ teaspoon salt
1 can pineapple slices, drain and preserve ¾ cup juice
1 small jar maraschino cherries

Cream shortening and sugar; add eggs. Sift dry ingredients. Add to creamed mixture alternately with juice. Beat well. In 9″ skillet combine 4 tablespoons butter and 1 cup brown sugar. Simmer until smooth but *do not burn*. On top of sugar mixture place pineapple slices with cherry in center of each. Pour batter over all. Bake at 350° for 50 minutes. Let stand 5 minutes; then turn out on waxed paper and serve.

Apple-Date Dream Cake

2 cups sifted all-purpose flour
1 cup sugar
1½ teaspoons baking soda
1 teaspoon salt
1 teaspoon ground cinnamon
½ teaspoon ground allspice
2 eggs, slightly beaten
1 can apple pie filling (21 ounce)
½ cup cooking oil
1 teaspoon vanilla
1 cup chopped dates
¼ can chopped walnuts
whipped cream

Sift together flour, sugar, soda, salt, cinnamon, and allspice. Combine eggs, filling, oil, and vanilla. Stir into flour mixture and mix well. Stir in dates and nuts. Pour into greased 9″ x 13″ baking dish. Bake at 350° for 40 to 45 minutes. Cool. Cut into squares. Serve with dollop of whipped cream. Serves 12.

Golden Butter Sponge Cake

1 cup soft butter

1 cup sugar

6 egg yolks

2 cups sifted cake flour

$\frac{1}{2}$ teaspoon baking powder

$\frac{1}{2}$ teaspoon salt

6 egg whites

$\frac{3}{4}$ cup sugar

In electric mixer, cream butter with 1 cup sugar at medium speed until very light and fluffy. Add egg yolks, one at a time, beating well after each addition. Beat until mixture is very fluffy and smooth, about 5 minutes. Sift together flour, baking powder, and salt; stir into butter mixture. Beat egg whites until frothy; add $\frac{3}{4}$ cup sugar gradually, beating until very stiff; fold into butter mixture. Lightly grease bottom of 10″ tube pan; pour in batter. Bake at 350° for 50 to 55 minutes. Invert to cool.

The Best
Sour Cream Chocolate Cake

$\frac{1}{2}$ cup butter (1 stick)

2 squares unsweetened chocolate

1 cup boiling water

2 cups sifted all-purpose flour

$\frac{1}{2}$ teaspoon salt

1 teaspoon baking soda

$1\frac{3}{4}$ cups brown sugar, firmly packed

2 eggs

$\frac{1}{2}$ cup sour cream

1 teaspoon vanilla

Butter and flour a 9″ x 5″ x 3″ loaf pan. Combine chocolate and boiling water in bowl and let stand until cool. Sift flour, salt, and baking soda together. Cream butter until soft and fluffy, add brown sugar gradually beating until light and creamy. Add eggs one at a time, beating hard after each addition. Add chocolate. Stir in flour until smooth, add sour cream and vanilla. Bake at 325° for 50 to 60 minutes. Cool on rack 5 minutes, turn out and cool completely, then frost.

CHOCOLATE ICING

2 ounces unsweetened chocolate, melted

2 tablespoons butter

¹/₄ cup hot water, cream, or coffee

¹/₈ teaspoon salt

2 to 2¹/₂ cups powdered sugar

1 teaspoon vanilla

Mix together chocolate and butter, add hot water. Add remaining ingredients and mix well.

Sour Cream Pound Cake

3 cups sifted flour

1 teaspoon salt

¹/₄ teaspoon baking soda

1 cup butter

2³/₄ to 3 cups sugar

6 eggs

1 teaspoon vanilla

1 teaspoon almond extract

1 cup dairy sour cream

powdered sugar

Sift flour, salt, and baking soda. Cream butter and sugar until light and fluffy. Add eggs, 1 at a time, beating well after each addition. Add extracts (total beating time 10 minutes). Add dry ingredients alternately with sour cream, beating well after each addition. Put into a well-greased 10″ or 12″ fluted tube pan. Bake at 325° for 1 hour or until done. Cool in pan on rack 10 minutes. Remove and cool. Dust with powdered sugar. Serves 12.

Spice Cake—1

2½ cups sifted cake flour
1 teaspoon baking powder
1 teaspoon baking soda
1 teaspoon salt
1 teaspoon cinnamon
½ teaspoon ground cloves
½ cup soft butter
½ cup light brown sugar
1 cup sugar
2 eggs
1 teaspoon vanilla
1¼ cups buttermilk

Grease and flour two 8″ x 1½″ square pans or one 13″ x 9″ x 2″ pan. In a large bowl beat at high speed butter, sugar, egg, and vanilla, until light and fluffy. Sift remaining dry ingredients together. At low speed, add flour mixture alternately with buttermilk into the sugar mixture. Beat 1 minute until smooth. Bake at 350°, the square pans for 30 to 35 minutes and the oblong pan for 40 to 45 minutes. Cool in pan for 10 minutes. Remove and cool completely before frosting.

SEAFOAM FROSTING

¼ cup egg white
1½ cups light brown sugar
1 tablespoon light corn syrup
⅛ teaspoon cream of tartar
1 teaspoon vanilla
⅓ cup water

Combine in top of double boiler all ingredients except vanilla. Beat 1 minute over rapidly boiling water. Beat constantly for 7 minutes, until stiff peaks form. Remove from heat, add vanilla, beat until thick enough to spread, about 2 minutes. Frosting is very thick.

Spice Cake—2

2¼ cups cake flour
1 cup sugar

1 teaspoon baking powder

1 teaspoon salt

3/4 teaspoon ground cloves

3/4 teaspoon cinnamon

2 1/4 teaspoons baking soda

3/4 cup brown sugar

3/4 cup shortening

1 cup buttermilk

3 eggs

Sift the first 7 ingredients together, add brown sugar, shortening, and buttermilk. Beat with electric mixer on slow speed for 2 minutes. Add eggs and beat 2 more minutes. Pour into 2 round greased and floured 9″ cake pans. Bake at 350° for 30 minutes. Cool cakes and frost with caramel frosting.

CARAMEL FROSTING

1/4 cup sweet cream

1/4 cup butter

1/4 cup plus 2 tablespoons brown sugar

2 cups confectioners' sugar

1/4 teaspoon salt

1 teaspoon vanilla

Mix cream, butter, brown sugar, and salt, and place over low heat. Stir until sugar is dissolved. Do not boil. Remove from heat; stir in powdered sugar and vanilla. Stir until cool enough to spread.

Individual Upside-down Cakes

For 6, melt 1/4 cup butter and mix with 1/2 cup brown sugar. Divide among 6 individual pie pans. Put 1 slice pineapple in each pan, with a cherry in the center hole. Make up a small package of yellow cake, pour over the pineapple slices to within 1/2″ of the top (use remaining batter for cupcakes), and bake at 375° for 20 minutes. Cool 1 minute, then turn out of pans, making sure that all the syrup is poured over the pineapple. Serve with whipped cream or vanilla ice cream if you wish.

Best Applesauce Cake

½ cup shortening
2 cups sugar
1 large egg
1½ cups applesauce
2½ cups flour
1½ teaspoons baking soda
1½ teaspoons salt
¾ teaspoon cinnamon
½ teaspoon cloves
½ teaspoon allspice
½ cup water
½ cup nuts
1 cup raisins

Sift the dry ingredients together and set aside. Cream the shortening and add the sugar. Thoroughly beat in the egg, then add the applesauce. Stir in the dry ingredients, then add the water. Mix in the nuts and raisins and bake in a tube pan at 350° for 40 minutes or until tester comes clean. "Tastes best when made with the freshest spices available."

Helen's* Pecan Butterscotch Cake

¼ cup butter
1 cup dark brown sugar
1¼ cups hot milk
½ cup shortening
¾ cup dark brown sugar
¼ teaspoon salt
3 eggs, separated, whites beaten until stiff
3 cups cake flour
3 teaspoons baking powder
½ cup chopped pecans

Melt butter, add 1 cup brown sugar and milk. Cool. In another bowl cream shortening and ¾ cup brown sugar, add egg yolks. Sift together flour, salt, and baking powder. Add to sugar mixture alternately with butter mixture. Fold in beaten egg whites. Pour batter into 3 greased and floured 9″ cake pans. Sprinkle pecans over top of batter in each pan. Bake at 325° for 15 to 20 minutes.

*The "Helen" in this and other recipes is Helen Gilchrist, who for 20 years was a part of the Benner family.

ICING

3 tablespoons shortening
2 tablespoons butter
1 cup dark brown sugar
⅛ teaspoon salt
¼ cup milk
2 to 3 cups powdered sugar

Cook shortening, sugar, salt, and milk for 3 minutes. Add enough powdered sugar to spread.

Caramel-Walnut Cake

½ cup butter
1 cup sugar
2 eggs
2 to 3 cups chopped black walnuts
2 teaspoons orange rind
2¼ cups cake flour
2 heaping teaspoons baking powder
¼ teaspoon salt
¾ cup whole milk

Cream sugar and butter. Add eggs and beat thoroughly. Add nut meats and grated orange rind. Sift dry ingredients together and add alternately with milk. Bake at 375° for 25 minutes.

FROSTING

Mix 3 tablespoons of butter, 4 teaspoons of burnt sugar, and 4 tablespoons of milk. To this mixture add powdered sugar until it is of consistency to spread on cake.

Orange Cakes

3 eggs, separated
1 cup sugar
3 tablespoons hot water
1 rounded teaspoon baking powder
pinch salt
1 tablespoon vinegar
1 cup flour
powdered sugar

Beat egg whites. Set aside. Beat yolks. Add sugar, hot water, and baking powder to yolks and beat thoroughly. Add salt and vinegar. Beat again. Fold in whites and add flour. Pour into muffin tins and bake at 350° for 25 minutes. When cool, split and fill with orange filling. Roll in powdered sugar. Makes 16.

FILLING

grated rind and juice of 1 orange
¹/₂ cup sugar
2 tablespoons flour
1 cup cold water

Combine flour and sugar, then add liquids and rind. Cook until thick. Cool.

Butter Cake
with Quick Broiled Icing

¹/₂ cup butter
1 cup sugar
2 eggs
¹/₂ cup milk
1¹/₂ cup cake flour
1¹/₂ teaspoon baking powder
¹/₄ teaspoon salt
1 teaspoon vanilla

Cream butter and sugar, add beaten yolks. Sift flour, baking powder, and salt together. Add alternately with milk. Fold in beaten egg whites. Bake at 325° in square or oblong pan 8" x 11" for 25 to 30 minutes. Keep in pan and spread with icing and broil under broiler with low fire. Watch constantly.

BROILED ICING

3 tablespoons melted butter
5 tablespoons brown sugar
2 tablespoons cream
1/2 cup coconut

Mix ingredients until smooth. Spread icing on cake and place under broiler until icing bubbles all over and is light brown. Watch constantly.

Lemon Jell-O Cake

1 package yellow cake mix
1 1/2 teaspoons lemon extract
4 eggs
3/4 cup salad oil
1 cup boiling water
1 three-ounce package lemon Jell-O
1 1/2 cups powdered sugar
lemon juice

Dissolve Jell-O in boiling water. Let cool. Put cake mix in large mixer bowl. Add eggs 1 at a time while mixing; add cooled Jell-O, oil, and lemon extract. Beat hard 2 minutes. Pour into a Bundt pan and bake at 350° for 1 hour, or pour into a well-greased 9" x 13" x 2" pan and bake at 350° for 35 to 45 minutes. Test with toothpick. Mix together powdered sugar and lemon juice for syrup. Punch holes in cake with fork. Dribble syrup over cake.

COOKIES & BARS
Seasoning with love...

*O*ne *of the most rewarding events in our home is the annual
Christian Life Christmas dinner. We serve a buffet dinner
to all Sunday School teachers and their spouses early in December.*

*Preparation begins immediately following Thanksgiving
by decorating the Christmas tree and getting the house in order.
We prepare Christmas candy and cookies early and freeze them.
Because of the size of this group, it is necessary to serve the meal
at three different times on the selected weekend. One group is
served on Friday evening, and two groups on Saturday, one at
5:00 and the other at 7:00.*

*Probably the most valuable side benefit is that this early
December activity has helped us get all of the baking and decorating done early so that the rest of December can be enjoyed to
the fullest!*

—Marion Snyder
Shawnee Mission, Kans.

Carrot Cookie Squares

2 eggs, beaten
1 cup sugar
¾ cup corn oil
1 cup flour
1 teaspoon baking soda
1½ teaspoons cinnamon
½ teaspoon salt
1½ cups carrots, grated fine
¾ cup flaked coconut
¾ cup chopped nuts

Mix eggs and sugar. Sift flour with soda, cinnamon, and salt; add this and corn oil alternately to egg mixture. Mix well; stir in carrots, nuts, and coconut. Spread in greased 13″ x 9″ x 2″ pan. Bake at 350° for 25 to 30 minutes. Cool and spread with frosting (see below), then cut into squares and remove from pan. Store in covered container in refrigerator. May be frozen.

ORANGE CREAM CHEESE FROSTING

1 tablespoon orange juice
grated rind of 1 orange
1 three-ounce package of cream cheese
1½ to 2 cups confectioners' sugar

Let cream cheese soften at room temperature, then beat well with orange juice and rind; add confectioners' sugar, a little at a time, until frosting is of good spreading consistency.

Chocolate Peppermint Bars

4 squares semisweet chocolate
2 sticks butter or margarine
4 eggs
2 cups sugar
1 cup flour
1 cup chopped nuts

Melt chocolate and margarine. Cool. Beat eggs, add sugar, flour, and then chocolate mixture. Add chopped nuts. Line a 11″ x 16″ sheet cake pan with foil. Spread batter. Bake at 350° for 25 minutes. Cool thoroughly and then add topping.

TOPPING

3 cups powdered sugar

6 tablespoons soft butter or margarine

1 tablespoon cream

2 teaspoons peppermint extract

¼ teaspoon vanilla, plus a few drops green food color

Combine and spread as smoothly as possible on cooked mixture. Refrigerate until chilled and add icing.

ICING

3 squares semisweet chocolate

3 tablespoons butter or margarine

Melt chocolate and butter together. Brush on top of chilled mix. Cut into small bars. Makes 10 to 12 dozen bite-size cookies or 5 dozen regular-size.

Molasses Crunches

¾ cup shortening

1 cup brown sugar

1 egg

½ cup light molasses

2¼ cups flour

¼ teaspoon salt

2 teaspoons baking soda

1 teaspoon cinnamon

1 teaspoon ginger

½ teaspoon ground cloves

Cream shortening and sugar. Add egg and molasses. Sift dry ingredients and blend with sugar mixture. Chill dough. Roll into 1″ balls. Roll into sugar. Place on greased baking sheet. Bake at 350° for 12 to 15 minutes.

Date-Nut Torte

⅓ cup sifted flour
½ teaspoon baking powder
¼ teaspoon salt
1 cup pitted dates, chopped
¾ cup pecans or walnuts, chopped
1 teaspoon grated lemon peel
3 egg yolks
¾ cup sugar
3 egg whites
whipped cream

Preheat oven to 325°. Lightly grease an 8″ x 8″ x 2″ baking pan. On sheet of waxed paper, sift flour with baking powder and salt. Add dates, pecans, and lemon peel; toss well. Set aside. In medium bowl, beat egg yolks with ¼ cup sugar until very thick and light. With rubber scraper, fold in flour mixture just until combined. In large bowl, beat egg whites at high speed just until soft peaks form when beater is slowly raised. Add remaining sugar, 2 tablespoons at a time, beating well after each addition. Continue beating until stiff peaks form when beater is raised. With rubber scraper, fold flour mixture into egg whites until well combined. Bake at 325° for 50 minutes, or until surface springs back when gently pressed with fingertip. Let cool in pan on wire rack. To serve: Cut into rectangles. Top with whipped cream. Serves 8.

Black Bottom Cakes

1½ cups sifted flour
1 teaspoon baking soda
1 cup sugar
½ teaspoon salt
¼ cup unsweetened cocoa
1 cup water
⅓ cup cooking oil
1 tablespoon vinegar
1 teaspoon vanilla

Sift dry ingredients into mixing bowl, add remaining ingredients, beat until well blended, fill lined muffin cups one-third full with batter. Pour filling on top.

FILLING

1 eight-ounce package cream cheese
1 egg
¹/₃ cup sugar
¹/₈ teaspoon salt
1 cup chocolate pieces
chopped almonds

Combine cream cheese, egg, sugar, and salt. Beat well. Stir in chocolate pieces. Put a heaping tablespoon of mixture on batter in each muffin. Sprinkle with sugar and chopped almonds if desired. Bake at 325° for 20 or 30 minutes. Makes at least 20 cups.

Coconut Oatmeal Cookies—1

1 cup butter
1 teaspoon vanilla
1 cup white sugar
1 cup brown sugar
2 eggs, unbeaten
1 cup flour
1 teaspoon baking soda
¹/₂ teaspoon baking powder
pinch of salt
2 cups quick uncooked oatmeal
1 cup crumbled cornflakes or Rice Krispies cereal
1 cup coconut

Fluff butter with mixer, add 1 cup white sugar gradually, and then 1 cup brown sugar. Add vanilla; add eggs, one at a time, and mix well. Next add flour, soda, baking powder, and salt and mix well.

To the above mixture, add the dry oatmeal, cornflakes or Rice Krispies, and coconut. Mix well. Drop by teaspoonfuls on greased cookie sheet, about 1″ apart (cookies spread). Bake at 350° for 12 to 15 minutes. Makes 3 to 3¹/₂ dozen cookies.

Coconut Oatmeal Cookies—2

1/2 cup shortening
1/2 cup sugar
1/2 cup brown sugar, packed
1 egg
1/2 cup flour, sifted
1/2 teaspoon baking powder
1/2 teaspoon baking soda
1/4 teaspoon salt
1 cup shredded coconut
1 cup quick oats
1 teaspoon vanilla

Blend shortening and both sugars. Add unbeaten egg and mix well. Sift together flour, soda, baking powder, and salt. Add to shortening mixture. Stir in coconut, oatmeal, and vanilla. Drop from teaspoon onto greased cookie sheet. Bake at 350° for 8 minutes. Makes 9 dozen small cookies.

Flo's Sugar Cookies

4 cups flour
1 teaspoon baking powder
1 cup shortening
1 cup sugar
2 eggs, beaten
1 teaspoon baking soda
1/3 cup milk
1/2 teaspoon salt
1 teaspoon vanilla
1/2 teaspoon lemon juice
1/4 teaspoon almond extract

Mix flour, baking powder, salt, and shortening as for pie. In another bowl add soda to sugar, when blended add beaten eggs, milk, and flavorings. Pour sugar into flour mixture and mix until smooth. Chill. Roll out on floured board, cut into desired shapes. Bake at 325° for 8 to 10 minutes.

Spice Bars

1 cup raisins
1 cup water
1/2 cup shortening
1 cup sugar
1 egg, slightly beaten
1 3/4 cups flour, sifted
1/4 teaspoon salt
1 teaspoon baking soda
1 teaspoon cinnamon
1 teaspoon nutmeg
1 teaspoon allspice
1/2 teaspoon cloves
1/2 cup walnuts, chopped

Boil raisins and water. Remove from heat. Stir in shortening. Cool until lukewarm. Stir in sugar and egg. Sift dry ingredients, beat into raisins. Stir in nuts. Bake in a 13" x 9" x 2" pan at 375° for 20 minutes. When cool, dust with confectioners' sugar. Makes 2 dozen. "A moist, cakelike bar."

Lemon Love Notes

1/2 cup butter
1 cup flour, sifted
1/4 cup powdered sugar
1 cup sugar
2 tablespoons flour
1/2 teaspoon baking powder
2 eggs, beaten
2 tablespoons lemon juice
2 teaspoons grated lemon rind

Combine the first 3 ingredients, mix well, and press into an un-greased 8" square pan. Bake at 350° for 8 minutes. Cool in pan. Combine sugar, flour, and baking powder. Add eggs, lemon juice, and rind. Mix well. Pour over crust. Bake at 350° for 25 minutes. Cool. Sprinkle with powdered sugar, cut into squares. Makes 16.

Oatmeal Cookies—1

1 cup seedless raisins
1½ cups boiling water
2 cups sifted all-purpose flour
2 teaspoons baking powder
½ teaspoon salt
1 teaspoon cinnamon
½ teaspoon allspice
½ teaspoon cloves
2 cups quick-cooking oats
1 cup chopped walnuts
1 cup shortening
1 cup sugar
3 eggs, well beaten

Cook raisins in boiling water 5 minutes. Drain, keep ¼ cup raisin liquid. Sift flour, baking powder, salt, and spices. Add oats and nuts with flour mixture. Cream shortening and sugar, add eggs and beat well. Add flour-oats mixture alternately with raisin liquid. Drop by teaspoons on greased sheet and bake at 400° for 12 to 15 minutes. Makes 4 dozen.

Oatmeal Cookies—2

½ cup brown sugar
½ cup granulated sugar
½ cup shortening
1 egg, beaten
½ teaspoon vanilla
¼ teaspoon salt
½ teaspoon baking soda
½ cup sifted flour
½ cup raisins
½ cup dates

½ cup chopped pecans

½ cup coconut

2 cups uncooked oatmeal

Cream together sugar and shortening. Add egg and vanilla. Sift together salt, baking soda, and flour; add to creamed mixture. In another bowl mix together remaining ingredients; then add flour mixture. Mix well. Drop by teaspoons onto a greased cookie sheet. Bake at 325° for 10 minutes. "The cookies fall some after leaving the oven."

Wilma's Christmas Cookies

⅓ cup sugar

¼ cup butter

2 eggs, beaten

1½ cups sifted flour

½ teaspoon allspice

½ teaspoon cinnamon

¼ teaspoon ground cloves

¼ teaspoon salt

1 teaspoon lemon juice

½ teaspoon vanilla

¼ teaspoon baking soda dissolved in one tablespoon water

⅓ cup orange juice

½ pound candied cherries, chopped

½ pound candied pineapple, chopped

1 pound pitted dates, cut in thirds

¾ pound whole pecans

½ pound chopped walnuts

Cream butter and sugar. Add egg, orange juice, lemon juice, and vanilla. Mix well. Sift flour and spices. Add to creamed mixture. Add soda mixture, nuts, and fruit. Drop by teaspoonfuls on an ungreased cookie sheet. Bake at 350° for 15 minutes. Makes 3½ dozen. "Wonderful."

Chocolate Nut Chewies

⅔ cup shortening
2 cups brown sugar
3 eggs
1 teaspoon vanilla
2 cups flour
½ teaspoon salt
1 teaspoon baking powder
1 cup walnuts, chopped
1 six-ounce package semisweet chocolate chips

Cream shortening and sugar, add eggs and beat well. Add vanilla. Sift dry ingredients, add to sugar mixture, and beat until smooth. Stir in walnuts and chocolate chips. Bake in a greased 10″ x 15″ pan at 350° for 25 minutes. When almost cool, cut into squares. Makes 3 dozen.

Christmas Oatmeal Party Cookies or Sandies

1 cup butter
1 cup confectioners' sugar
2 teaspoons vanilla
2 cups sifted flour
½ teaspoon salt
1 cup quick-cooking oats

Cream butter, sugar, vanilla, and salt until light and fluffy. Stir in flour and oats. Use 2 tablespoons of dough for each, shape into 1″ balls or 1½″ logs. Bake on ungreased cookie sheet at 325° for 20 minutes, or until done. Cool.

CHOCOLATE DIP

Melt 6 ounces (1 cup) semisweet chocolate pieces, put over hot water, remove, dip tops of round cookies or end of log in chocolate, then in finely chopped walnuts. Let set overnight before stacking to store. Makes 4½ dozen.

M&M Specials

1½ cups flour
1 teaspoon baking soda
1 teaspoon salt
1 teaspoon instant coffee
1 cup margarine or butter (or half butter and half margarine)
¾ cup brown sugar
¾ cup granulated sugar
2 eggs
1 teaspoon vanilla
½ cup chopped walnuts
2 cups rolled oats
½ cup coconut
1 twelve-ounce package chocolate bits or M&M's

Sift flour, measure, and sift again with soda and salt. Add instant coffee. Cream butter with both sugars. Beat eggs into butter-sugar mixture. Add vanilla and mix well. Stir in dry ingredients. Add nuts, oats, coconut, and chocolate bits and mix thoroughly. Drop on aluminum-foil-lined cookie sheet, about 1 tablespoon of batter for each cookie. Bake at 350° for 10 minutes or until light brown. Makes 5 to 6 dozen cookies.

Church Windows

1 large package semisweet chocolate chips
1 stick margarine
1 cup chopped nuts
1 large package colored miniature marshmallows
1 cup coconut

Melt chocolate chips and margarine in top of double boiler. Put in large bowl and let cool. Add other ingredients and mix well together. Make rolls about 1½″ thick and 10″ long by rolling between pieces of waxed paper. Mixture makes about 4 rolls. Wrap tight in waxed paper and refrigerate until hard. Slice in circles. Note: Coconut may be reserved and each roll can be rolled in it before being wrapped in waxed paper. "These freeze very well and are good for Christmas."

Lemon Date Squares

½ cup butter

¼ cup powdered sugar

1 cup flour

1 teaspoon grated lemon rind

2 eggs

1 cup sugar

2 tablespoons flour

½ teaspoon baking powder

½ teaspoon salt

1 cup flaked coconut

½ cup pitted dates, chopped

1 tablespoon lemon juice

Cream together butter and powdered sugar until fluffy. Blend in 1 cup flour and lemon rind. Pat into a buttered 8″ square pan. Bake at 350° for 20 minutes. Beat eggs until foamy. Add sugar gradually and beat until thick. Blend in remaining ingredients. Spoon over baked crust. Bake at 350° for 25 minutes. Cool on wire rack.

Lemon Crumb Squares

1 cup soft butter

2 cups flour

½ cup powdered sugar

¼ teaspoon salt

TOPPING

4 eggs

2 cups sugar

¼ cup lemon juice

¼ cup flour

Mix together first 4 ingredients. Spread in 10″ x 14″ pan. Bake at 325° for 25 minutes. For topping, beat eggs slightly; then, with fork, mix in other topping ingredients. Pour over the prebaked crust. Return to 325° oven and bake an additional 25 minutes. Remove and sprinkle lightly with powdered sugar. Cool. Cut into 2″ squares. Makes 35.

Date and Nut Squares

2 eggs
¹/₂ cup sugar
¹/₂ teaspoon vanilla
¹/₂ cup flour
¹/₂ teaspoon baking powder
¹/₂ teaspoon salt
1 cup chopped pecans
2 cups dates, finely cut
¹/₂ cup confectioners' sugar

Beat eggs, sugar, and vanilla. Blend in flour, baking powder, and salt. Stir in nuts and dates. Spread in greased 8″ x 8″ x 2″ pan and bake at 325° for 25 to 30 minutes. Cut into 2″ squares and sprinkle with confectioners' sugar. Makes 16.

Date Bars

3 eggs, well beaten
1 cup sugar
1 cup flour
¹/₄ teaspoon baking powder
1 teaspoon salt
1¹/₂ cups (1 small package) sliced dates
1 teaspoon vanilla
1 cup chopped nuts

Mix all ingredients together and bake in buttered 9″ x 12″ pan at 350° for 30 minutes. Makes 2 dozen.

German Almond Cookies

1 cup butter or margarine
1 cup sugar
1 egg, separated
1 teaspoon almond extract
2 cups flour
1 tablespoon sugar (additional)
¼ teaspoon cinnamon
½ cup blanched almonds, slivered or sliced

Cream together butter and 1 cup sugar; add egg yolk and almond extract; stir in flour. Press into an ungreased 10″ x 15″ jelly-roll pan. Beat egg white and spread over dough. Top with mixture of 1 tablespoon sugar, cinnamon, and almonds. Bake at 350° for 20 to 25 minutes. Cool 10 minutes and cut on the diagonal. Cool completely and remove cookies from pan. Cookies freeze well.

Double Chocolate Drops

½ cup nuts
1 six-ounce package semisweet chocolate pieces
1 cup sifted all-purpose flour
½ teaspoon baking soda
½ teaspoon salt
½ cup shortening
½ cup sugar
1 egg
¼ cup warm water

Preheat oven to 350°. Chop nuts coarsely. Melt half the semisweet chocolate pieces in a saucepan over hot water. Sift flour, soda, and salt together. Work or cream shortening until it feels creamy. Then add sugar gradually, beating until smooth. Stir in unbeaten egg and the cool melted chocolate. Mix in the flour mixture and warm water alternately. Stir in nuts and remaining solid pieces of chocolate and drop by teaspoonfuls onto an ungreased baking sheet. (Allow for spreading during baking.) Bake 12 to 15 minutes. Makes 3 dozen.

FBI Brownies

2 eggs

1 cup sugar

½ teaspoon vanilla

2 squares of chocolate or ⅔ cup cocoa

½ cup butter

½ cup flour

½ cup nuts

Beat eggs until light. Add sugar and vanilla and beat until thick. Melt chocolate with butter. Add egg mixture and beat until smooth. Add flour and nuts and spread on 8″ x 11″ greased shallow pan. Bake at 325° for 30 minutes. Cut in squares when cool. No icing needed. Makes about 20.

Cinnamon Sugar Star Cookies

1½ cups sifted powdered sugar

1 cup butter

1 large egg

1 teaspoon vanilla

½ teaspoon almond flavoring

2½ cups sifted all-purpose flour

1 teaspoon cinnamon

1 teaspoon baking soda

1 teaspoon cream of tartar

mixture of 2 tablespoons sugar and 1 teaspoon cinnamon for topping

Mix sugar and butter. Add egg and flavorings and mix until well blended. Sift dry ingredients including cinnamon and stir into butter mixture. Cover dough well and refrigerate for 2 to 3 hours. Preheat oven to 375°. Roll dough on floured board to about ¼″ thick. Cut into star shapes. Bake 7 to 8 minutes on center rack of oven. While baking mix 2 tablespoons sugar and 1 teaspoon cinnamon. Sprinkle on hot cookies. This makes 2½ dozen cookies.

Swedish Ginger Cookies

1 cup butter
1½ cups sugar
1 egg
1½ tablespoons grated orange peel
2 tablespoons dark corn syrup
1 tablespoon water
3¼ cups sifted flour
2 teaspoons baking soda
2 teaspoons cinnamon
1 teaspoon ginger
½ teaspoon cloves
almond halves

Cream butter and sugar well. Add egg and beat until light and fluffy. Add peel, syrup, and water. Mix well. Sift dry ingredients, stir into creamed mixture. Chill dough overnight. Roll dough to ⅛" thick on lightly floured surface. Sprinkle with white or colored sugar. Press lightly with rolling pin. Cut into shapes. Place 1" apart on an ungreased cookie sheet. Top with 1 almond half. Bake at 350° for 8 to 10 minutes. Makes 6 dozen. "I like to use a daisy flower cookie cutter."

Cheesecake Diamonds

5 tablespoons butter
⅓ cup brown sugar
1 cup sifted all-purpose flour
¼ cup chopped nuts
½ cup white sugar
1 eight-ounce cream cheese, softened
1 egg
2 tablespoons milk
1 tablespoon lemon juice
½ teaspoon vanilla

Cream butter and brown sugar, add flour and nuts and mix well. Set aside 1 cup of mixture for topping. Press remainder in bottom of 8" x 8" x 2" pan. Bake at 350° for 12 to 15 minutes. Blend white sugar and cream cheese until smooth. Add egg, milk, lemon juice, and vanilla. Beat well, spread over crust, sprinkle with reserved 1 cup topping. Return to oven, bake 25 minutes more. Cool, then chill. Cut into diamonds. Makes 16.

Helen's Sour Cream Cookies

2 cups brown sugar
1 cup shortening
½ teaspoon salt
2 eggs
1 cup sour cream
1 teaspoon baking soda
4 teaspoons baking powder
4½ cups flour
1 cup raisins
1 cup chopped walnuts

Cream sugar, shortening, and salt. Add eggs, mix well. Add sour cream, raisins, and walnuts. Sift remaining dry ingredients and combine into the raisin mixture. Mix well. Drop by spoonfuls onto a greased cookie sheet. Bake at 375° for 10 minutes.

Christmas Cookies

1 pound butter
1 cup powdered sugar
1 cup chopped nuts
4 cups flour, sifted
½ cup each red and green candied cherries

Cream together butter and sugar. Add remaining ingredients and mix with hands. Form into round rolls, 2" wide while still soft. Decorate each with a cherry. Refrigerate overnight. Slice ¼" thick. Bake on ungreased cookie sheet at 350° for 10 minutes. Makes 5 dozen.

PIES & PASTRIES

Seasoning with love...

*H*ospitality *in our home for dinner or a snack has been the key to ministering to people who would otherwise be alone.*

Because we believe that no one should be left alone on holidays, we usually invite people to share our activities on Memorial Day, July 4th, Labor Day, Easter—and always Thanksgiving. Bridal showers, fellowship parties, and other group meals are often held in our home. And asking someone over after church is routine. Whether we have fancy food and elaborate decorations, or plain home cooking, it doesn't matter. It's the warmth and welcome that count.

Inviting guests without expecting a return favor has enriched our lives. Nothing could reward us better than the deepened friendships we've gained.

—Yvonne Spencer
Franklin, Mich.

Pecan Pie

1 cup white corn syrup
1 cup dark brown sugar
$\frac{1}{3}$ teaspoon salt
1 teaspoon vanilla
$\frac{1}{3}$ cup melted butter
3 eggs, slightly beaten
1 cup shelled whole pecans

Combine syrup, sugar, salt, butter, and vanilla, and mix well. Add slightly beaten eggs. Pour into a 9″ unbaked pie shell. Sprinkle pecans over all. Bake in preheated 350° oven for about 45 minutes. "This is my best."

My Favorite Pumpkin Pie

5 eggs
2 cups whole milk
1½ cups white sugar
3½ cups Libby's pumpkin
1 teaspoon cinnamon
½ teaspoon ginger
⅛ teaspoon cloves
⅛ teaspoon allspice
⅛ teaspoon nutmeg
1 teaspoon salt
¼ cup cream
¼ cup melted butter

Beat eggs, add milk, and strain. Add pumpkin, sugar, spices, salt. Mix, do not overbeat. Add cream and then the melted butter last. Pour into 2 pie pans lined with pastry rolled a bit thicker than usual. Bake at 400° for 10 minutes, reduce heat to 300° and bake for 60 minutes. Let set 1 or 2 hours before cutting. "You can use 9″ or 8″ pie pans. Long, slow cooking gives the finest flavor. The filling may be kept in the refrigerator several days."

Mincemeat

2½ pounds chuck beef, or rump roast (4 to 5 pounds uncooked will equal 2½ pounds cooked)
4 pounds tart apples (pared and cored)
5¼ cups seedless raisins
5 cups currants
½ pound ground suet (ground at store)
4 teaspoons salt
2 tablespoons nutmeg
2 tablespoons cinnamon
2 tablespoons powdered cloves
4 cups sugar
2 cups fruit juice (cider or 1 cup coffee)
2 cups meat stock

Cook meat until tender, cool in meat juice. Put through food chopper (the coarse grind). Put apples through the same grind. Add ground meat, ground apples, suet, and remaining ingredients. Cover and simmer slowly for at least 1 hour in oven. Pack in clean hot sterilized jars at once and seal. "May be frozen, but will keep at least 2 weeks in refrigerator. If canned, will keep 1 or 2 years." Makes 10 pints.

Editor's note: Happy were the recipients of Audrey Benner's holiday mincemeat—all done up in a holly-bedecked Mason Jar.

TO MAKE PIE

To 1 pint of mincemeat, add 1 or 2 small peeled and chopped apples, about ¼ cup sugar, and ½ cup of any fruit or spice juice. Bake at 425° for 40 minutes. "This is an old Iowa recipe."

Boysenberry Pie

4 to 5 cups frozen boysenberries
¾ cup sugar
3 tablespoons flour
1 tablespoon butter

Mix together sugar and flour. Add berries. Pour into an unbaked 9″ pie shell. Dot with butter. Cover with lattice top crust. Bake at 450° for 10 minutes. Reduce heat to 350° and bake for 30 to 35 minutes.

Black Raspberry Pie

2 cans black raspberries
³/₄ cup white sugar
¹/₄ cup flour
1 tablespoon butter

Drain raspberries and reserve ²/₃ cup juice. Mix together sugar and flour, add reserved juice. Mix well. Fold in raspberries. Place in a 9″ pastry shell. Dot with butter. Fold top pastry under lower pastry and crimp edges. Slit top. Bake at 450° for 10 minutes. Reduce heat to 350° and continue to bake for 25 minutes.

Gooseberry Pie

2 cans gooseberries
³/₄ cup gooseberry juice
1 cup, 2 tablespoons sugar
3¹/₂ tablespoons, flour
dash of salt
1 tablespoon butter

Blend together sugar, flour, and salt. Mix with berries and juice. Place in an unbaked pie shell. Dot with butter. Cover with lattice crust. Bake at 450° for 10 minutes. Reduce heat to 350° and bake 30 to 35 minutes.

Grape Crumb Pie

3¹/₂ cups Concord grapes
1 cup sugar
¹/₄ cup flour
¹/₄ teaspoon salt
1 tablespoon lemon juice
1¹/₂ tablespoons melted butter

Slip skins from grapes. Bring pulp to boiling. Press through a sieve to remove seeds, add skin. Combine sugar, flour, and salt. Add lemon juice, butter, and grapes. Pour into a 9″ unbaked pie shell. Sprinkle crumb topping over top. Bake at 400° for 40 to 50 minutes.

CRUMB TOPPING

¾ cup flour
½ cup sugar
⅓ cup butter

Blend together and mix well.

Blue Plum Pie

2½ pounds Italian blue plums
1½ cups sugar
3 tablespoons flour
pinch of salt
½ teaspoon nutmeg
juice of ½ lemon

Fill unbaked crust with plums, halved and seeded. Start lining crust around edges placing plum cut-side up. When crust is full, stack halves cut-side up in center of pie. Sift together the sugar, flour, and salt. Scatter over plums. Sprinkle nutmeg and lemon juice over pie. Cover with top crust and place foil under pie to catch juice overflow. Bake at 450° for 10 minutes, reduce heat to 350° and bake 30 minutes more.

Rhubarb Pie

3 egg yolks
1½ cups sugar
2 tablespoons flour
¾ cup cream
dash salt
1 teaspoon vanilla
1½ cups diced rhubarb

Mix together egg yolks, sugar, and flour. Add cream, salt, vanilla, and rhubarb. Pour into an unbaked pie shell. Place lattice dough strips on top of pie. Bake at 350° for 1½ hours.

Dutch Peach Pie

1 quart peeled, sliced fresh peaches
1 cup sugar
1/4 cup flour
1/4 teaspoon salt
1/4 teaspoon cinnamon
1/8 teaspoon nutmeg
3/4 cup evaporated milk
2 tablespoons butter, melted

Arrange sliced peaches in bottom of 9" unbaked pastry shell. Blend together in a small mixing bowl the sugar, flour, salt, and spices. Add milk and melted butter. Mix thoroughly and pour over the peach slices. Bake at 400° until peaches are tender, about 45 minutes. Cool before serving. Serves 6 to 8.

Deep-dish Apple Pie

10 cups Jonathan apples, peeled and thinly sliced
1 cup sugar
1 tablespoon flour
1/2 teaspoon cinnamon
1/4 teaspoon nutmeg
1/4 teaspoon salt
3 tablespoons butter
1 cup sifted flour
1/8 teaspoon salt
1/3 cup shortening
2 to 3 tablespoons cold milk

Place apples in 12" x 8" x 1" baking dish. Combine sugar, 1 tablespoon flour, and spices. Sprinkle over apples, mixing lightly. Dot with butter. Sift together flour and salt. Cut in shortening, add milk gradually, stirring with a fork. On a lightly floured board, roll to 1" larger than the size of the baking dish. Place dough on top of apples. Brush with milk, cut steam slits. Sprinkle with granulated sugar. Bake at 400° for 45 to 50 minutes. "Serve with ice cream."

Deep-dish Cherry Pie

¾ *cup sugar*
¼ *cup flour*
pinch of salt
1 cup cherry juice and water
½ *teaspoon almond extract*
4 cups sour cherries
1 tablespoon butter
red food coloring

Mix flour, sugar, and salt in pan. Add juice, mix well. Heat and cook 5 minutes. Add almond extract, food coloring, and cherries. Pour into a 10″ x 6″ x 2″ baking dish. Dot with butter. Fit the pastry crust tightly on top of cherries. Press sides with fork. Brush top with milk. Bake at 450° for 25 to 35 minutes.

PASTRY

Cut ⅓ cup shortening into 1 cup flour and a dash of baking powder and salt. Add 4 tablespoons cold water. Roll pastry ⅛″ thick to cover the top of the baking dish. Make air vents in pastry. Place on top of cherries.

Dutch Apple Pie

6 medium apples, peeled, sliced
3 tablespoons unsifted flour
1 cup sugar
¼ *teaspoon cloves*
1 cup sour cream
½ *teaspoon cinnamon*
1½ *tablespoons sugar*

Fill unbaked 9″ pie crust with apples. Set aside. Combine flour, 1 cup sugar, and cloves. Add sour cream. Mix thoroughly and pour over apples. Combine cinnamon and 1½ tablespoons sugar. Sprinkle over sour cream mixture. Bake pie for 10 minutes at 450°. Reduce heat to 350° and bake an additional 40 minutes.

Old-fashioned Grape Pie

3½ cups Concord grapes
1 cup sugar
3½ tablespoons flour
⅛ teaspoon salt
½ teaspoon grated lemon peel
2 teaspoons grated orange peel
2 tablespoons butter

Slip skins from grapes. Heat pulp to boiling. Then through a sieve to remove seeds. Mix skins and sugar, add flour, salt, and lemon and orange peel. Add to pulp. Pour into a 9″ unbaked pie shell. Dot with butter. Cover with top crust. Bake at 450° for 10 minutes, then at 350° for 30 minutes. Decorate with baked crust grape leaves.

Wilma's Pecan Pie

6 eggs
1 cup sugar
2 cups dark Karo syrup
1 teaspoon vanilla
⅓ cup cream
2 teaspoons cornstarch
4 tablespoons butter (melted)
pinch of salt

Beat eggs, add sugar mixed with cornstarch. Add syrup, cream, and then the melted butter, vanilla, and salt. Pour into unbaked crust and sprinkle 1 cup pecans on top. Bake at 350° for 45 minutes.

Christina's* Strawberry Pie

1 quart strawberries
1 cup water
1 cup sugar

3 tablespoons cornstarch

1 tablespoon lemon juice

red food color, if desired

Wash, drain, and hull strawberries. Simmer 1 cup of berries with ⅔ cup water until berries start to break up, about 3 minutes. Blend sugar and cornstarch with remaining ⅓ cup water and lemon juice, stir into boiling mixture, boil 1 minute, stirring constantly. Cool. Put remaining 3 cups berries in baked pie shell, cover with glaze. Refrigerate until firm, about 2 hours. Top with whipped cream. "A blue-ribbon pie."

*Mrs. Christina (Ralph) Barton, Riverside, Calif.

Special Lemon Pie

1⅓ cups sugar

1½ cups water

½ teaspoon salt

½ cup cornstarch

¼ cup water

4 egg yolks, slightly beaten

½ cup fresh lemon juice

3 tablespoons butter

1 tablespoon grated lemon peel

4 egg whites

¼ teaspoon salt

½ cup sugar

Mix together the first 3 ingredients, heat to boiling. Mix together cornstarch and ¼ cup water to a smooth paste. Add to boiling mixture, stirring constantly, cook until thick. Mix egg yolks and lemon juice. Slowly stir into thickened mixture. Heat and cook, stirring constantly, until mixture bubbles again. Remove from heat, stir in butter and peel. Cover and cool until cooled to lukewarm.

MERINGUE

Beat egg whites and salt until foamy. Gradually add sugar, beat until it forms peaks. Stir in 2 rounded tablespoons of meringue to lukewarm lemon filling. Pour into a 9" pie shell. Spread meringue on top of filling. Bake at 325° for 15 minutes or until lightly browned. Cool for at least 1 hour before cutting.

Cherry Supreme Pie

| 1 fourteen-ounce can sweetened condensed milk, chilled |
| 1/2 pint whipping cream, chilled but not whipped |
| 1 sixteen-ounce can drained sour pitted cherries, chilled |
| 1/3 cup fresh lemon juice |
| 1 cup chopped pecans |
| 1 teaspoon lemon extract |

Mix milk, cream, and lemon juice together and fold in remaining ingredients. Pour into baked and cooled 9″ graham cracker pie crust. Chill until served. This dessert may be made up the day before or the morning of the party, but it should be chilled at least several hours.

Lemon Meringue Pie

| 1¼ cups sugar |
| 3 tablespoons cornstarch |
| 3 tablespoons all-purpose flour |
| dash salt |
| 1½ cups hot water |
| 3 egg yolks, slightly beaten |
| 2 tablespoons butter |
| 1/2 teaspoon grated lemon peel |
| 1/3 cup lemon juice |
| 3 egg whites |
| 1 teaspoon lemon juice |
| 6 tablespoons sugar |

In saucepan, mix first 4 ingredients; gradually stir in hot water. Quickly bring to boil, stirring constantly. Reduce heat; continue cooking and stirring 8 minutes. Stir small amount hot mixture into egg yolks, then return to hot mixture. Bring to boiling, cook 4 minutes, stirring constantly. Add butter and lemon peel. Slowly stir in 1/3 cup lemon juice. Pour into cooled 9″ pastry shell. Cool to room temperature. For meringue, beat egg whites with 1 teaspoon lemon juice to soft peaks. Gradually add 6 tablespoons sugar, beating until stiff peaks form and sugar has dissolved. Spread meringue over filling. Bake at 350° for 12 to 15 minutes. Cool thoroughly before serving.

Double Lemon Velvet Pie

1⅓ cups sugar

6 tablespoons cornstarch

2 cups boiling water

1 teaspoon grated lemon rind

⅓ cup lemon juice

2 egg yolks, beaten

1 cup evaporated milk

1 tablespoon vanilla

2 egg whites, beaten stiff

unflavored gelatin

Mix sugar and cornstarch; add boiling water. Cool until thick. Add lemon rind and juice. Add egg yolk and cook slowly a few minutes. Reserve 1 cup of mixture to use for top layer of pie. Add 1 tablespoon of unflavored gelatin to ¼ cup of cold water, let soak for 15 minutes. Stir in lemon filling slowly. Add evaporated milk and vanilla. Chill until mixture starts to set, then fold in egg whites. Pour into a baked pie shell and top with the 1 cup reserved lemon sauce. Chill. "My best!"

Chocolate Cream Pie

1 cup sugar

3 egg yolks

2½ tablespoons cornstarch

2 cups milk

4 squares chocolate

¼ teaspoon salt

2 tablespoons butter

1 teaspoon vanilla

Combine sugar, egg yolks, and cornstarch. Add milk and mix well until the mixture begins to thicken. Add chocolate and stir until it melts. Add butter and vanilla and pour into pie shell. To make meringue beat 3 egg whites for about 4 minutes, gradually adding ½ cup sugar and ½ teaspoon vanilla, until stiff peaks form. Top the pie with the meringue. Bake at 350° about 5 minutes until the meringue is light brown.

Lemon Sour Cream Pie

1 cup sugar

3 tablespoons cornstarch

dash of salt

1 cup milk

3 egg yolks, beaten

¼ cup butter

1 teaspoon grated lemon peel

¼ cup lemon juice

1 cup dairy sour cream

3 egg whites

¼ teaspoon cream of tartar

½ teaspoon vanilla

6 tablespoons sugar

Combine 1 cup sugar, cornstarch, and dash of salt. Slowly stir in milk. Cook and stir until mixture is boiling and thickened. Blend small amount of hot mixture into beaten egg yolks; return to hot mixture. Cook and stir 2 minutes. Add butter, lemon peel, and lemon juice. Cover; cool. Fold in sour cream. Spoon into baked 9″ pastry shell. Beat egg whites with cream of tartar and vanilla to soft peaks. Gradually add sugar, beating to stiff peaks. Spread meringue over pie, sealing to edge. Bake at 350° for 12 to 15 minutes or until golden. Cool.

Lemon Pie

1½ cups granulated sugar

½ cup all-purpose flour

2 tablespoons cornstarch

½ teaspoon salt

2¼ cups boiling water

3 eggs, separated

6 tablespoons lemon juice

3 tablespoons grated lemon rind

6 tablespoons sugar

Combine 1 cup of sugar with flour, cornstarch, and salt in a double boiler. Add boiling water, stirring constantly. Cook until smooth and thickened, about 15 minutes. Beat egg yolks with ½ cup sugar and pour hot mixture over egg mixture while stirring. Return to double boiler and cook 5 minutes longer. Just before removing from the heat, add lemon juice, the rind, and 1 tablespoon butter. Let mixture cool and pour into pie shell. Top it with meringue. To prepare the meringue beat the egg whites gradually adding sugar until stiff peaks form. Bake the pie about 30 minutes at 350°.

Burnt Sugar Pie

¾ cup granulated sugar
¾ cup boiling water
3 tablespoons granulated sugar
4 tablespoons flour
2 tablespoons cornstarch
½ teaspoon salt
½ cup cold milk
2 cups scalded milk
3 eggs
2 tablespoons butter
1 teaspoon vanilla
3 tablespoons sugar

In a heavy skillet, put the ¾ cup sugar and heat slowly until light brown. Add boiling water and cook until it forms a syrup. Remove from heat and cool.

Sift together the 3 tablespoons sugar, flour, cornstarch, and salt into a heavy saucepan. Gradually add the ½ cup cold milk, blending until smooth. Add caramel syrup and mix well. Gradually add the scalded milk. Place over low heat, stirring constantly, and cook until thick.

Separate the eggs and beat the yolks well. Stir a small amount of the hot mixture into the beaten egg yolks and blend. Add to remaining hot mixture. Return to low heat and cook for 2 minutes. Add butter and vanilla and pour into baked pie shell.

Top with whipped cream or meringue, made from 3 egg whites and 3 tablespoons sugar. Bake in medium oven until the meringue is light brown.

Caramel Pie

| 4 eggs |
| 1¾ cups sugar |
| 2 teaspoons vanilla |
| 2 cups milk |
| 2 tablespoons butter |
| 5 tablespoons flour |

Beat 2 whole eggs and 2 additional egg yolks well. Add 1 cup sugar mixed with the flour, add milk, butter, and vanilla. Bring to a boil, stirring constantly until thick. Remove. Caramelize ¾ cup sugar, add to mixture, pour in baked pie shell. May be added either warm or cold. The 2 egg whites may be used as meringue. "I use a dab of whipped cream on top with pecans."

Ambassador Black Bottom Pie

CRUST

| 14 large gingersnaps |
| 5 tablespoons melted butter |

Roll the cookies fine, add melted butter, and mix well. Pat out evenly in a 9″ pie pan, and bake at 300° for 10 minutes. Cool.

FILLING

| 1 tablespoon gelatin |
| 4 tablespoons cold water |
| ½ cup sugar |
| 1¼ tablespoons cornstarch |
| 4 egg yolks |
| 2 cups milk, scalded |

CHOCOLATE CUSTARD LAYER

| 1½ squares melted chocolate |
| 1 teaspoon vanilla |

RUM-FLAVORED CUSTARD LAYER

4 egg whites
1/2 cup sugar
1/4 teaspoon cream of tartar
1 tablespoon rum-flavored extract

TOPPING

2 tablespoons powdered sugar
1 cup cream, whipped
1/2 square grated chocolate

Soak gelatin in cold water. Combine sugar and cornstarch, and add beaten egg yolks. Add the scalded milk slowly, and cook over simmering water in a double boiler, stirring occasionally, for 20 minutes, or until custard generously coats a spoon. Remove from heat and take out 1 cup of the custard. To this add the melted chocolate and beat well with rotary eggbeater. When cooled blend in vanilla and pour into cooled crust and chill. While remaining custard is still hot, blend in the softened gelatin and cool, but do not allow to stiffen. Make a stiff meringue by beating the egg whites until frothy, adding cream of tartar, and beating until stiff enough to hold a point; then gradually beat in the sugar. Beat until very stiff. While remaining custard mixture is still smooth and soft, fold in the meringue and blend in the rum flavoring. As soon as the chocolate custard layer has begun to set, cover it with the fluffy rum-flavored custard, and chill until set. Whip cream until firm. Gradually fold in powdered sugar and grated chocolate. Spread on top of chilled pie.

My Favorite Custard Pie

2 1/2 cups milk, scalded
4 eggs, slightly beaten
2/3 cup sugar
1/4 teaspoon salt
1 teaspoon vanilla
1/4 teaspoon nutmeg

Mix all ingredients except milk. Slowly stir in hot milk. Pour into a 9″ unbaked pie shell. Sprinkle top with nutmeg. Place on lowest rack in oven. Bake at 475° for 5 minutes. Reduce heat to 425° and bake for 10 minutes or until set. Do not cut pie for 1/2 hour after it has been removed from the oven.

Coconut Cream Pie

½ cup sugar	
3 tablespoons cornstarch	
3 tablespoons flour	
½ teaspoon salt	
2 cups milk	
1 egg, slightly beaten	
½ cup cream, whipped	
1 teaspoon vanilla	
2 or 3 drops of yellow coloring	
1 medium size package coconut	

Mix sugar, cornstarch, flour, and salt; add milk. Put in heavy pan over direct heat and bring to boil, stirring constantly. Lower heat, cook and stir until thick. Stir a little hot mixture into egg, return to hot mixture, again bring to boiling, stirring well. (Cook mixture about 5 minutes before adding egg.) Cool, then chill. Beat well with beater, fold in whipped cream and vanilla. Add coconut, two-thirds in pie and the rest on top.

For banana cream pie, omit coconut and put half of the filling in baked 9″ pie shell. Add 2 sliced bananas, then rest of the filling.

Butterscotch Pie

6 tablespoons butter, melted	
2½ cups scalded milk	
3 tablespoons cornstarch	
1½ cups brown sugar	
2 eggs	
¼ teaspoon vanilla	

Melt butter and brown sugar and cook until a rich brown. Add hot milk and heat until sugar is completely dissolved. Beat yolks slightly, add cornstarch, and pour milk mixture over it, stirring constantly. Add vanilla. Pour into an unbaked 9″ pie shell and bake at 450° for 10 minutes, and then at 325° for 30 or 35 minutes. Do not cut until 4 hours after baking.

Best Chocolate Pie

4 tablespoons cornstarch
1 cup sugar
1/2 teaspoon salt
3 squares unsweetened chocolate, broken
2 1/2 cups milk
3 egg yolks, beaten
1 tablespoon butter
2 teaspoons vanilla

Mix cornstarch, sugar, salt, and chocolate in pan. Gradually stir in milk. Cook over medium heat, stirring constantly, until thick and mixture comes to a boil. Boil 1 minute while stirring. Blend half the mixture into egg yolks, then stir into mixture in the pan. Cook 1 minute stirring constantly. Remove; stir in butter and vanilla. Chill or cool filling and pour into baked 9″ shell. Top with whipped cream.

Wilma's Sour Cream Pie

1 cup sour cream
1 cup raisins
1 cup sugar
2 tablespoons vinegar
3/4 teaspoon cinnamon
1/4 teaspoon ground cloves
1/4 teaspoon nutmeg
1/8 teaspoon salt
3 egg yolks

Cook all ingredients until thick. Cool slightly and pour into a 9″ baked pie crust. Spread with meringue. Bake at 300° for 25 to 30 minutes.

MERINGUE

Beat 3 egg whites slightly, add a dash of salt and 2 teaspoons lemon juice. Gradually add 4 tablespoons sugar. Beat until stiff.

CANDY & SWEETS

Seasoning with love...

*W*herever you go, someone needs a listening ear. As my husband says in one of his speeches, *"Everyone has a hurt, is hurting, or will hurt sometime in his life."*

We are on both ends of the ministry of hospitality—giving and receiving. In either case, mealtime or snack time usually ends up the same way, because God seems to have led us into empathy for people struggling with various frustrations. We encourage them to open up and let us share their thoughts and feelings, because Jerry and I are continually thanking God for struggles that have made us better people, more attuned to His will for us. Passing along this perspective has encouraged others along the way and has helped us, too.

God has given us two ears for listening, but only one mouth.

—Jewel Oliver
Aurora, Colo.

Wilma's Chocolate Fudge

4½ cups sugar
¼ pound butter
1 large can condensed milk

Bring above to full rolling boil and boil only 7 minutes.

In a large bowl combine:

1 cup chopped walnuts
1 quart marshmallow topping
2 twelve-ounce packages chocolate chips
1 teaspoon vanilla

Pour hot mixture over ingredients in bowl, stir until well dissolved and blended. Pour into buttered 9″ x 13″ pan. Place in refrigerator to set. Keep refrigerated. Makes 5 pounds.

Chocolate-Coconut Candy

1 stick butter
1 fifteen-ounce can sweetened condensed milk
2 one-pound boxes powdered sugar
7 ounces flaked coconut
1 pound nuts, finely chopped
8 ounces semisweet chocolate
1 5″ x 3″ bar of paraffin

Mix together butter, condensed milk, and powdered sugar. Knead until smooth. Add coconut and nuts. Form into balls the size of walnuts. Refrigerate ½ to 1 hour. Make a chocolate coating by combining semisweet chocolate and paraffin in the top of a double boiler. Melt them over hot water, stirring occasionally, until ingredients are well blended. Dip candy balls in melted chocolate. Keep chocolate over hot water while dipping. With tongs or forks, lift balls out of chocolate and lay on waxed paper. Put candy in refrigerator to harden. Store in tightly sealed container. May be frozen. Makes a generous amount.

Cream Caramels

2 cups sugar
3/4 cup light corn syrup
1/2 cup butter
2 cups cream

Bring the first 3 ingredients and 1 cup of the cream slowly to a boil, stirring constantly. Gradually stir in the other cup of cream. Stir frequently as mixture begins to thicken; more constantly as it darkens. Cook to 254°. (Test by dropping a little mixture into cold water. It is ready when it forms a hard ball.) Pour into buttered 7″ square pan with 1/2 cup broken nuts scattered over the bottom. When cold, cut into squares. Makes 5 dozen.

Strawberry Candy

2 small or 1 large package strawberry gelatin
3/4 cup flaked coconut
3/4 cup nutmeats, finely chopped
3/4 cup condensed milk
red and green colored sugar

Mix the dry gelatin with the remaining ingredients except for colored sugar. Form into berries. Dip small end in red sugar, large end in green sugar. Makes 2 dozen.

Can't Fail Divinity

2 cups sugar
1/2 cup water
pinch salt
1 pint marshmallow creme
1/2 cup chopped nuts

Combine the sugar, water, and salt and bring to a hard boil. Place the creme in a large bowl and pour in the hot syrup all at once. Mix with a spoon until it begins to lose its gloss. Stir in nuts and drop by a buttered teaspoon onto waxed paper. Makes about 2 dozen pieces with about 140 calories each.

Nut Crunch

1 cup butter
1 cup granulated sugar
3 tablespoons water
¾ cup crushed pecans
4 ounces chocolate chips, melted
¼ cup finely chopped pecans

In a heavy iron skillet melt together butter, sugar, and water. Stir constantly over high heat for about 10 minutes until mixture is dark brown. Stir in crushed pecans, then pour into a buttered 9″ x 13″ pan. When almost cool, spread melted chocolate chips over top and immediately sprinkle chopped pecans. Allow to harden. Break into pieces. "I am not a candy maker, but this recipe has never failed me. Makes nice Christmas gifts."

Wilma's Molasses Popcorn Balls

5 quarts popcorn, popped and unsalted
⅔ cup molasses
1½ cups sugar
½ cup water
¼ teaspoon vinegar
¼ teaspoon salt
2 tablespoons butter
2 teaspoons vanilla
1½ teaspoons baking soda

Without stirring, cook together molasses, sugar, water, vinegar, and salt, to a light crack stage. Remove, and add butter, vanilla, and soda (soda may cause syrup to bubble up). At once pour over popcorn and stir with a fork. With buttered hands shape into balls the size of baseballs.

OTHER DESSERTS
Seasoning with love...

*C*onversation—with shoes kicked off. That's my idea of good hospitality. Unless, of course, what the guest really needs is a long soak in a hot bath without talking to anybody!

A friend once mentioned a beautiful home she had stayed in while on tour—peaceful surroundings, wonderful food. The thing that impressed her the most was that the owners were not home when the guests arrived. They had opened their home to tired strangers, an expression of trust and hospitality that left my friend a lasting example of Christian love.

Come to find out, the beautiful home was my parents' home, and the wonderful hosts were my mom and dad!

—Yvonne Mercer
Rochester, N.Y.

*B*illy called."

"Again? That's the third time, isn't it?"

Seems unusual to me because our son, Billy, generally took things in stride. Besides, Dallas was a long way from North Carolina. But, Billy was concerned about his parents and their *home on the water as Hurricane Diana pounded the Carolina beaches—the eye of the storm barely 30 miles away.*

We are not really his parents. You see, Billy had grown up in our family. Starting when he was about eight, Billy and his dad just shared Thanksgiving dinner with us. Billy needed a mom and a family. We provided that. Ever since, he has been a special blessing to us.

It is part of my heritage to keep a warm hearth and a boiling pot. I had learned to share whatever we had in my childhood home, known to some as Horner Hotel long ago in Wisconsin. No mere menu makes the fellowship sweet, but the blessings, great and small, come from opening the heart as well as the home.

—Miriam H. Wilfong
Hampstead, N.C.

Strawberry Angel Delight

½ cup flour
¼ cup brown sugar
¼ cup butter
⅓ cup chopped pecans
2 tablespoons lemon juice
7 ounces marshmallow creme
1 sixteen-ounce package frozen sliced strawberries
1 cup heavy cream, whipped

Combine flour and sugar. Cut in butter, add pecans. Press into a 9″ springform pan. Bake at 250° for 20 minutes. Gradually add lemon juice to marshmallow creme, mixing until well blended. Stir in strawberries. Fold in whipped cream. Pour over crust and freeze. Serves 8 to 10.

Frozen Lemon Dessert

3 cups crushed lemon cookies
1 tablespoon butter
1 cup sugar
6 eggs, separated
8 tablespoons fresh lemon juice
grated rind of 4 lemons (just yellow part)
2 cups heavy cream, whipped
4 tablespoons sugar

Spread half of crushed cookies evenly over bottom of a buttered 8″ x 12″ pan, or a round 9″ springform pan. Set aside. Beat together sugar and egg yolks; add lemon juice and rind. Cook this mixture in the top of a double boiler over hot but not boiling water until thick, stirring constantly. Cool. Fold in whipped cream. Beat egg whites just until soft peaks form; add sugar gradually and continue beating; fold into lemon and cream mixture. Pour evenly over crust; sprinkle with remaining lemon cookies. Freeze 6 to 8 hours or overnight. Remove from freezer 5 to 10 minutes before serving. Serves 12 to 15.

My Favorite Ice Cream

6 eggs
2½ cups sugar
1½ quarts milk
1 pint half-and-half cream
1 pint heavy cream
¾ teaspoon salt
2½ tablespoons vanilla

Heat milk and 1½ cups sugar in a double boiler to just below the boiling point. In a bowl, beat egg yolks and 1 cup sugar, then add to hot milk. Stir until mixture thickens or coats a spoon. Remove from heat, add vanilla and salt. Cool. Add the remaining cream and beaten egg whites. Freeze. Makes 1 gallon. "My best ever."

Home-made Ice Cream

3 tablespoons cornstarch
6 cups whole milk
2⅔ cups sugar
4 large or 5 small eggs
¾ teaspoon salt
1 thirteen-ounce can evaporated milk
1 pint whipping cream
3½ tablespoons pure vanilla extract
25 pounds crushed ice

Mix cornstarch with ½ cup milk. Add 1½ cups milk and cook in double boiler until thick and smooth, beating constantly to avoid lumps. Blend sugar, eggs, salt, and evaporated milk in electric mixer. Add hot cornstarch mixture and beat well. Add whipping cream, remaining milk, and vanilla extract. Pour into gallon electric or hand freezer. Pack with layer of crushed ice and layer of ice cream salt until entirely covered. Freeze until firm and remove paddle. Be careful to pour off excess water. Add more crushed ice and salt. Cover freezer tightly and store. If you wish to store in food freezer, it is best to put ice cream into another container that has first been thoroughly chilled. Makes 1 gallon.

Coffee Ice Cream—Dissolve 3 tablespoons instant coffee into 1 cup water and 2 teaspoons vanilla.

Peach—2 cups fresh crushed peaches, 1 tablespoon vanilla, ½ teaspoon almond extract.

Strawberry—3 cups fresh crushed strawberries, 1 tablespoon vanilla, and evaporated milk.

Chocolate—2 squares melted chocolate, omit vanilla.

Pumpkin—2 cups canned pumpkin, 1 tablespoon vanilla, ½ teaspoon cinnamon.

Lemon Ice Cream

1 cup sugar
3 tablespoons lemon juice
2 teaspoons grated lemon rind
1 pint light cream
2 drops yellow food coloring

Mix together thoroughly the sugar, lemon juice, and grated rind. Gradually stir in cream and yellow food coloring. Pour the mixture into a refrigerator tray and freeze for 3 hours without stirring. Makes 1 pint.

Cranberry Sherbet

4 cups cranberries (1 pound)
2 cups boiling water
1 teaspoon unflavored gelatin
½ cup cold water
2 cups sugar
1 pint ginger ale

Cook cranberries in water until skins pop. Press through fruit press. Add gelatin softened in cold water and sugar. Cool. Add ginger ale. Freeze until mushy consistency. Put in bowl and beat, then freeze until firm. Use as side dish with turkey dinner. Serves 10. "My husband's favorite."

Lemon Crunch Freeze

½ cup coarsely chopped walnuts
1 cup sifted all-purpose flour
¼ cup firmly packed dark brown sugar
½ cup melted butter or margarine
2 eggs, separated
1 fourteen-ounce can sweetened condensed milk
½ cup fresh lemon juice
1 teaspoon grated lemon peel
¼ cup granulated sugar

Heat oven to 350°. In a medium-sized bowl combine flour, brown sugar, and walnuts. Pour in butter and stir until well blended and mixture is crumbly. Put mixture on a cookie sheet and with a fork break it up into small crumblike particles. Bake 20 minutes, stirring occasionally, until crumbs are crisp and golden brown. Cool crumbs. Spread two-thirds of the crumb mixture in the bottom of a 9″ x 5″ x 3″ loaf pan. In a medium-sized bowl, beat the 2 egg yolks until thick and lemon-colored. Add condensed milk, lemon juice, and lemon peel, and stir until mixture thickens. In a small bowl beat the 2 egg whites until soft peaks form. Gradually add the ¼ cup granulated sugar and beat until stiff peaks form. Fold egg whites gently into the lemon mixture until well blended. Pour over the crumbs in loaf pan and sprinkle remaining crumbs over top. Cover with aluminum foil and freeze until firm, about 4 to 6 hours. Spoon into sherbet glasses. Serves 6 to 8.

Fancy Lemon Fluff

¼ cup butter
⅓ cup brown sugar
1½ cups wheat flakes
⅓ cup chopped nuts
3 egg whites
1 cup heavy cream, whipped
½ cup sugar
juice and grated rind of 1 lemon
3 egg yolks

Melt butter and brown sugar. Boil to hard ball stage. Add wheat flakes and nuts. Spread on foil to cool. Crumble. Beat egg whites with sugar until it forms stiff peaks. Beat egg yolks with a fork, then add to egg whites. Fold into whipped cream, lemon juice and rind. Place half of the wheat flake crumbs into a buttered square pan. Pour whipped cream mixture over top. Sprinkle with remaining crumbs. Freeze. Serves 8.

Lemonade-Apricot Parfait

1 six-ounce can frozen lemonade concentrate, undiluted
1/2 cup apricot jam
1 quart vanilla ice cream
1/2 cup heavy cream, whipped

Combine lemonade and jam. Pour a spoonful in the bottom of parfait glasses. Add a scoop of ice cream. Continue to alternate until lemonade-jam mixture is used completely. Top with whipped cream. Freeze. Serves 4.

Janet's Key Lime Frozen Dessert

1 cup fine graham cracker crumbs
3 tablespoons butter
2 eggs, separated
1 fifteen-ounce can sweetened condensed milk
1/2 cup fresh lime juice
1 teaspoon vanilla
1/4 cup sugar
3 or 4 drops green food coloring

Combine crumbs and butter. Press on the bottom of an 8″ x 8″ square pan. Chill. Beat egg yolks until thick; combine with sweetened condensed milk. Add lime juice, rind, and vanilla. Stir until mixture thickens. Add food coloring. Beat egg whites into soft peaks. Gradually add sugar; beat until stiff. Fold into lime mixture. Pour on top of crumbs. Freeze.

Frozen Maple Mousse

1 cup maple syrup
1/4 cup granulated sugar
4 egg yolks
1 pint whipping cream
1 teaspoon vanilla
1 cup pecans (whole or broken)

Beat maple syrup, sugar, and egg yolks together; cook in a double boiler until it thickens, then set aside to cool. Whip the cream and add vanilla and pecans; beat with the maple mixture. Pour into refrigerator pan and quick freeze. After 1 hour stir and continue freezing.

Apricot Mousse

2 1/2 cups canned apricots
2 egg whites
1 1/2 cups cream, whipped
1/2 cup sugar

Drain canned apricots and press through sieve, making sure you have at least 2 1/2 cups pulp. Place in freezer tray in freezer 45 minutes. Remove from tray, turn into bowl containing the unbeaten egg whites. Beat until light and fluffy. Whip cream, gradually adding sugar. Fold cream into beaten apricot mixture. Return to tray and freeze. Serves 8 to 10.

Janet's Creamy Chocolate Icebox Pie

PIE CRUST

1 1/2 cups finely crushed chocolate wafers
1/3 cup butter or margarine, melted

Combine wafers and melted butter or margarine. Press onto bottom of 9″ pie pan; bake at 325° for 10 minutes.

PIE FILLING

1 eight-ounce package cream cheese, softened
1/2 cup sugar
1 teaspoon vanilla
2 eggs, separated
1 six-ounce package semisweet chocolate bits
1 cup heavy cream, whipped
1/4 cup commercial sour cream
3/4 cup chopped pecans

Combine cream cheese, 1/4 cup sugar, and vanilla; mixing until well blended. Stir in beaten egg yolks. Melt chocolate bits and add to cream cheese mixture. Beat egg whites until soft peaks form. Add remaining 1/4 cup sugar while still beating. Add egg whites to chocolate mixture. Fold in whipped cream, sour cream, and pecans. Pour over crumb crust and freeze. Decorate as desired with whipped cream and whole pecans. The pie freezes in 45 minutes and has an ice cream consistency. Serves 8 to 10.

Frozen Fruit Slush

1 six-ounce can frozen lemonade
1 six-ounce can frozen orange juice
1 eight-ounce box frozen sliced strawberries
1 No. 2 can unsweetened crushed pineapple
1 small bottle maraschino cherries cut in halves, with juice
3 bananas, diced
2 1/2 cups water
1 cup sugar
1/2 teaspoon wild cherry flavoring (optional)

Thaw frozen ingredients to slush stage. Combine all items. Refreeze, stir periodically for even distribution of fruits. When at slush stage, place in plastic container or containers, for storage. Remove from freezer 1/2 to 1 hour before serving (according to size of container). May be served in medium-sized punch bowl, along with small cookies.

Apple Betty

6 cups sliced apples, peeled
⅓ cup granulated sugar
¾ cup hot water
¼ cup shortening
2 tablespoons butter
½ cup brown sugar
1 cup flour
½ teaspoon cinnamon
1 teaspoon baking powder
¼ teaspoon salt

Place apples into a saucepan with granulated sugar and water. Simmer 10 minutes. Pour into a greased 9″ square pan. Blend shortening, butter, and brown sugar until creamy. Sift flour, cinnamon, baking powder, and salt. Add to butter mixture. Mix well and sprinkle over apples. Bake at 350° for 40 minutes. Serve with whipped cream or ice cream. Serves 6. "It is economical, easy to make, and very good to eat."

Basic Fruit Cobbler

2 cups sliced fruit (peaches, apples, etc.)
1 tablespoon lemon juice
1¾ cups sugar
½ cup butter
¾ cup flour
2 teaspoons baking powder
¾ cup milk

In saucepan, cook fruit with lemon juice and 1 cup sugar over moderate heat until fruit softens. Reserve. Preheat oven to 350°. Place butter or margarine in baking dish and allow to melt in oven. Meanwhile make batter of remaining ¾ cup sugar, flour, baking powder, and milk, beating until smooth. Remove baking dish from oven and carefully pour batter over melted butter. Do not stir. Gently spoon fruit mixture over batter. Again, do not stir. Bake 25 to 30 minutes until top is browned. Serves 6 to 8. Serve with unwhipped heavy cream or ice cream.

Shortcake

3 cups flour
2 tablespoons sugar
3½ teaspoons baking powder
¾ teaspoon salt
¼ teaspoon baking soda
1 teaspoon grated lemon rind
½ cup shortening
1½ cups buttermilk
2 tablespoons melted butter

Sift flour, salt, sugar, soda, and baking powder into bowl. Add lemon rind. Work shortening into dry ingredients as you do for pie crust. Add buttermilk all at once. Stir with fork until well blended. Drop dough into 6 or 8 mounds on a greased cookie sheet. Take fork and flatten slightly. Brush with melted butter and sprinkle sugar on each one. Bake at 450° for 12 minutes or pour batter in round or 9″ x 9″ cake pan and bake 20 minutes at 450°.

Cherry Puff Tarts

2 cups flour
1 cup (2 sticks) butter
1 cup plus 2 tablespoons water
2 teaspoons almond extract
3 eggs
1 can cherry pie filling

Measure 1 cup flour into bowl. Cut in ½ cup (1 stick) butter. Sprinkle with 2 tablespoons water and mix with fork. Divide dough into 6 equal pieces. Pat each piece into a 4½″ round and place on ungreased baking sheet. In saucepan, bring remaining ½ cup butter and 1 cup water to rolling boil. Remove from heat; stir in almond extract and remaining 1 cup flour. Stir until smooth and thick, then add 1 egg at a time, beating well after each addition, until smooth. Drop batter in small amounts from a teaspoon all around dough round, to form a pastry edge. Bake pastry shells 30 minutes in preheated 400° oven. When baked, quickly spoon cherry pie filling into each shell and bake an additional 10 minutes, or until puff edge is done.

Sour Cream Tarts

| 3 egg yolks, well beaten |
| 1 cup sour cream |
| 1 cup sugar |
| 1 tablespoon flour |
| 1 cup steamed raisins |
| 1/4 teaspoon cloves |
| 1/2 teaspoon nutmeg |
| 1 teaspoon cinnamon |

Prepare a favorite pie crust dough. Roll out 1/4" thick. Cut dough in 3" circles. Press circles in muffin tins (2½" diameter). Prick dough. Bake at 400° for 10 to 15 minutes or until golden brown. Beat egg yolks. Mix together sugar, flour, and spices. Add to egg yolks gradually. Mix well. Stir in sour cream. Add raisins. Cook filling in top of double boiler 15 to 20 minutes or until mixture is thick. Stir occasionally. Spoon filling into tart shells. Top with whipped cream and garnish with a piece of candied cherry.

Winter Tart

| 2 eight-ounce packages cream cheese |
| 1 cup confectioners' sugar |
| 1 tablespoon grated lemon peel |
| 1/2 cup light cream |
| canned pineapple slices |
| canned mandarin oranges |
| bananas (dipped in lemon juice first) |
| strawberries, in season |
| grapes, fresh or canned and halved |
| apricot preserves |

Make your favorite pie crust. On pizza pan or jelly-roll pan, roll it into the shape you want your tart to be—round like a pizza or rectangular. Fold dough up 1/2" and down 1/4" all around to make an edge. Prick with fork. Bake until golden at 450° for 10 to 12 minutes. Let cool. Mix together cream cheese, confectioners' sugar, lemon peel, and light cream. Beat until smooth. Refrigerate until needed. When crust is cool, spread it carefully with cheese filling. Drain fruit well. If using a rectangular-shaped crust, start in the middle with 2 rows of bananas that overlap. Next place 2 rows of oranges on each side of bananas. Continue until filling is covered with fruit. If making a pizza pattern, make a design in the center with 1 fruit and continue to make rows out from the center. Heap apricot preserves and, using a pastry brush, cover tart with this glaze.

Strawberry Spectacular

1½ cups all-purpose flour
1 teaspoon baking powder
½ teaspoon salt
6 egg yolks
6 egg whites
1½ cups sugar
⅓ cup cold water
2 teaspoons vanilla
1 teaspoon lemon juice
½ teaspoon cream of tartar
3 cups whipped cream, sweetened to taste
1 quart washed and hulled strawberries (reserve 20 whole berries and slice the rest)
¼ cup currant jelly

Preheat oven to 325°. Blend flour, baking powder, and salt, and set aside. Beat egg yolks in a small bowl until very thick and lemon-colored. Pour beaten egg yolks into ingredients alternately at low speed with water and flavorings. In a large bowl, beat egg whites and cream of tartar until stiff. Gradually fold egg yolk mixture into beaten egg whites. Pour into ungreased tube pan 10″ x 4″. Bake 60 to 65 minutes. Turn pan upside down with tube over neck of funnel or bottle. Cool and remove from pan. Slice across the cake making 3 even layers. On bottom layer spread some of the sweetened whipped cream and top with sliced berries. Put on next layer and repeat with whipped cream and berries. Put on top layer, cover top and sides with remaining whipped cream. Melt currant jelly over low heat. Reserve about 20 whole strawberries and dip point of the berries into the jelly. When cool, decorate with berries point up on cake.

Walnut Cherry Delight Dessert

1 cup shelled walnuts
1¼ cups sifted flour
½ cup butter, softened
½ cup packed brown sugar
½ cup flaked coconut
1 eight-ounce package cream cheese (softened)
⅓ cup sugar
1 egg
1 teaspoon vanilla
1 can cherry pie filling (1 pound, 5 ounce)

Chop ½ cup of walnuts coarsely, set aside for top. Chop remaining walnuts fine. Combine flour, brown sugar, and butter, blend until fine crumbs form. Add coconut and finely chopped walnuts. Mix well. Set aside ½ cup of this mixture. Pack remainder onto the bottom of a greased 9″ x 13″ pan. Bake at 350° for 12 minutes or until edges are very lightly browned. Beat cream cheese with white sugar, egg, and vanilla until very smooth. Spread over hot baked walnut layer. Bake 10 minutes longer. Remove from oven. Spread cherry pie filling over top. Sprinkle with coarsely chopped walnuts and reserved flour-brown sugar mixture. Bake 15 minutes longer or until golden brown. Cool before cutting into 3″ squares. Makes 12.

My Favorite Apple Dumplings

1¼ cups sugar
2 cups water
½ teaspoon cinnamon
¼ cup butter
6 apples
2 tablespoons chopped raisins
2 tablespoons chopped walnuts
1 tablespoon honey

DOUGH

2 cups enriched flour
1 teaspoon salt
²/₃ cup shortening
¹/₃ cup cream

Mix sugar, water, and cinnamon. Cook 5 minutes, add butter. Pare and core apples, fill with mixture of raisins, nuts, and honey mixed together. Place apples on 6″ squares for small apples, 7″ squares for larger ones. Mix flour and salt into bowl, cut in shortening, add cream a tablespoon at a time, roll ¼″ thick, cut in squares 6″ or 7″ depending on size of apple. Sprinkle with spices, butter. Fold corners over apple after first spreading all edges with cream to adhere better, and pinch edges. Make 2 round tops of dough; no smaller than the other to fit on top. Brush with cream before placing on top to hold dough. Place in greased baking pan or individual baking dishes and pour sauce over. Bake at 375° for 35 minutes.

Editor's note: Many who have eaten in the Benner home recall this delectable dessert with great delight.

Banana Split

2 cups graham cracker crumbs
³/₄ cup melted margarine
¹/₄ cup sweetened condensed milk
2 cups powdered sugar
³/₄ cup melted margarine (additional)
1 one-pound can crushed pineapple, drained
7 to 8 sliced, firm bananas
1 nine-ounce container whipped topping
chopped nuts for garnish
maraschino cherries for garnish

Combine the graham cracker crumbs and the ¾ cup melted margarine. Press into a 9″ x 13″ cake pan and bake 5 to 8 minutes in a 350° oven. Beat together the condensed milk, powdered sugar, and additional ¾ cup melted margarine. When crust has cooled, pour the beaten ingredients into it. On top of the beaten ingredients, layer in order, the pineapple, sliced bananas, and topping. Sprinkle nuts on topping and garnish with cherries. Refrigerate overnight before serving.

Snowballs

1 seven-ounce package flaked coconut

1 large box vanilla wafers

1 cup crushed pineapple, drained

½ cup sugar

½ cup pecans, finely chopped

10 large marshmallows, cut in small pieces

1 cup whipping cream

Finely crush 7 vanilla wafers. Add drained pineapple, sugar, nuts, and marshmallows. Mix well. Let stand about 1 hour. Then whip cream. Spread pineapple filling on a vanilla wafer. Top with another wafer and spread again with filling. Top with third wafer. Repeat process for additional snowballs. Frost sides and top of wafer sandwiches with whipped cream. Sprinkle with coconut. Chill in refrigerator overnight. To serve top with a maraschino cherry. Both the whipped cream and coconut can be tinted, if desired. Makes 8 to 10 balls.

Date Torte

2 egg whites

¼ teaspoon salt

¾ cup firmly packed brown sugar

⅔ cup finely crushed cornflakes

2 egg yolks

½ cup chopped walnuts

1 cup chopped pitted dates

Beat egg whites and salt until foamy throughout. Gradually add ½ cup of sugar and beat until mixture will form stiff shiny peaks. Fold in half of the cereal. Beat egg yolks until thick and lemon-colored; gradually add remaining sugar and beat until blended. Fold in remaining cereal. Add to egg white mixture. Then fold in nuts and dates. Pour into a 9″ square pan that has been greased and floured. Bake at 350° for 30 to 35 minutes. Remove from oven and cool. Cut into squares. Serve with lemon sauce.

LEMON SAUCE

⅔ cup sugar
1 tablespoon cornstarch
⅛ teaspoon salt
1 cup water
1 tablespoon butter
1 teaspoon grated lemon rind
2 tablespoons lemon juice

Combine sugar, cornstarch, and salt in saucepan; mix well. Add water gradually, stirring constantly. Cook and stir over medium heat until mixture comes to a boil. Boil 3 minutes, stirring constantly. Remove from heat. Add butter, lemon rind, and juice. Serve warm or cold over torte. Makes about 1¼ cups sauce.

Raspberry Creme Tarts

1 ten-ounce package frozen raspberries, thawed
¼ cup sugar
2 tablespoons cornstarch
1 tablespoon lemon juice
¼ teaspoon almond extract
1 three-ounce package cream cheese
¼ cup powdered sugar
2 tablespoons milk

Drain raspberries. Add enough water to raspberry syrup to measure 1 cup. Combine sugar and cornstarch. Stir into syrup. Cook, stirring, until thickened and clear. Add lemon juice and almond extract. Combine cream cheese with powdered sugar and milk. Spread inside bottoms of tart shells. Arrange raspberries over cream cheese layer; top with glaze. Chill. Fills 1 to 1½ dozen small tarts.

TART SHELLS

Combine 1⅓ cups sifted flour, 2 tablespoons sugar, and ½ teaspoon grated lemon peel. Cut in ½ cup butter. Stir in 2 egg yolks until pastry forms ball. Divide dough into small portions and press into 2½″ tart shells. Prick with fork. Bake at 425° for 8 to 10 minutes. Cool.

Frozen Raspberry Mousse

1 cup hot water

1 three-ounce package raspberry gelatin

1 package frozen raspberries, thawed and mashed

1 tablespoon lemon juice

2 egg whites

1/4 cup sugar

1 cup whipping cream

Dissolve gelatin in hot water. Add raspberries and lemon juice. Chill until partially set. Beat egg whites until stiff; add sugar. Beat whipping cream. Fold egg white mixture and whipped cream into gelatin mixture. Pour into a 5-cup salad mold or dish. Place in freezer and serve frozen. Serves 8 to 10.

Blitz Torte

1/2 cup butter

1 cup sugar

4 egg yolks

1 cup flour

1 teaspoon baking powder

3 tablespoons milk

1 teaspoon vanilla

4 egg whites

1/2 teaspoon cream of tartar

1 cup sugar

1 teaspoon vinegar

1 teaspoon vanilla

1/4 cup slivered almonds

Grease and flour 2 round cake pans, 9" or 10" type. Cream butter and sugar; add egg yolks. Sift flour and baking powder and add alternately with combined milk and vanilla, beating well after each addition. Divide mixture evenly into 2 cake pans and set aside. Beat egg whites until foamy. Add cream of tartar and beat until soft peaks form. Add sugar and beat until stiff peaks hold. Add vanilla and vinegar and blend well. Spread on top of each layer of batter and sprinkle with almonds. Bake at 350° for 30 minutes; cool.

FILLING

1 cup sugar
1 tablespoon flour
4 egg yolks
1 cup dairy sour cream

Combine sugar and flour in top of double boiler. Add sour cream and slightly beaten egg yolks. Cook over hot water until thick. Cool. Place one layer on cake plate; cover with all of cooled filling and top with second layer. Whip 1 cup of heavy cream and frost torte completely. Refrigerate at least 3 to 4 hours before serving. "It tastes better if done a day ahead."

Cherry-Topped Cheesecake

1 cup graham cracker crumbs
3 tablespoons melted butter
1 eight-ounce package cream cheese
¾ cup sugar
2 eggs
1 teaspoon vanilla
1 cup sour cream
1 can cherry pie filling (21 ounce)

Mix cracker crumbs, 2 tablespoons sugar, and butter. Pat mixture in the bottom of a 9″ cake pan, with removable bottom, or over the bottom and sides of a 9″ pie pan. Bake at 325° for 10 minutes. Remove and set aside. Reset oven to 375°. For filling: cream the cheese until light, beat in 8 tablespoons (½ cup) of the sugar, add eggs 1 at a time beating until well blended. Add ½ teaspoon vanilla. Spread filling in baked shell, bake at 375° for 18 minutes, or until mixture is barely set when pan is jiggled. Remove from oven.

TOPPING

Mix sour cream, the remaining 2 tablespoons sugar, and ½ teaspoon vanilla. Spread over the filling and return to oven for 5 minutes. Cool to room temperature, then spread cherry pie filling over top and chill for at least 4 hours, or overnight. Serves 6 to 8.

Peach Cobbler

2 cups sliced, peeled peaches
1 tablespoon lemon juice
1¾ cups sugar
½ cup butter
¾ cup flour
2 teaspoons baking powder
¾ cup milk

Cook fruit with lemon juice and 1 cup sugar until just tender but not soft. Set aside. Melt butter in an 8″ square pan. Mix in a bowl remainder of sugar, flour, baking powder, and milk. Beat until smooth. Pour batter over melted butter—do not stir into butter. Spoon fruit over batter—do not stir into batter. Bake at 350° for 25 to 30 minutes. Serve with ice cream.

Date Delight

1¼ cups graham cracker crumbs
⅓ cup melted butter or margarine
½ pound dates, cut up
½ cup chopped nuts
½ cup crushed pineapple, drained (optional)
4 egg yolks
3 cups milk
⅔ cup sugar
3 tablespoons cornstarch
vanilla to taste
⅛ teaspoon salt

Mix together graham cracker crumbs and butter. Press into a 9″ square pan. Reserve a few crumbs for topping. Spread dates over bottom of crust. Sprinkle chopped nuts and pineapple over dates. Set dish aside. Beat egg yolks. Mix together sugar, cornstarch, and salt. Add gradually to yolks, mixing well, stir in milk and vanilla. Cook in top of double boiler 15 to 20 minutes, stirring occasionally. Pour custard over date, nut, and pineapple mixture. Top with meringue. Sprinkle a few crumbs over meringue. Bake at 350° for 25 minutes. Serve with whipped cream.

MERINGUE

4 egg whites
8 tablespoons sugar

Beat egg whites until stiff but not dry. Gradually add sugar. Beat until whites hold soft peaks.

❧ ❧

Pineapple Date-Nut Pudding

1 No. 2 can pineapple chunks, drained; reserve liquid for sauce
1 cup chopped California walnuts
1 cup chopped dates
½ cup enriched flour
1 teaspoon baking powder
½ teaspoon salt
3 egg yolks
1 teaspoon vanilla
¾ cup sugar
3 egg whites, stiffly beaten

Combine pineapple, nuts, and dates. Add to sifted dry ingredients; mix well. Beat egg yolks and add vanilla and sugar; stir into fruit mixture. Fold in stiffly beaten egg whites. Bake in greased 9″ x 13″ baking pan at 325° for 35 minutes. Serve warm or cold with pineapple sauce.

PINEAPPLE SAUCE

1 cup pineapple syrup
2 tablespoons orange juice
1 tablespoon cornstarch
1 tablespoon butter or fortified margarine

Combine ingredients and mix well. Cook until thickened, stirring constantly.

Date-Nut Cream Pudding

2½ tablespoons cornstarch
¼ cup sugar
½ teaspoon salt
2 cups milk
2 eggs, beaten
1 tablespoon butter
1 teaspoon vanilla
¾ cup chopped dates
⅓ cup chopped walnuts

Mix together cornstarch, sugar, and salt. Add milk, and cook in a double boiler until thick. Add mixture to eggs slowly. Cook until thickened. Remove from heat, add butter and vanilla. Cool. Stir in dates and walnuts. Serves 4 to 6.

Rice Pudding

½ cup long grain rice
½ teaspoon salt
1¾ cups boiling water
2 eggs
⅓ cup sugar
¼ teaspoon salt
1 teaspoon vanilla
1 tablespoon butter
2 cups milk

Cook rice, salt, and water in double boiler until rice is tender and water has been absorbed. In a greased 1-quart casserole, slightly beat the eggs, sugar, salt, and vanilla. Scald the milk and add the butter. Add this to the hot rice and egg mixtures and sprinkle a little cinnamon and nutmeg over the top. Place casserole in shallow pan and fill it almost to the brim with hot water and bake at 350° for 60 to 75 minutes. Cool on a wire rack and serve warm or cold with nutmeg sauce.

NUTMEG SAUCE

1¼ cups boiling water
¾ cup sugar
1¼ tablespoons flour
½ teaspoon nutmeg
1 teaspoon vanilla
1 tablespoon butter
dash salt

Put the sugar, salt, flour, and nutmeg through a sifter and add to the boiling water to which the butter and vanilla have been added. Stir to mix and cook until it comes to a rolling boil, then remove. Serve warm or cold. "Good and fast."

Fruit Spice Pudding

1 cup sugar
¼ cup shortening
1 cup water or fruit juice
2 cups chopped, seedless raisins
1 teaspoon cinnamon
1 teaspoon nutmeg
½ teaspoon cloves
1¾ cups flour
1 teaspoon salt
½ teaspoon baking soda
1 cup chopped dates
½ cup chopped dried apricots
½ cup broken California walnut meats

Cook sugar, shortening, water, raisins, and spices for 3 minutes; cool. Add flour sifted with salt and baking soda. Stir in fruits and nut meats. Bake in 8″ x 12″ waxed-paper-lined cake pan at 325° for 50 to 60 minutes. Cool. Serve with whipped cream. Cut into 2″ x 3″ pieces. Makes 16.

Favorite Plum Pudding

1 cup currants
1 cup raisins
³/₄ cup bread crumbs
3 eggs
1 cup sugar
1 cup shortening
1 teaspoon salt
1 teaspoon nutmeg
1 teaspoon cinnamon
1 teaspoon ground cloves
¹/₂ teaspoon allspice
2 teaspoons baking powder
1 cup milk
2¹/₂ cups flour
¹/₂ cup figs
¹/₂ cup chopped nuts
1 teaspoon baking soda, dissolved in 1 tablespoon water

Cream together currants, raisins, bread crumbs, eggs, sugar, shortening, salt, spices, and milk. Sift flour and baking powder 3 times, then add to creamed mixture. Add soda and beat well. Steam 3 hours. Serve with hard sauce or lemon sauce.

LEMON SAUCE

1 cup sugar
2 tablespoons cornstarch
¹/₂ teaspoon salt
1 cup boiling water
1 tablespoon butter
2 tablespoons lemon juice from fresh lemons
¹/₂ teaspoon grated lemon peel

Mix sugar, cornstarch, and salt. Add boiling water. Cook until clear, add butter, lemon juice, and peel.

Wilma's Chocolate Pudding

1/2 cup sugar

3 tablespoons cocoa

2 tablespoons cornstarch

1 tablespoon butter

pinch salt

1 cup boiling water

1/2 cup whipping cream, whipped

1 teaspoon vanilla

Mix dry ingredients, add boiling water, cook until thick, add butter. Cool, add vanilla and the whipped cream. May be put into serving dishes at this time. Chill. Serve with a dab of whip cream and a cherry if desired. Serves 4 or 5.

Old-fashioned Raisin-Rice-Custard Pudding

1/2 cup rice

1 quart milk

1/2 cup seedless raisins

3 tablespoons butter

3 eggs, beaten

2/3 cup sugar, rounded

1 teaspoon vanilla

1/4 teaspoon salt

nutmeg

Mix rice with 2 cups of milk in top of double boiler, cook over hot water until tender. Add raisins and butter. Combine eggs, vanilla, salt, and remaining milk. Strain, add sugar. Stir into hot rice mixture. Pour into a greased 1 1/2-quart baking dish. Sprinkle with nutmeg. Set in pan filled half full of warm water, bake at 325° for 45 to 50 minutes, or until set. Serves 6. "Good either warmed or chilled."

Flan

4 eggs
⅔ cup sugar
3½ cups evaporated milk
1 teaspoon vanilla
⅛ teaspoon salt

Beat egg slightly, add milk and strain. Add sugar, salt, and vanilla. Set aside. Melt ¾ cup sugar slowly, to a good caramel color, not too dark a color. Add 3 tablespoons boiling water, stirring well. Pour into a straight-sided 1-quart casserole dish, keep tilting dish until bottom and half of sides are coated. Carefully pour custard into dish. Set into a pan of cold water. Bake at 350° for 50 to 60 minutes. "This light dessert is served all over the world. A favorite with many."

Flan (Creme-Caramel)

CARAMEL BASE

1 cup sugar
⅓ cup water

Cook sugar and water in a small saucepan over moderately high heat, stirring constantly until the mixture caramelizes or turns golden. This will take about 8 to 10 minutes. Using the caramel base, coat the bottom and sides of a 6-cup mold, 8 individual custard cups, or a 1½-quart oven-proof dish. Place the dish or cups in cold water a few minutes to set.

CUSTARD

3 cups milk
4 whole eggs plus 3 egg yolks
½ cup sugar
2 teaspoons vanilla

Preheat the oven to 350° and heat 1" of water in a shallow roasting pan while making the custard. This is the Bain-Marie in which the custard will bake in its dish. Scald the milk in a medium saucepan and set aside to cool. Beat the eggs and egg yolks together with the sugar. With the beater on, add a little of the scalded milk, then add the remaining milk and the vanilla. Beat until foamy and pour into the prepared dish or custard cups. Place in the Bain-Marie and bake until knife inserted in the middle comes out clean, 40 minutes or more. Cool and refrigerate. Unmold and run a knife around the sides of the custard. Place a serving platter over the top and invert onto the platter. Serve chilled but not ice-cold. Surround the cream with fresh fruit. Serves 6 to 8.

Lemon Sponge Pudding

1 cup sugar
3 tablespoons flour
3 tablespoons lemon juice
1/8 teaspoon salt
2 egg yolks
1 cup milk
1 tablespoon melted butter
2 egg whites, stiffly beaten

Combine sugar, flour, lemon juice, and salt. Add egg yolks, milk, and butter. Fold in egg whites. Pour in 6 custard cups, place in a pan of water. Bake at 325° for 40 minutes or until cake part on top springs back to touch. Place in glass sherbet dishes and sprinkle with toasted almonds.

Chocolate Dream Squares

1¹/₃ cups fine graham cracker crumbs
1 cup butter
2 cups powdered sugar
3 eggs
3 squares semisweet chocolate
1¹/₂ cups chopped nuts
1 teaspoon vanilla

Line an 8″ square pan with about half of the graham cracker crumbs. Cream butter, add powdered sugar. Beat in eggs, one at a time. Beat in semisweet chocolate, melted and slightly cooled. Stir in nuts and vanilla. Spread in pan and cover with balance of crumbs. Refrigerate overnight. Serves 12. "Use only 5 squares of chocolate if you double the recipe while using one mixing bowl. 6 squares seem to be too strong."

Raspberry Bavarian

1 three-ounce package black raspberry gelatin

1 ten-ounce package frozen raspberries, thawed

1/2 cup sour cream

1 cup boiling water

Dissolve gelatin in boiling water. Drain raspberries, reserving liquid. Add enough cold water to liquid to make 1 cup; combine with dissolved gelatin. Chill until thickened to consistency of egg whites. Using low speed of mixer or blender, mix sour cream and thickened gelatin until smooth. Fold in drained raspberries; pour into a 3-cup mold and chill until set. Serves 5 to 6.

Baked Prune Whip

1 cup cooked prunes, pitted

1/4 cup sugar

2 tablespoons lemon juice

3 egg whites, stiffly beaten

1/4 cup sugar

Mash prunes, add 1/4 cup sugar. Add lemon juice to beaten egg whites and gradually beat in 1/4 cup sugar. Fold in prunes. Pour into ungreased 7" casserole. Bake at 325° for 40 minutes or until set. Cool. Serve with custard sauce (use the leftover yolks) or whipped cream. Serves 4 to 6.

Cherry Jumble

1 No. 2 can (2 1/2 cups) sour red cherries, drained

1/2 cup sugar

1/2 cup cherry syrup

1 tablespoon butter or fortified margarine

1 cup enriched flour

1 teaspoon baking powder

1/4 teaspoon salt

½ cup sugar
½ cup water

Combine cherries, ½ cup sugar, and syrup; heat to boiling. Add butter. Remove from heat. Sift dry ingredients into mixing bowl. Add water and beat well. Pour into well-greased 9″ square pan; top with hot fruit mixture. Bake at 400° for 40 minutes. Serves 6 to 8.

❧ ☙

Purple Cow

1 pint vanilla ice cream
¼ cup milk
2 tablespoons frozen grape juice concentrate
1 tablespoon frozen lemonade concentrate
frozen whipped dessert topping, thawed
mint leaves

In blender container, combine ice cream, milk, and frozen juice concentrates. Cover and blend until smooth. Serve in tall glasses with straws. Garnish with whipped dessert topping and mint leaf, if desired. Makes 2 cups.

❧ ☙

Strawberry Mousse

2 egg whites
salt
½ cup sugar
8 large strawberries
1 cup cream, whipped to stiff peaks

In a bowl beat 2 egg whites with a pinch of salt until they hold soft peaks. Beat in sugar, 2 tablespoons at a time, and continue to beat until stiff and shiny. In a blender puree strawberries and fold the puree into the meringue. Fold in cream. Pour into stemmed glasses and chill at least 3 hours.

Caramel Cup Custard

1 cup sugar
½ cup water
2 eggs
2 cups milk
½ cup sugar
½ teaspoon vanilla
dash of salt
dash of nutmeg

Place 1 cup sugar in saucepan over low heat. Stir until entirely melted, stirring constantly. Add water. Boil mixture until it becomes a thin syrup. Pour 1 tablespoon syrup in each custard cup. Beat remaining ingredients in a bowl. Rest a spoon over syrup, then pour the custard slowly over spoon into custard cups. Bake at 350° for 35 minutes.

Caramel-Raisin Pudding

¾ cup seedless raisins
½ cup brown sugar
½ cup milk
1 cup enriched flour
2 teaspoons baking powder
½ teaspoon salt
2 teaspoons butter or fortified margarine
3 cups boiling water
1 cup brown sugar
1 tablespoon butter or fortified margarine
½ teaspoon vanilla

Soak raisins 5 minutes; drain. Combine sugar and milk; add sifted dry ingredients, raisins, and 2 teaspoons butter. Combine remaining ingredients; heat to boiling and cook 5 minutes; pour into greased 8" x 12" baking pan and drop batter from spoon over hot sauce. Bake at 350° for 30 minutes. "This is a pudding that makes its own sauce."

Favorite Fudge Sauce

½ cup light corn syrup

1 cup sugar

1 cup water

3 one-ounce squares chocolate

1 teaspoon vanilla

¾ cup evaporated milk

Combine syrup, sugar, and water. Cook 30 minutes or to firm ball stage. Remove and add chocolate. Stir until melted. Add vanilla. Slowly add evaporated milk. Mix well. Cool. "This may be heated for hot fudge sundaes. It's wonderful."

Chocolate Sauce

2 tablespoons butter

1 square unsweetened chocolate

¼ cup cocoa

¾ cup sugar

½ cup cream or evaporated milk

⅛ teaspoon salt

1 teaspoon vanilla

Melt butter and chocolate in a saucepan. Mix together cocoa and sugar, then blend into butter. Slowly stir in cream. Bring to a boil stirring well with a wire whip for 10 seconds. Remove from heat. Add salt and vanilla.

Butterscotch Sauce

¾ cup brown sugar

⅓ cup light corn syrup

2 tablespoons butter

⅛ teaspoon salt

⅓ cup cream

Mix sugar, syrup, butter, and salt. Heat and cook to soft ball stage (236°). Remove and cool, stir in cream. Makes 1 cup.

Praline Sauce

1 tablespoon butter

2 tablespoons slivered almonds

2 tablespoons butter

1 cup brown sugar

¼ cup light corn syrup

½ cup evaporated milk

dash of salt

In saucepan melt 1 tablespoon butter and sauté almonds until lightly browned. Add butter, sugar, syrup, and salt. Cook over low heat, stirring constantly until sugar is dissolved. Slowly blend in milk. Remove from heat. Cool. Serve over coffee ice cream. Makes 1¼ cups.

Fresh Cranberry Sauce

4 cups (1 pound) fresh cranberries

3 cups sugar

2 cups boiling water

1 tablespoon grated orange rind

Wash cranberries, removing stems. Combine with remaining ingredients in 3½-quart saucepan; let stand 5 minutes. Simmer, covered, 5 minutes. Remove from heat; let stand 5 minutes. Then simmer covered, 5 minutes longer. Remove from heat. Cool; then refrigerate until well-chilled—several hours or overnight. Makes 1 quart.

BEVERAGES

Seasoning with love...

*K*en and I have never looked for extra members for our family, but sharing our home has been a large and exciting
part of our hospitality. God has put many beautiful people with
great potential on our doorstep, and sometimes they have needed
to stay a while. As their faces march across my mind, I get all
blessed thinking, "Who's next, Lord?"

—Betty Rice
Winter Haven, Fla.

*M*y dear friend, Marion Boykin, taught me how to have a
crowd over with little pain or strain. Set a date, invite
several people, some old friends and some new friends. Usually
we have 12, counting us. Assign each couple an item to bring:
vegetable, Jell-O salad, green salad, or dessert. Then you make
the house spiffy. Prepare the main dish, the bread, and the drink.

Somehow people feel more at home if they've had a part. So,
with their part, and your part—honey, you've got a party!

—Paulette Woods
Sacramento, Calif.

Janet's Party Punch

3 quarts unsweetened pineapple juice
juice of 8 lemons
juice of 8 oranges
juice of 3 limes
2 cups sugar
1 cup mint leaves
4 quarts dry ginger ale
2 quarts carbonated water

Combine fruit juices, sugar, and mint leaves; mix thoroughly; chill. Just before serving, add ginger ale and carbonated water. Pour over large cake of ice in punch bowl. Float thin slices of lemon and lime, and fresh summer blossoms for a party touch. Serves 35.

Cranberry Sparkle

4 cups cranberry juice cocktail
2$^1/_4$ cups pineapple juice
$^1/_2$ cup orange juice
$^1/_4$ cup lemon juice
4 to 6 tablespoons sugar
1 quart ginger ale

In a large bowl combine first five ingredients, cover bowl; chill. When ready to serve, pour over ice in a punch bowl. Add 1 quart of chilled ginger ale. Makes about 11 cups punch.

Frosty Fruit Cocktail

1 bottle ginger ale (28 ounce)
1 six-ounce frozen tangerine juice concentrate
3$^1/_2$ cups salad fruits, chilled and drained
1 ten-ounce package frozen cantaloupe balls, thawed and drained

Combine ginger ale and tangerine concentrate. Stir until dissolved. Pour into refrigerator tray and freeze only to mush, about 1 hour. Combine fruits and cantaloupe balls. To serve, put a spoonful of frozen juice in each glass, then fruits and last more frozen juice, top with cherry or strawberry and a sprig of mint. Serves 8.

Ruby Cocktail

pineapple sherbet
cranberry juice

Place 1 scoop of pineapple sherbet in juice glass, then fill with chilled cranberry juice. Serve with pineapple tidbits and maraschino cherries on toothpicks. "For a first course."

Apricot Punch

2½ cups apricot nectar
3 tablespoons lemon juice
1 cup orange juice
¼ cup light corn syrup

Combine all ingredients. Chill half in refrigerator. Place remainder in freezer tray to form a mush. Just before serving, blend together. Garnish with lemon or orange slices. Serves 4. "Good for a first course served in the living room."

Eggnog Coffee

2 pints coffee ice cream
2 quarts eggnog
5 cups cold coffee
1 pint whipping cream, whipped

Blend together eggnog and coffee; fold in whipping cream. Place into punch bowl; float ice cream balls in punch. Sprinkle with nutmeg. Serve at once. Serves 30 half-cup servings. For individual servings: fill ⅔ cup cold coffee in glass, then add two scoops coffee ice cream, fill glass to top with eggnog.

Pineapple Mallowade

24 large marshmallows
1 cup water
2 cups unsweetened pineapple juice
¼ cup lemon juice
⅛ teaspoon salt
3 cups ginger ale

Place marshmallows and water in top of double boiler. Heat over boiling water until marshmallows are melted; stir occasionally. Blend in fruit juices and salt. Mix well; chill in refrigerator. Add ginger ale just before serving. Pour into ice-filled glasses. Garnish with fresh mint leaves, if desired. Serves 6 to 8.

Hot Mulled Cider

½ cup brown sugar
1 teaspoon whole allspice
1 teaspoon whole cloves
¼ teaspoon salt
dash nutmeg
1 cinnamon stick
2 quarts apple cider

In a large saucepan, combine the above ingredients. Slowly bring cider to boiling. Cover and simmer for 20 minutes. Strain to remove spices; pour hot cider over clove-studded orange wedges and cinnamon sticks in warm mugs. Good go-alongs: glazed doughnuts, crisp sugar cookies, or crackers and corn chips. If you like, you can "mull" it ahead, then reheat at serving time.

Fluffy Mocha-Cream

1 tablespoon instant coffee
1/4 cup hot water
1 3/4 cups cold water
1 pint chocolate ice cream
1/8 teaspoon almond extract
1/2 cup heavy cream, whipped
nutmeg

Dissolve instant coffee in hot water; add cold water. Chill. Add ice cream and stir until nearly melted. Fold almond extract into whipped cream. Float on top of mocha beverage. Sprinkle with nutmeg. Makes 1 quart.

INDEX

MEAT AND MAIN DISHES

Baked Lemon Pork Chops / 56
Baked Pork Chops / 55
Baked Stuffed Pork Chops / 56
Barbecued Pork Chops / 57
Beef Stroganoff / 49
Butterfly Pork Chops / 54
California Steak / 48
Chicken Fried Steak / 47
Chili Hamburger Pie / 66
Chow Mein / 62
Crockpot Roast / 52
Eggplant and Sausage Casserole / 64
Favorite Meat Loaf / 74
Fiesta Meatballs in Almond Sauce / 69
Glazed Baked Pork Chops / 58
Glazed Ham Loaf / 60
Hamburger and Noodles in Sour Cream / 65
Ham Loaf / 60
Ham Squares / 61
Ham Stroganoff / 59
Hungarian Pork-n-Kraut Goulash / 63
Little Barbecue Loaves / 73
Lynn's Beef and Cheese Pie / 74
Lynn's Meatball Stroganoff / 68
Marinated Chuck Roast / 51
Meatball Casserole / 70
Meatballs / 68
Meatballs and Spaghetti Sauce / 72
Meat-n-Potato Pie / 65
Minute Steak Scramble / 48
My Favorite Ham Loaf / 58
Norwegian Meatballs / 70
Not Just Steak / 47
Oven Barbecued Ribs / 53
Pepper Steak / 50
Quick Chow Mein / 62
Roast Ribs of Pork Loin / 54
Roast Sirloin Tip / 46
Sausage, Sauerkraut, and Tomato
   Casserole / 64
Sausage Soufflé / 66
Savory Short Rib Dinner / 52
Spanish Round Steak / 50
Standing Rib Roast of Beef / 46
Steamed Beef Brisket / 49
Stuffed Green Peppers / 67
Stuffed Pork Chops / 57
Swedish Meatballs / 72
Swedish Meat Loaf / 75
Sweet-and-sour Pork Chops / 55
Swiss Steak / 51
Upside-down Ham Loaf / 59
Vegetable Pot Roast Au Jus / 53
Wilma's Swedish Meatballs with
   Parsley Spaghetti / 71

OTHER DESSERTS

Apple Betty / 256
Apricot Mousse / 254
Baked Prune Whip / 274
Banana Split / 261

Basic Fruit Cobbler / 256
Blitz Torte / 264
Butterscotch Sauce / 277
Caramel Cup Custard / 276
Caramel-Raisin Pudding / 276
Cherry Jumble / 274
Cherry Puff Tarts / 257
Cherry-Topped Cheesecake / 265
Chocolate Dream Squares / 273
Chocolate Sauce / 277
Cranberry Sherbet / 251
Date Delight / 266
Date-Nut Cream Pudding / 268
Date Torte / 262
Fancy Lemon Fluff / 252
Favorite Fudge Sauce / 277
Favorite Plum Pudding / 270
Flan / 272
Flan (Creme-Caramel) / 272
Fresh Cranberry Sauce / 278
Frozen Fruit Slush / 255
Frozen Lemon Dessert / 249
Frozen Maple Mousse / 254
Frozen Raspberry Mousse / 264
Fruit Spice Pudding / 269
Home-made Ice Cream / 250
Janet's Creamy Chocolate Icebox Pie / 254
Janet's Key Lime Frozen Dessert / 253
Lemonade-Apricot Parfait / 253
Lemon Crunch Freeze / 252
Lemon Ice Cream / 251
Lemon Sponge Pudding / 273
My Favorite Apple Dumplings / 260
My Favorite Ice Cream / 250
Old-fashioned Raisin-Rice-Custard
   Pudding / 271
Peach Cobbler / 266
Pineapple Date-Nut Pudding / 267
Praline Sauce / 278
Purple Cow / 275
Raspberry Bavarian / 274
Raspberry Creme Tarts / 263
Rice Pudding / 268
Shortcake / 257
Snowballs / 262
Sour Cream Tarts / 258
Strawberry Angel Delight / 249
Strawberry Mousse / 275
Strawberry Spectacular / 259
Walnut Cherry Delight Dessert / 260
Wilma's Chocolate Pudding / 271
Winter Tart / 258

PIES AND PASTRIES

Ambassador Black Bottom Pie / 238
Best Chocolate Pie / 241
Black Raspberry Pie / 228
Blue Plum Pie / 229
Boysenberry Pie / 227
Burnt Sugar Pie / 237
Butterscotch Pie / 240
Caramel Pie / 238

SOUPS AND STEWS

VEGETABLES AND FRUIT

YEAST BREADS